MEET ME AT THE
BILTMORE

100 YEARS AT
PROVIDENCE'S MOST
STORIED HOTEL

AMANDA QUAY BLOUNT

Meet Me at the Biltmore:
100 Years at Providence's Most Storied Hotel
Copyright © 2022 Amanda Quay Blount

Produced and printed by Stillwater River Publications.
All rights reserved. Written and produced in the
United States of America. This book may not be reproduced
or sold in any form without the expressed, written
permission of the author and publisher.

Visit our website at
www.StillwaterPress.com
for more information.

First Stillwater River Publications Edition

ISBN: 978-1-958217-22-1

Library of Congress Control Number: 2022918271

1 2 3 4 5 6 7 8 9 10
Written by Amanda Quay Blount.
Cover & interior book design by Matthew St. Jean.
Published by Stillwater River Publications,
Pawtucket, RI, USA.

Names: Blount, Amanda Quay, author.
Title: Meet me at the Biltmore : 100 years at Providence's
most storied hotel / Amanda Quay Blount.
Description: First Stillwater River Publications edition. |
Pawtucket, RI, USA : Stillwater River Publications, [2022] |
Includes bibliographical references.
Identifiers: ISBN: 9781958217221 | LCCN: 2022918271
Subjects: LCSH: Providence Biltmore Hotel--History. |
Hotels--Rhode Island--Providence--History. |
Providence (R.I.)--History.
Classification: LCC: TX909.2.R42 P76 2022 |
DDC: 910.46097452--dc23

For Dane and Barrett.

CONTENTS

MEET ME AT THE BILTMORE

THANKS AND ACKNOWLEDGEMENTS

This project began because I wanted to read a book about the Providence Biltmore Hotel. What started as a few internet searches turned into a veritable treasure chest of information about the hotel, about Rhode Island, and about the amazing, bizarre, and intriguing people who have been a part of the Biltmore's story. I am deeply indebted to everyone who has been supportive of this project throughout its development. I am sure that I will forget a name here, so please know that if you are someone who listened to me wax poetic about the importance of the Biltmore or of hotels and their places in history, I am so grateful to have had your ears.

I would like to, first and foremost, thank my grandmother, Joan Stewart Hicks, for being one of the early champions of this book and for finding the topic as fascinating as I do. I wish she could be here today to read it, but I am forever grateful that I had an opportunity to read her some of the early drafts.

Historical research is an incredibly complicated endeavor, and the study of history is only possible because of the patience, diligence, and dedication of librarians, research staff, and preservationists who digitize and archive materials. To that end, this book would never have been written without the outstanding people at the Community College of Rhode Island who provided me access to *The Providence Journal*'s historical archives (especially Chris Peterson and Jillian Lang, who suggested I try the parking lot Wi-Fi when the building was closed due to COVID-19—it worked! And I spent more than 300 hours in your parking lot over two years). Thanks to everyone who contributed to the project from the Rhode Island Historical Society and the Providence Athenaeum. Thanks to Rachel Robinson from the Providence Preservation Society; Ray McCue and the Johnson and Wales University's Culinary Arts Museum team; and the whole team at the Providence Public Library. Thank you for your excitement and your support of this idea from day one. Many thanks to my cousin Kristen Hicks for her genealogy research and for following me down far too many obscure rabbit holes in my search for the people of the Biltmore's past.

Thank you to the people who let me interview them for this project, and for those who shared their stories to enrich this book: Dick Brush (for your many hours of interviews and your enthusiast support, in addition to your stories), the Schrott family, Jimi Pugliese, Steve Lautieri, Ray McCue, Donna Hoffmeister, Michael Babb, David Lee Black, Scott Williams, and the countless individuals who shared their stories of experiences and employment at the hotel with me. A special thanks to Fallon Masterson for your early support of this project and for fact-checking some of my key points. Many thanks to Katherine Furman who let me pick her brain about publishing, and to Amanda Kallis for helping me hone my craft.

I would also like to say thank you to my editor and publisher, Steven Porter of Stillwater River Publications and Stillwater Books, who has answered a lot of questions over the past year and who has been incredibly patient with me as I figured out how to put this project into book form. We are so lucky to have such a dedicated local bookstore and press in Rhode Island.

To my husband Dane, for whom this book is dedicated and who put up with two straight years of complaints about this project—you are my hero and anchor. To my personal cheer squad: Liz Miele, Angela Grosso-Burke, Amanda Amaro, Angineh Djavadghazaryans,

Ashley Navin, Nicole Seigert, and Kristen Williams—I would have given up a hundred times if it weren't for your constant encouragement. A lifetime of gratitude for my mother, Libby Hicks, and her endless support of my writing over the past 30 years. Thanks also to her husband, Steve, and my amazing siblings and their partners—Branton, Melinda, Lindsay, Will, Barry, and Chrissy. Thanks for rooting for me the whole way. Thanks to Mel Perone for loving this hotel as much as I do and for being the first person I sat down to have a drink with at the Biltmore's bar.

Last but not least, thank you to my father, Barry Blount, Sr. This book would never have been made if it weren't for you calling me the first weekend I lived in Providence and saying, "Oh, you have to go downtown and check out the historic Biltmore Hotel. It's really cool." Of all the advice you ever gave me in life, Dad, I think this one got the most mileage.

PART I
THE CITY'S HOTEL

1

DREAMING OF A FIRST-CLASS

PUBLIC HOUSE

On July 21, 1921, an Irish American taxi driver named Frank Gilligan sat in his jitney cab on Washington Street in downtown Providence, Rhode Island. His passenger, Dr. William Jordan, grumbled impatiently in the back seat. The traffic in the downtown section of Exchange Place had become unbearable with the recent installation of new trolley lines that zigzagged out across the city from Union Station. Frank had just left a steady job in carpet sales at the Outlet Company to set out on his own as a jitney driver, but had already run into a string of bad luck. Earlier that year, his brakes had given out on a delivery in the Silver Lake neighborhood, sending him and his cab crashing through a glass picture window of a streetfront pharmacy, badly injuring a nearby pedestrian. Frank had not even begun to pay off the fine from that accident before this fateful day, when yet again he would be faced with the perils of the newly bustling automobile traffic in the crowded manufacturing hub of Providence.

The early 20th century had witnessed extensive expansion and consolidation of America's railway system, with new lines connecting

Westminster Street at the turn of the century. Courtesy of the Providence Public Library Digital Collections, Rhode Island Photograph Collection.

once distant cities and towns. As shipping by rail increased the efficiency and affordability of commerce, and as more convenient travel between cities became commonplace, urban centers boomed. Providence, already leading in shipping and trade thanks to its position along a complex system of rivers, ports, and waterways, was easily positioned to leverage the new industrial advances. In the decades immediately following the Civil War, Rhode Island's economy tripled. The textile and metal industries flourished, increasing their output and advancing their technological skill. Complex mill campuses were rapidly built and updated all around the city and state.

William McLoughlin writes in his history of the state that, "Rhode Island's humming mills and belching factories turned out such technically skilled work that at last it was able to enter the world market in competition with British and other European manufacturers…If the United States in those years finally achieved international status as a world power, as a manufacturing nation, shouldering its way into every market around the world as well as meeting the enormous needs of its own expanding empire, then Rhode Island was not only playing its part, but was at the forefront."

During this time, Providence was rivaled only by Philadelphia in its production of highly sought-after goods: wool, worsteds, silver, cotton, and jewelry. Local mills churned out textiles while the factories were some of the nation's largest producers of rubber, steam engines, and metal products. If it could be mass produced, it was being produced in Rhode Island. The state's textile companies were known all across the US for being of the highest quality and technicality, and local company brands such as Fruit of the Loom became household names. Meanwhile, manufacturers of other products became synonymous with the best in their class: Corliss steam engines, Gorham silver, Manton ship windlass, Household sewing machine, Cottrell printing, American Screw Company, and Perry Davis's patented medicinal Pain Killer.

To meet the labor needs of the mills and factories, Rhode Island attracted the highest number of immigrants of any state in the country. By 1920, Rhode Island was the most diverse state in the Union, with 71 percent of Rhode Islanders being of "foreign stock," either born abroad or having at least one parent who was born abroad. This was the highest percentage of immigrants in any state population, with Massachusetts coming in second with 66 percent. As the number of people in the labor market increased, profits to investors increased as well. With the surge in population, Providence's middle class expanded dramatically. The number of people needed to serve the growing population drove an increase in wholesalers, retailers, lawyers, nurses, doctors, ministers, shopkeepers, publicans, and innkeepers to the city. New city infrastructure went up just as quickly: banks, storefronts, newsstands, theaters, taverns, offices, schools, and hospitals all followed suit. Transportation networks became critical to moving goods and people across the capital, leading to incredible congestion in the downtown area.

This was the situation in Providence that Frank Gilligan found himself inching through on that hot July day. Just as Frank saw some movement ahead, a sign that the trolleys had cleared and the jitneys could pass, his luck ran out. Thirteen stories above him, looming over Washington street, a welder had just lost his grip on his massive wrench. A flaming hot rivet slipped from the steel construction, careening past the work crews to the ground below. With the jitney

Biltmore Hotel under construction. Courtesy of the Providence Public Library Digital Collections, Rhode Island Photograph Collection.

trapped in motionless traffic, the scalding piece of metal easily tore through its soft roof, landing on Frank's pant leg and badly burning him before ricocheting onto his passenger. Both men suffered injuries in the freak accident. *The New York Times* reported the next day that the injured parties were treated at Rhode Island Hospital, and that construction continued on schedule at the new Biltmore Hotel.

Providence's newest hotel construction was a long time in the making. Luxury hotels of the early 20th century had become the social epicenter of the cities they inhabited. They not only provided tony apartments for the rich and famous, but they served a commercial and civic function as well. Large dining rooms provided ample space for political meetings and charitable fundraisers. The hotel was the great neutralizer, with enough rooms and meeting spaces for opposing political groups to host overlapping meetings. The palatial hotels of this era became gathering places where big decisions were made; where new ideas were debated; and where people from all levels of society converged.

The great wealth of the Progressive Era also brought a newfound proclivity toward leisure and recreation. Rhode Island, in particular, pioneered "the new consumer art of summer vacations, resort places, and of tourism," writes McLoughlin. Thanks to its stunning, unbridled coastline and easy accessibility between Boston and New York, Rhode Island emerged as the playground for the rich and famous. Known as Rhode Island's "resort era," this time was marked by seemingly endless construction of mansions up and down the Narragansett Bay coast. The development of Newport as a destination town was both intentional and exclusive. Guided by the shrewd hand of Caroline Astor, the wife of William Backhouse Astor and the leading socialite in New York City, the powerful wives of New York millionaires devised a vision for a summer retreat town where they would dominate all aspects of society. Partially in response to the overabundance of "new money" in New York, this tightknit group of society women built a village of opulence and grandeur in Newport the likes of which had never been seen in the world. McLoughlin, in his text, referred to Newport as "the most palatial, extravagant, and expensive summer resort the world had seen since the days of the Roman Empire." Mansion after mansion was built, with competition for the most expensive architects at an all-time high. It was a time of such exorbitant wealth that the contemporary sociologist Thorstein Veblen coined the term "conspicuous consumption" to describe the lifestyles he observed in Newport. Mark Twain referred to Newport in his autobiography as a "breeding place—that stud farm, so to speak—of aristocracy; aristocracy of the American type."

A lot of money was traveling through Providence on its way to Newport in those summer months—in addition to the incredible wealth of Rhode Islanders themselves, whose sweeping estates dotted the thoroughfares of the city. As Providence's popularity grew, so did the need for accommodations and entertainment. Several hotels went up in downtown Providence at the turn of the century, including the Narragansett Hotel, City Hotel, Hotel Dorrance, the Blackstone Hotel, and Hotel Dreyfus, to name a few. Vaudeville theaters began popping up all over the city with saloons in close pursuit. Before widespread theater became popular, Providence hosted numerous "public lecture halls." Shakespeare Hall came first, located on Dorrance Street. Later, Howard Hall was built on its footprint. The great halls hosted renowned orators such as Jenny Lind, Sam Houston, Tom Thumb, and Edgar Allan Poe. The Providence Opera House, opened in 1871 at Dorrance and Pine streets, continued in its popularity through the early years of the 20th century.

Among the most popular theaters in Providence in the early part of the century was the Albee Theater. The theater's proprietor, Edward F. Albee, had a keen understanding of Providence's entertainment business. He saw the businessmen from New York, Connecticut, and Massachusetts coming into the city on trains each day and leaving before dinner each night. He knew that Providence had to do something more to attract these wealthy patrons to its theaters,

*Albee Theater in downtown Providence. Courtesy of the Providence Public Library
Digital Collections, Rhode Island Photograph Collection.*

halls, opera houses, and stages. Providence needed something to make them stay. New York City, the epicenter of the luxury hotel, already boasted dozens of expensive hotels such as the Plaza, the Commodore, and the Waldorf-Astoria. In order to attract those in high society—the Vanderbilts, Astors, Morgans, Rockefellers, and others—a city needed a high-class hotel. In 1919, Albee wrote to Providence's Mayor Joseph H. Gainer, and the message was clear: it was time for luxury accommodations in downtown Providence.

This was not the first request from local businessmen to improve the hospitality options in the bustling manufacturing city. In a 1915 article in *The Providence Journal*, it was reported that the Providence

Chamber of Commerce had met at the Narragansett Hotel, a modest 250-room hotel located at the corner of Dorrance and Weybosset Streets, to discuss the city's needs. Henry A. Carpenter, president of the Chamber, presided over the meeting, which covered a broad range of topics from support of ship subsidies to criticisms of William Jennings Bryan. The reporter noted that when Carpenter mentioned that a new hotel was proposed in the city, it was "greeted with much applause." The Narragansett Hotel, the city's most prestigious hotel at that time and still a considerably modest one in the parlance of the day, was not up to the standards of the types of people the Chamber of Commerce wanted to attract to the city. However, plans for a new hotel were delayed, due in part to the war effort that consumed the United States in 1917.

When planning resumed, the Chamber of Commerce committee charged with pursuing and financing the new hotel cut no corners when approaching hotelmen to explore the new project with the city. The country's most prominent hoteliers were approached, including John McEntee Bowman (General Manager of the New York Biltmore) and E.M. Statler (of the Statler Hotels Corporation).

Statler's high-efficiency luxury hotels, most notably the newest Hotel Pennsylvania in New York City, were gaining notoriety across the United States, and he was the early frontrunner to manage the new hostelry in Providence. Early plans with Statler were postponed in 1915 but resumed with gusto in post-war 1919, when the Chamber of Commerce pushed to move forward with their aim for the luxury hotel. Statler told the Chamber that he would only be interested in moving forward with the plan if the hotel was to be the sole hotel project in the city. Given Statler's propensity for standardization across his hotels, he also was less interested in a rebuild of the existing Narragansett Hotel, which was the initial aim of the Chamber. It was during discussions with Statler that the Chamber resolved to pull the plug on rebuilding the Narragansett Hotel and focus instead on new construction.

Photograph of Butts Block, site chosen for construction of Providence's new luxury hotel. Photograph taken in 1915. Courtesy of the Providence Public Library Digital Collections, Rhode Island Photograph Collection.

The Chamber explored several locations for a new hotel, ultimately landing on a piece of land then known as Butts Block, a triangular plot at the intersection of Washington Street and Dorrance Street owned by the estate of George W. Butts. On the site presently were a number of small stores, including Reiner's Pharmacy. The plot was across the street from City Hall and cater-corner to the city's central train and trolley hub, Union Station. The proximity to the train station was key. All successful luxury hotels of this era were built in close proximity to train stations. The first known book on hotel management, written in 1848 by an African American abolitionist, pastor, and community organizer by the name of Tunis G. Campbell, outlined the railway-hotel connection explicitly. After working as the head waiter at the Howard Hotel in New York City early in his life, Campbell published the seminal work *Hotel Keepers, Head Waiters, and Housekeepers' Guide.* In it, Campbell insisted that every hotel manager must be intimately familiar with the networks of transportation and accommodation in his region. A.K. Sandoval-Strausz notes in his book, *Hotel: An American History,* that Campbell pioneered modern hospitality service, which recognized the integral role that hotel managers must play in the comprehensive travel experience of each guest. Campbell advised that the dining room at any hotel "should be ready an hour before any rail-road cars or steamboats start…and for an hour after the arrival of the same."

Drawing of Tunis Campbell from his book, Hotel Keepers, Head
Waiters, and Housekeepers Guide, *1848.*

Indeed, this intersection of transit and hospitality persisted.
Menus from some of the most famous hotels in New York City
not only listed the evening's dining options, but also listed the train
schedules on the very first page. This trend continued throughout
the early part of the 20th century. At the end of Prohibition, when
the Commodore Hotel in New York City constructed a 125-foot
bar (self-proclaimed the longest in the world), they also erected an
enormous, illuminated board behind the bar that showed all the local

train schedules. A newspaper reported at the time that, "for safety, the clock [behind the bar] will always be set five minutes ahead."

Thus, the choice of Butts Block for Providence's newest hotel was perfect. *The Providence Journal* printed in October 1919 that the Chamber committee assigned to the project, chaired by Alfred L. Aldred, had completed negotiations for land to build a "first-class house" in downtown. *The Journal* applauded the choice of site for the hotel, noting that the triangular lot on Exchange Place would allow for an optimal amount of rooms to have outward facing windows, fresh air, and be out of the traffic of other, busier streets. It also noted that the hotel would be "just steps" from Union Station.

The Chamber, while securing the location, continued to vet hotel operators across the country for bids to operate the hotel. Continuing to show interest in the project, E.M. Statler made a visit to Providence from New York in October 1919 to review the chosen site for the hotel. John McEntee Bowman visited shortly thereafter, after returning from Cuba where he was working on the development of the Havana Biltmore. Reporting at the time made clear that the negotiations for management of this new hotel were highly competitive, and the Providence Chamber was persistent in choosing the most qualified visionary for their project.

When the Journal reported that the new hotel was "assured" in October 1919, they noted that "the establishment will be adapted first to the needs of businessmen stopping in the city, but it will not be lacking in facilities to care for any social demands that may be upon it." Early projections estimated that a hotel of this stature would cost the city $3,000,000. Just a few days after the paper reported that the building was assured, they announced that the debate over hotel operators was over: John McEntee Bowman of the Biltmore-Bowman Hotel Corporation and partner, Lou C. Wallick, would own and operate the hotel on a 15-year lease. The President of the Chamber proudly told the paper that the glamorous hotel would be "the last word in a modern commercial hotel." The Providence Biltmore

John McEntee Bowman. Photo courtesy of the Library of Congress.

Hotel Company was formed shortly thereafter for the express purpose of building, owning, and operating the hotel in Providence, incorporating on June 10, 1920 under the general corporation law in the state of Delaware, and marking the beginning of the iconic hotel brand in downtown Providence.

Though Bowman was well known in the hotel world, his notoriety was still less than the famed E.M. Statler. Why, then, did the Chamber decide to snub Statler and the national reputation that he brought with him? While the details of this decision remain a mystery, it is likely due to the nature of the hotels that Bowman was constructing around the country. Far more luxurious and palatial than the standardized Statler hotels, Bowman's newly formed hotel corporation was stretching the imagination of luxury-seekers across the country. Bowman was also known to be quite the charmer, and this could not have hurt negotiations with Providence's business leaders.

Gustav Baumann, President of the Beaux-Site Hotel Corp. and Proprietor of Holland House. Photo courtesy of Cornell University Library.

Born in Toronto in 1875, John McEntee Bowman came to the United States at the age of 17, alone and with barely enough money for taxi fare. His first hotel job landed him at the Waumbeck summer resort on Saranac Lake, New York. But when the season ended, he found himself without a job. He traveled to New York City, the epicenter of hostelries in the United States, to pursue his dream of working in larger hotels. He began by writing letters to several leading hotel men in the city. The letters were in vain, and young John worked odd jobs for nearly five years, including as a horse-handler and, later, a trainer at Durland's Riding Academy on Columbus Circle. It was here he would meet Gustav Baumann, an established hotelman in the city. It was this introduction that would gain John a minor position at Baumann's Holland House hotel on 5th Avenue.

John Bowman was kindhearted and likable, not to mention

strikingly good looking, with a handsome and strong build. His winning smile and congeniality were contagious, and his loyalty gained him the trust and respect of fellow hotel workers. During his first few months at Holland House, John would walk the hotel from the lower kitchen to the roof, almost daily. He was deeply invested in learning the intricate workings of the hotel, and his determination gained him respect from Gustav Baumann, who promptly promoted John to hotel secretary. In the years that followed, the friendship between Gustav and John would be called a "father-son relationship" by *Maclean's* magazine, which later featured John at the height of his ascension in the hotel world.

A reporter for *Maclean's* wrote in 1917 that "not a great many years ago the Holland House patronage outgrew the hotel's capacity to accommodate it and Baumann began to consider the erection of a new hotel. His attention was directed to a site at the corner of Fifth Avenue and Twenty-fifth Street, which was at the time regarded as pretty well up-town. Many of his friends favored this location and urged him to build there, but [John] Bowman was dead against it. His bump of foresight warned him that Twenty-fifth Street would soon be left far behind in the rapid movement of business northward. He had already seized upon the fact that the Grand Central terminal zone was the strategic point for large hotel developments and in the end he was able to persuade Mr. Baumann to the same belief."

It was at John's direction that Baumann pursued the area adjacent to Grand Central Station for the new hotel, resulting in the birth of the very first Biltmore Hotel. While the hotel is described as John's brainchild, it was sponsored by Gustav's riches. The Beau-Site Company was organized under Gustav to erect the Biltmore, easily attracting investors who trusted Gustav due to his long history in successful hotel management. John Bowman became the general manager and VP of the company upon its formation.

The new hotel was financed in large part by the New York Central Railroad, the colossus company of railroad magnate Cornelius

"Commodore" Vanderbilt. When the company's realty division agreed to finance hotels in New York City, they chose the Vanderbilt family name to brand their new investments. The name "Biltmore" originated from the Asheville, North Carolina estate of one of Cornelius's heirs, George Washington Vanderbilt II. The name combined the Dutch *De Bilt* (Vanderbilt's ancestors' place of origin in the Netherlands) with *more* (*mōr*, Anglo-Saxon for "moor," an open, rolling land).

While G.W. Vanderbilt's siblings were building palatial mansions in Newport, the younger of the Vanderbilt heirs preferred the rolling hills and bucolic peacefulness of his mother's beloved Asheville. The Biltmore estate became a choice destination for America's celebrity socialites, and included visits from US Presidents, senators, giants of Wall Street, and notable writers and artists, thus sealing the reputation and iconic brand of the Biltmore name. Leveraging this fame seemed like an obvious choice to the Central Railroad investors. By naming the New York hotel after the already-famous estate, they aimed to draw the same elite crowd that had already been accustomed to the opulence of the Vanderbilt estate in Asheville to the new hotel.

With the financial backing of the Central Railroad and the esteemed leadership of Gustav Baumann, the New York Biltmore was destined for greatness. Baumann secured the architectural firm Warren and Wetmore, who had designed the adjacent Grand Central Train Station, in the design and construction of the hotel. The New York Biltmore was a tremendous success from its first days in operation. Ads ran across the country highlighting its prime proximity to the major train station and one's ability to enter the hotel from an entrance within the station, eliminating the need for taxis or walking along the busy New York streets. The hotel boasted a massive ballroom, various restaurants, and every amenity imaginable for men and women of the time. What came next, however, shocked the hotel community.

On the morning of October 14, 1914, Gustav Baumann was making his usual rounds of the hotel, chatting with employees. After a brief discussion with an employee in the carpentry shop, Baumann walked out to the 22nd floor balcony overlooking the rooftop gardens below. Exactly what occurred in the following moments remains a mystery, but just minutes later the 61-year-old hotel magnate was found dead by a hotel waiter, his body having fallen 11 stories onto the garden path.

It is not unlikely that Gustav Baumann threw himself from the New York Biltmore's 22nd floor on that fateful day. Despite the prevailing account that he had lost his balance while leaning over the three-foot parapet, it was reported a few weeks later that his estate at the time of his death was worth $190,000, down from $4 million just two years prior. If only he'd known that the recession of 1914 would soon be ending, and perhaps with it would have come a turnaround in the hotelman's fortunes. Given their close relationship, Baumann's death must have come as a painful shock to John Bowman, who was quickly moved into general management of the hotel by the investors. But if his heart ached in grief for his mentor, John didn't have much time to lament the loss. Very shortly after becoming the General Manager of the New York Biltmore, Bowman dissolved Gustav's Beau-Site Company, replacing it with his own, newly formed Bowman Hotel Company. In the latter part of 1915, the Bowman Hotel Co. took over full management of the New York Biltmore.

Maclean's dubbed John Bowman the "fairy prince" of the hotel world and noted that he was introducing a brand-new system of hotel management into the operation of the Biltmore. Managers of other hotels around the country were following his lead, making him a trendsetter. "Instead of trying to handle the bulk of the work with one or two assistants," the reporter wrote, "he has surrounded himself with what might be called a 'cabinet' of assistants, each one of whom, as manager, is responsible for someone department of the hotel organization. These men are chosen for their particular fitness for their work, with the result that the entire system runs smoothly and efficiently, each department standing on its own bottom, its head being responsible to the chief himself...Mr. Bowman belongs to a new race of hotel managers."

Bowman was building a veritable hotel empire when he was approached by Arthur Aldred, President of Gladding's Department Store and the Providence City Chamber of Commerce, to consider a new project in the manufacturing hub of New England. With projects in development all across the country and in Cuba, Bowman needed a partner to help with the Providence deal. Lou C. Wallick was less known than John Bowman but no less qualified. Lou came from a long line of hotel men, his father W.L. Wallick having owned and operated hotels in Ohio, Pennsylvania, and New York. Lou was one of five boys in his family, all of whom had business connections in the hotel industry. He was formal partners with his brother, London Wallick, with whom he operated the famous Cadillac Hotel in New York before selling it to focus on the Providence Biltmore. Lou was, perhaps, most famous for his ownership of the Secor Hotel in Toledo, OH, and later the Deschler Hotel in Columbus. He and his wife ultimately settled in New Jersey, however, and while he remained President of the Providence Biltmore, operations of the hotel were left mainly up to his son until the hotel changed hands two-and-a-half decades later.

Maclean's took note of the team. There was a time, they wrote, when a hotelkeeper, "while often a very worthy citizen, was looked down upon by the better classes in the community. Hotelkeeping was not exactly a genteel business. Today, the profession, if such it may be called, is being raised to a dignity and importance more in keeping with its standing in the business world. The management of such huge establishments as the Biltmore and the Commodore is the work of no ordinary man. It requires genius of a high order to control their complex operation." Genius was exactly what Providence was looking for, and in Bowman and Wallick, that is precisely what they got.

2

BE A BOOSTER!

"It seems to me a matter of regret that the name to be applied to the new hotel to be erected in Providence should not be one to perpetuate some strictly local historical name. I would suggest the name of Roger Williams be given consideration at the present time. There are of course many other Providence and Rhode Island names that could be applied with equal interest but the name of Roger Williams is in my opinion the very best that could be applied."

—*Letter to the Editor,* The Providence Journal
November 1919, Henry S. Robinson, Barrington, RI.

While Bowman and Wallick retained the right to name the hotel, the Biltmore name was not without controversy. Providence has always been a city proud of its heritage. It makes sense, then, that the city's first luxury hotel, which was financed largely by the city's denizens themselves, commanded pride and ownership from city residents.

Op-ed pieces like the one quoted above from as early as 1919 expressed the residents' discontent with these "out-of-towners" placing a foreign brand on the city's newest development. The Chamber of Commerce responded in March 1920 to what had obviously

Advertisement from 1920 encourages the citizens of Providence to invest in the Biltmore. Obtained from The Providence Journal *historic archives.*

become a growing public concern over the Biltmore's name. In a half-page ad in *The Providence Journal* entitled, bluntly, "Why Call It The Biltmore?," the Chamber wrote:

> "Local history is rich in names that could be applied to the proposed new hotel with all propriety. Why, then, call it the Biltmore? The

value and prestige of a name that is known the world over for service and excellence in hotel management. The Biltmore in New York—the Biltmore in Providence, and, before many years have passed, Biltmore Hotels in other large cities in the United States will be recognized for their high standards by the traveling public, even as the trademark on a piece of merchandise is a guide to assured quality in any corner of the map. When the Providence Biltmore is completed, it will have no peer in New England. Through its presence in our city, Providence will take its rightful place among the most progressive cities on this continent."

A follow-up statement made by Alfred Aldred to the paper in January 1920 assured that while the architects and managers were from out of state, preference would be given to local businesses on contract work in connection with erection of the structure. That settled it. The Providence Biltmore would be named as such, with the belief that its name would carry the city to its rightful place among the greatest cities in America and beyond.

While the building was being designed and lawyers were carefully mapping out the capitalization plan, the Chamber of Commerce began to realize the challenges they would have in financing the construction of the hotel. By December 1919, the approximate cost of the hotel was suggested to be $3,500,000. By the end of January, the estimate had gone up a million dollars, to $4,500,000. The initial contract included that Bowman and Wallick would finance a portion of the hotel from their own assets—approximately $700,000—for which they would be paid second preferred stock on par with their investment. In January 1920, it was announced that the Chamber would hold a four-day drive for stock subscriptions to the 7 percent cumulative first preferred stock, in which the citizens of Providence and surrounding territory would be urged to participate.

Costs continued to climb. Before the public fundraising effort began, the cost of construction exceeded $5,000,000. In order to reach as many Providence denizens as possible for the campaign, the Chamber enlisted the support of fraternal organizations and brokerage houses, encouraging all businesses to contribute as well as to spread the word. To begin the fundraising campaign, the hotel corporation issued 25,000 first preferred stock at $100 a share. The stock would begin to accumulate on July 1, 1922. The second preferred stock was to be issued solely to Bowman and Wallick for their investment in furnishing the hotel. The pair purchased an additional $250,000 in second preferred stock to safeguard against the chance that the first preferred stock was not sufficient to pay the mortgage and for the land and construction. The second preferred stock was not able to be "retired until the mortgage and first preferred stock are paid off or retired," according to reporting in the *Journal*.

The public campaign was launched in March 1920 at the direction of a Public Financing Campaign committee, headed by Howard J. Greene. The committee was made up of more than 130 individuals, divided into 10 teams that would solicit different districts of the city. This strategy ensured that every possible citizen could be reached with the campaign prospectus. The Chamber of Commerce minced no words in their encouragement of the city's residents to partake in the public campaign. On March 12, 1920, they ran a strongly worded half-page advertisement that read:

Night after night the trains carry away from Providence those who find it impossible to secure a night's lodging here. Back they come in the morning—these men and women whose wares our merchants must buy—whose ideas our manufacturers must know of— whose money would help to make better business in Providence. A fine taste of hospitality they get! A wonderful impression of progressiveness they conceive of us! You can imagine what travelling men say—how the news is spread as they while away time in the smokers! Even Pullman porters, ever ready to advertise the first time visitor, put the jinx mark on our doorstep with their stories of the lack of hotel facilities here. This must be stopped! Not by continued grumbling at conditions as they are, but by a real, earnest effort to put through the plan which public-spirited men have labored long and arduously to bring to a head. You'll have your chance next week. You'll have the chance to help wipe out the city's greatest blot. Look eagerly for news of the Providence-Biltmore Hotel and the campaign which opens next Tuesday. Get a copy of the prospectus—all details are contained in it. Most banks and the Chamber of Commerce in Providence have a supply ready for you.

The scathing advertisement was bordered by a poem:

If you want to live in the kind of town,
Like the kind of town you like,
You needn't pack your clothes in a grip,
And start on a long, long hike,
For you'll only find what you left behind,
For there's nothing that's really new,
It's a knock at yourself when you knock your town,
It isn't your town—it's you!

—

Be a Booster!
Providence will be more like the kind of town you want it to be if you help to put up the Providence Biltmore.

—

The onslaught of public advertising worked. Public interest was strong on the first day of the campaign. *The Journal* published detailed instructions on how people could get in on the first preferred stocks, advising them that they only had four days to do so. Included on the ads were a coupon that could be filled out with one's request for stock and sent, with cash or check, to the Rhode Island Hospital Trust Company, care of the Campaign.

The Outlet Co., one of Providence's largest department stores, cashed in on the public interest in the campaign by running a contest. The first baby born in Providence on March 16, 1920 (the opening day of the campaign) would be awarded the very first preferred stock in the Providence Biltmore Hotel Company. Thus, at 6:30 a.m. on that morning, baby Thomas B. Carville was born and became the first shareholder in the new hotel. The management of the Outlet Co. called the Health Commissioner to confirm which baby was deemed "the day's first," and then submitted the name of Thomas B. (for Biltmore) Carville to the paper. The Outlet Co. would continue to play a pivotal role in the life of the hotel throughout the 20th century, even saving it from assured destruction more than 50 years later.

Further efforts to incentivize investment on opening day of the campaign included the sale of "trips" up the Biltmore's brand-new elevators to the roof garden atop the hotel. These elevator excursions were advertised for sale in the Journal for $100 a trip, payable in five installments of $20. Of course, this was before anyone knew what sort of menagerie the Wallick family had in mind for the Biltmore roof. Even without that knowledge, the trips were eagerly scooped up by well-heeled adventure seekers in the city.

Despite the onslaught of advertisements, contests, and gimmicks in the paper, the four-day campaign fell significantly short of its goal. The Chamber extended the campaign by several weeks. Then on April 7th, Mayor of Providence, Joseph Gainer, extended it himself, requesting that the financing committee not let the project fall short when fundraising had already achieved nearly 85 percent of its goal. However, despite these efforts, *The Providence Journal* again reported that the project had stalled, and the $2,500,000 in first preferred stock had not been scooped up by the public as anticipated. In a desperate printed plea, Chamber committee leader Howard Greene implored the public to find out which of their friends had not yet purchased stock and to encourage them to do so for the good of the city.

When the citizens of the city failed to purchase all the necessary stock, Chamber representatives Aldred and Greene traveled to New York to find out about alternative funding options. After a long series of meetings, Aldred sent the message back to Rhode Island that "interested parties in New York" would foot the remainder of the bill. In total, 21,000 shares of first preferred stock were sold to over 1,800 individuals and corporations. On May 7th, the citizens of Providence received the final word. "The Providence Biltmore Hotel is Assured!," the front page of the *Journal* proclaimed.

After the sale of stock was completed, the committee arranged a mortgage through Metropolitan Life Insurance Company to provide the remaining $1,900,000 needed for the land and building. The deal was secured and the hotel project, after much fanfare and public drama, would finally be moving forward. The Chamber's campaign that ensured the success of the hotel was hailed as "the greatest single achievement of Chambers of Commerce in the United States" at the Annual Meeting of the National Organization of Chamber of Commerce Secretaries in October 1920.

3

PALACES OF THE PEOPLE

When the Providence Biltmore was signed into existence by the Chamber of Commerce, the Chamber's President announced that the Biltmore would be all things to all people. It did not disappoint. In a statement to *The Providence Journal*, Chamber President Aldred stated, "The Committee came to the conclusion that what was needed most was a first-class commercial hotel in the heart of the city and was of the opinion that such an establishment, while accommodating the many transients stopping in the city, could also provide living quarters for many permanent guests." Designing a hotel to meet all of these needs would be a feat in and of itself.

Hotels, in the form we know them today, are uniquely American by design. When the transportation boom of the mid-19th century occurred, hospitality houses began popping up all along the roads, waterways, and later, the train lines that dotted America's northeast, midwest, west, and south. The hotel became the contemporary outgrowth of the taverns and inns of the Revolutionary period, intended to provide not just a modest bed but an experience to be remembered.

The first luxury hotels were heralded as "palaces of the people," with their popularity growing rapidly in early 19th century Boston,

New York, and Washington DC. From these early beginnings, four variations of hotels took shape: the resort hotel, often built in rustic, bucolic settings and offering an escape for upscale patrons to get away from the hustle and bustle of city life; the commercial hotel, which targeted merchants, salesmen, and other businesspeople for whom travel was essential to their trade and which often provided "sample rooms" for merchants to showcase their wares; middle-class hotels, which were designed more modestly and intended to accommodate respectable but less affluent travelers; and lastly, the luxury hotel—far less in number but capturing the imagination of all who saw them as the "opulent manifestation" of what a hotel should be. These included sprawling residential apartments, luxurious guestrooms, private baths, expansive ballrooms, and decadent dining.

Author Julie Satow notes in her book *The Plaza* that, beginning around the 1890s, the elite of society had used hotels as a setting to show off their wealth and success. The 300-foot marble corridor at the Waldorf-Astoria in New York City was named Peacock Alley and provided the setting for which New York's upper crust flaunted their prestige. With the new phenomenon of luxury hotel-apartments, Satow noted, "it became popular to go out to restaurants and eat among strangers, and to spend evenings ballroom dancing to an orchestra with hundreds of other couples. The Plaza and its compatriots became preeminent places to show off, enjoy one's wealth, and cement one's status in high-society." In luxury hotels, one "could march through the lobby in the latest fashion and be assured of appearing in the society column, the hotel hallway being clogged with reporters in search of gossip to fill the next day's papers."

The Providence Biltmore was one of a small class of new luxury hotels that aimed to combine the myriad functions of its predecessors. Like its New York predecessor, the Biltmore was designed in the Beaux-Arts style of the time by prominent architectural firm Warren and Wetmore. Whitney Warren and his partner Charles Delevan Wetmore were already world-renowned, having designed

Women of high society at Mrs. Astor's Society Tableaux. New York, 1919.
Photo courtesy of the George Grantham Bain Collection of The Library of Congress.

Grand Central Station in New York City; the Ritz–Carlton, Biltmore, Commodore, and Ambassador Hotels in New York; the Vanderbilt Hotel in Puerto Rico; multiple train stations under the New York Central Railroad, of whom they were the preferred architects; the Newport Country Club; and countless other buildings and terminals. Warren was a cousin to the Vanderbilt family and spent 10 years at the École des Beaux–Arts in Paris, as exemplified in his design of the Providence Biltmore. Wetmore was a lawyer by trade and one of Warren's earliest clients. Warren then convinced Wetmore to join him as a partner in his firm to run the business side of Warren and Wetmore. Warren's close society connections through his family ties led his firm to secure many lucrative and steady clients, particularly projects funded in whole or in part by the Vanderbilts.

The 1921 Warren and Wetmore plans stated that the new hotel in Providence was to be 19 stories high with 560 guest rooms, with the first floor being occupied exclusively by merchant shops,

WHITNEY WARREN   3695-2

Biltmore architect Whitney Warren. Courtesy of the George
Grantham Bain Collection of the Library of Congress.

totaling 12,000 square feet of commercial space. The decadent lobby would occupy the second floor, lifting the guests from the hustle of the streetscape to a literal and figurative higher ground within the hotel. The grand staircase was marble, adorned with decorative urns. And, nodding to the recent Egyptology craze, the ornate ceiling was adorned in Egyptian-style carvings, as well as mythical creatures such as griffins. The lobby, office, lounge, main dining room, café, and kitchen were all to be housed on floor two. Above, a writing room, private dining rooms, auditor's office, housekeeping office, valet, barber shop, women's hair salon, manicurist, and toilet rooms would meet the varying needs of the guests. The fourth floor consisted of "sample rooms," a popular innovation of the contemporary hotel, which were spaces for traveling salesmen to present their wares to the public. Each sample room was equipped with a bedroom and bath for the merchant.

The 5th through 17th floors were to be guest rooms, with the "L" shaped design of the hotel allowing for every single guestroom to have a window and outside view. This was virtually unheard of in that time, when many hotels included "inside rooms," void of natural light and air flow. On the 12th floor were suites, larger rooms equipped with parlors featuring fortepianos, reading desks, and writing desks. There were also salon rooms which consisted of living rooms and a bedroom connected to a smaller auxiliary room. All other standard guest rooms featured a large double bed or two twin beds.

The top floor of the Biltmore was to be its most luxuriant. A two-story ballroom was designed with massive windows, allowing for sumptuous air flow even in summer's warmest months and cozy, scenic dining in the cold of winter. This design mimicked the New York Biltmore's famous Cascades Ballroom, which doubled as a roof garden in summer months and was transformed seasonally to meet the needs of the hotel guests. The Providence Biltmore was to include the most technologically advanced hotel features available in that time, including elevators in multiple sizes that were separated entirely from the guestrooms to reduce noise pollution; vacuum cleaning systems; telautograph systems; a system to signal for maid service; pneumatic tube systems; compressed air and ventilating systems; a refrigeration plant; and a garbage incinerator. As originally promised by the Chamber of Commerce, the majority of supplies and materials for construction of the Biltmore came from Rhode Island's own family-run businesses.

Photo from the Providence Evening Bulletin *featuring the Biltmore under construction in 1921.*

The building was constructed to be "fireproof," in the terms of the day. It was supported by a steel frame built with 2,500 tons of steel from Hedden Iron Construction Company. New England Granite Works supplied the granite. It was then enclosed with limestone and covered in Harvard brick, made in Rhode Island. The steel trimmings were believed to protect the structure from the fires that had plagued hotels in other cities. Indeed, the modern construction did not go unnoticed by the hotel industry. In the June 1922 edition of industry magazine *The Hotel World,* the author noted that the Providence Biltmore was, without a doubt, the most fireproof modern structure of its day.

The belief in its fireproof nature held up when, in January 1928, a massive fire in the sub-basement storeroom engulfed a large area, sending billows of smoke outward that overcame more than 20 firefighters. Despite the flames and smoke, the fire never spread outside the storeroom, credit being given to the intentionally fireproof design of the building. So confident were the managers in the fireproof nature of the hotel that they never alerted the guests, and no one was asked to leave the building during the three-hour battle against the blaze. According to a report in *The Boston Daily Globe*, not even a whiff of smoke reached the lobby.

"The exterior is a masterpiece," read *The Hotel World* in its June 1922 issue. "And the interior is a work of art. Rare and costly rugs adorn the floors, and the ceilings and walls are covered with exquisite designs of the decorator's taste and genius. Potted palms and flowers in profusion lend softness to the foyers, making them inviting and restful."

The Biltmore's interior rooms and suites were so well-appointed that they served as natural advertisements for the city's local businesses. Ads were placed in *The Providence Journal* drawing attention to certain aspects of the hotel and noting where you could purchase those goods in the city. One such ad, placed by Phillips Lead & Supply, noted that guests of the Biltmore would no doubt marvel

Postcards depicting the Biltmore Hotel's lobby on opening day in 1922.
Courtesy of the Graduate Providence.

at the "shining beauty" of the plumbing fixtures in the bathrooms—
and one could easily procure such fixtures for their own homes by
contacting Phillips Lead & Supply Co. at their South Main Street
office. Everything about the Biltmore was to be leveraged for the
benefit of the city and its commerce—all the way down to the toilet
drains. Total construction of this opulent landmark took 18 months
and 14 days, at a cost of over $5,000,000 for land, equipment, and
construction.

Advertisement from June 1922 showcasing rugs being used at the new Biltmore hotel.
The Providence Journal, *1922.*

4

OPENING DAY

"The opening of this wonderful hotel is an epoch. It was brought to a realization through the energy, progressive spirit and civic pride of the businessmen of the city."

—*The Hotel World,* 1922.

A brutal heatwave was extending across New England on June 6, 1922. The city was abuzz despite the heat, with throngs of people lining the grassy mall in front of the Providence Biltmore in the hot afternoon sun to catch a glimpse of the elite guests arriving on private Pullmans with the afternoon train. Opening day at the hotel was by invitation only, and the city's denizens packed the streets around Exchange Place to see who had made the cut. Men, women, and children clamored over one another, craning their necks to view the high society guests disembarking from the trains. The entire scene played out to the soundtrack of a live 50-piece orchestra, booming across the city from the Biltmore's second-story terrace.

The Hotel World had sent its editor, Charles Gerhring, to tour the hotel the day before its opening. He returned to New York to print the preliminary findings and then came back to Providence

Advertisement for opening day at the Providence Biltmore Hotel.
The Providence Journal, *1922.*

the following day with the delegation from that city. "The hotel is one of the first of Providence's sights as one steps onto the city's beautiful mall from the railroad station," wrote Gerhring. "When you step from your Pullman the ease with which you can go to the Providence Biltmore will be the first thing that gives you a thrill of delight. You eliminate cab drivers, taxis, guides, and run into no congestion of traffic."

In addition to Rhode Island Governor Emery J. San Souci, Providence Mayor Joseph Gainer; the City Council; the Secretary of State; the RI General Treasurer; President William Faunce of Brown University; the Mayors of Newport, Pawtucket, Central Falls, and Cranston; several prominent senators and representatives;

city and state judges; and the most prominent Rhode Island merchants and tradesmen, a delegation of highbrow guests from across New England and New York City were among those invited to attend. The New York delegation was scheduled to depart from Grand Central Station that morning, arriving at 3:35 p.m. in Providence's Union Station. Providence's eager spectators were made to wait and swelter in the late afternoon heat, however, because the train blew a flue in Stamford and a repair was needed. The out-of-town guests pulled into Union Station just past 4 o'clock.

Among those scheduled to arrive on the 3:35 p.m. train were:

- Charles A. Abbey
- Robert Adamson (a banker and PR professional who was the former Fire Commissioner of N.Y. City)
- Harry Alexander
- Harry Barth (president of Barth Hotel Corp. in NYC)
- George J. Bascom
- Paul B. Boden
- Frank A.K. Boland (of the New York City Hotel Association)
- John G. Boggs (proprietor of Laurelton Hotel in New York)
- H. H. Brown (of H. H. Brown Shoe Company)
- Charles E. Burchell
- John S. Buzzini (a hotel real estate broker)
- Frank Byrne
- B. A. Callingham
- Earle E. Carley (a prominent stockbroker and friend to the Vanderbilts and Goulds)
- Jean Cauchois (of the Cauchois Coffee Co., the leading provider of coffee, teas, and spices to luxury hotels)
- Henry Coucherie
- Charles Clark
- Col. Charles H. Consolvo (owner-operator of the Monticello Hotel in Norfolk as well as the Jefferson Hotel in Richmond)
- John Droham
- I. Fluegelman
- Edward C. Fogg (managing director of New York's Plaza hotel)
- Simon Friedberger (a mill-owner from Philadelphia)

- M. J. Gramont
- E.C. Green (President of the New York State Hotel Association)
- Thomas D. Green (manager of the Woodward Hotel)
- Thomas Gresham (a well-known businessman from Richmond, VA who held significant stock in a number of hotels)
- Albert Guggenheim (president of Kienzler Distillery Co. of New York)
- E. V. Hartigan
- August Houser
- Dr. William F. Healey (a prominent surgeon from New York)
- Mabel Keating Healey (William's wife)
- Walter L. Hopkins (a NY architect)
- James E. Johnson
- Mrs. M. B. Keating
- A B. Kelleher
- Albert Keller (President of the Ritz-Carlton Hotel Corp.)
- Henry Kelly Jr. (founder of George Ehlenberger & Co., a produce and dairy business in New York)
- Theodore Kemm (hotel manager and wine steward)
- George Ketcham
- Carl H. Klappert
- Herman E. Klappert
- J. Kooser
- Willard A. Krayer (fruit and vegetable purveyor from NYC)
- Robert Maffitt (a close friend of John Bowman and VP of the Bowman-Biltmore Hotel chain)
- Homer. R. Mallow (of the Hotel Sterling in Wilkes-Barre, PA)
- Nathan Sweitzer (a poultry and wild game supplier from NY)
- Raymond Silz (hotel proprietor)
- George Sweeney (the manager of Hotel Commodore in NYC)
- Edward M. Tierney (President of the American Hotel Association of the United States and Canada)
- Arthur Taylor (banker)
- E. H. Titus (treasurer of Lord & Taylor and friend of Lou Wallick)
- L. H. VanCleft
- London I. Wallick (brother and business partner of Lou Wallick)
- George Wallen (President of the Metropolitan Opera)
- Jules Weber (wholesale grocer and importer of culinary delicacies)
- Samuel P Haldenstein (real estate investor)

- William P. Merritt
- Julius Manger (owner and operator of Hotel Netherland in NYC)
- Walton H. Marshall (manager of the Vanderbilt Hotel)
- Frank Matchett
- E. D. Miller (secretary and treasurer of the Bowman Hotels)
- A. F. Morril
- Jack O'Brien (ex-boxer and proprietor of health centers in New York)
- Charles H. Nollman
- John J. Page (owner of Blackford's fish dealers)
- F. N. Bain-Williamson
- Capt. Louis W. Parent
- E. M. Patison
- L. A. Peech
- Lucian B Prince
- W. Johnston Quinn
- Henry R. Reischmann (president of M. Reischmann and Sons, a furniture manufacturer)
- Harold Richardson (Richardson & Sons, a cheese importer)
- John M. Riehle (theatre executive)
- H. J. Russell (banker)
- Jack Schneider
- A. R. Smith
- Ebenezer Steer (president of Gray & Lampel custom tailors)

Based on the affiliations of these guests, it is clear that opening day at the Biltmore was intended to sufficiently woo the businessmen who had a stake in her success. From poultry purveyors and renowned cheese mongers to furniture manufacturers and high-end tailors, the managers of the Biltmore Hotel must have known that they needed to ensure the proprietors of their supply chain were thoroughly impressed. Perhaps they'd even come down on their prices if they saw a long-term contract in the hotel's successful future. It wasn't just manufacturers, grocers, and importers that were in attendance. Prominent distillery owners, who had diversified their portfolios since the passage of Prohibition, also attended. And of course, there were hotel men. Friends, colleagues, and investment partners of John Bowman and Lou Wallick came from their own establishments in New York, Pennsylvania, Virginia, and beyond to see the finest new hotel in the country.

CITY HALL AND PROVIDENCE BILTMORE HOTEL FROM THE PARK. PROVIDENCE, R. I.

Historic postcard featuring the Providence Biltmore Hotel and City Hall.
Author's collection.

From the hotel balcony, as guests arrived, a band played a concert to onlookers in Exchange Place who lined the mall. After a brief concert for the crowd, Greystone and his band crossed Exchange Place at 4 p.m. to lead the delegation of guests arriving from New York from Union Station to the hotel's grand entrance in a veritable parade. To commemorate the day, souvenirs were sold in shops all across the city, including silver spoons stamped with the hotel's image on the handle, sold for $5 a piece.

Every shop owner and business in downtown Providence wanted in on the Providence Biltmore's expected success. Advertisements flooded the *Journal* declaring the relocation of important and prosperous downtown shops to the Biltmore. Larchar-Horton, a local advertising company, announced in the paper on opening day that their agency had been chosen to lead national advertising for the hotel. Below this, Providence Gas Co. prominently featured the Biltmore and its state-of-the-art kitchens in its advertisement for home gas grills. Krasnow's Fine Jewelry ran an ad for an inventory removal sale at their Washington Street location to reduce inventory

The Biltmore's Garden Room set for dinner. Postcard from author's private collection.

before they moved to their "sumptuous new headquarters" at the Biltmore. Likewise, Gay's Art Galleries ran an ad a few days prior to the hotel's opening informing its patrons that as of June 6th it would be relocating its world-renowned photographic studio to the lobby of the Biltmore. An invitation was extended to the public to visit the new studio and enjoy having their portrait done—either by photograph or paintbrush. Real estate agents advertised commercial buildings for sale based on their proximity to the new luxury hotel. John Robinson, a realtor, advertised for sale: "Fifty acres, 2 miles from the Biltmore, where the manufacturer can build his factory as he has planned—increasing efficiency, cutting down old 'Mr. Overhead' and assured of plenty of good light and fresh air! Both factories and hotels are essential to a growing city—Providence is forging ahead!" Strategic placement of local papers in all incoming trains allowed expected hotel patrons to peruse the hotel's features and amenities alongside their respective purveyors' names and numbers, before their train arrived in the city. In addition to the relocation of popular downtown shops, the Biltmore's opening also marked the beginning of Providence's WEAN radio station, which began operation on the same day, using a 300-foot tower stationed on the roof of the hotel.

No detail was left to chance on opening day, by management or by any of the city's prominent businessmen. Of all the well-heeled men and women that were present on the opening day, perhaps one of the most fascinating is one who is nearly forgotten by the history books today. At the time, however, he was known throughout the northeast and across the country. This man was Dutee Wilcox Flint, and he was a Biltmore man, through and through.

5

THE RISE AND FALL OF DUTEE FLINT

I f the Biltmore was to be the most modern and well-equipped hotel in America at the time of its opening, then Dutee Flint wanted to be connected to it. Flint, a native Rhode Islander, was, at the time of the hotel's opening, the largest Ford automobile dealer in the United States. An entrepreneur, Flint's incredible wealth had its roots in his ambitious pursuit of a partnership with Henry Ford in the early days of the Ford auto empire.

It all began when a young Dutee was thumbing through the pages of a magazine aboard a train from Chicago to Providence in 1904. This young man of 22 was just beginning to imagine a future for himself, and even then, he sensed that his future included greatness. The grandson of Dutee Wilcox, a wealthy jewelry merchant in Providence, Dutee Flint had sales in his blood. Naturally, when he flipped open the advertisement from a newly incorporated automobile manufacturing company, the Ford Motor Company, he was intrigued. The advertisement simply called for "qualified individuals" to apply to become the first dealers of Ford's new Model A automobiles. Needless to say, when the train stopped in Detroit, young Dutee stepped off and into his future.

After securing a substantial overnight loan from his grandfather,

Photograph of a Ford dealership display room, 1925.
Courtesy of the Library of Congress.

Dutee arranged to meet with Henry Ford himself and locked in his first contract to bring a Ford dealership to his native Rhode Island. The vastness and speed at which Dutee built his empire shocked Providence and impressed Henry Ford. "My idea was that the train I was riding on, when I read about Ford in a magazine, was on wheels, that the horseless carriage was on wheels, that the whole future of the country was on wheels," Flint said in a 1953 interview, "and I wanted to get in on it. I was sure I had the right thing. Gramps was sold enough to lend me the money right away, and that's how I got started."

In the same interview, Flint shared that in 1905 he was selling just 10 cars a year; by 1910, he was selling more than 200. From there, his dealership empire grew by leaps and bounds. He doubled sales each year and expanded his dealerships into New York and New Jersey. The rate of growth was so astounding that in a letter to

Flint from Henry Ford, Ford stated that he considered Flint the best agent that he had. "There is no reason you will not continue to represent me as long as the Ford Motor Company builds automobiles," Ford wrote.

If ever there were a way to jinx a man, a statement like that may have been it.

Dutee made an incredible fortune in 10 short years, and he spent it lavishly. He and his wife Rose purchased a 32-room mansion on the water in the Edgewood section of Cranston, Rhode Island. Outside of business, Dutee was known as a master sailor and yachtsman. He owned the massive 140-foot *Halcyon* motor yacht, one of the largest pleasure boats on the Narragansett Bay at the time. From the teak deck, equipped with a revolutionary telephone system, Dutee conducted business in style as he and Rose sailed up and down the Bay, from their mansion in Edgewood to their summer residence in Newport or to their farm on Aquidneck. Dutee remained close friends with Clara and Henry Ford during these years of prosperity. It was aboard one of his yachts that Rose and Dutee transported the

Photograph of the Halcyon, Dutee and Rose Flint's motor yacht.
Courtesy of the Providence Public Library, Rhode Island Photograph Collection.

Fords to a clambake on Prudence Island in 1914—along with 75 employees of the Flint business enterprises. This friendship was not simply a business arrangement. Even after his spectacular decline, Flint refused to speak an ill word of Henry Ford, their relationship seemingly unbreakable despite the immense complications of their business dealings.

Dutee Flint was still in his glory on June 6, 1922, when hundreds of the region's most prestigious businessmen descended on Providence to witness the unveiling of John Bowman's newest hotel. By then, Dutee was one of the richest and most extravagant denizens of Providence. Beyond his automobile empire, he owned 37 gasoline stations across southern New England and several Lincoln dealerships. He also retained the patents on several of his inventions, including an improved gas pump for filling stations. Dutee was the first to employ the use of a converted steamship to transport cars, which he used to move his inventory from a plant in New Jersey to his Rhode Island assembly factories and dealerships. Prior to this innovation, trains were the primary mode of transport. With the introduction of the steamship *Transford*, Dutee revolutionized mass transport of cars up and down the seaboard.

Rose and Dutee loved nothing more than to show off their good fortune. They were known as consummate hosts and entertainers, so it is no surprise that Dutee quickly inserted himself into the opening day festivities of the Providence Biltmore. As the Pullman cars whistled their entry into Union Station, a long line of Dutee's Fords awaited a select group of passengers. After a short but scenic drive through downtown, nearly 200 guests arrived at Rose and Dutee's expansive Edgewood mansion. Guests were welcomed inside to gawk at Rose and Dutee's well-equipped estate on the water, their expansive view of the Bay, and Dutee's prized 2,200-piece pipe organ that he had recently installed in his home for concerts. The guests were then treated to a reception of a late afternoon lunch before being motored back for a 5 p.m. "inspection" of the hotel.

Dutee Flint was experiencing his financial crescendo on that celebratory day in June. In the blistering heat, he could never have known how rapidly the decline would be, and how far he could fall. At the end of that downward spiral, however, it would be the Biltmore that caught the Flints before their total ruin.

6

"THE HOTEL IS OURS."

While hundreds of guests from out of state enjoyed a lavish welcome in Providence on opening day, the honor of being the Biltmore's first official guest went to the city's mayor, Joseph H. Gainer. The mayor proudly strode through the main entranceway on Dorrance Street, leading the procession, who stared in awe at the beautiful lobby and adorning shops. Pausing to marvel at the grand staircase before ascending to the second floor, the mayor found himself at hotel check-in. Alongside the front desk, a newsstand, cigar stand, telegraph office, and telephone booths dotted the grand, open foyer. The foyer had high columns and a vaulted ceiling, and it was wrapped on three sides by a balcony that afforded guests a pleasing view of the street-level shops below. The lobby provided a great reprieve from the scorching heat of the June afternoon, which was recorded to be near 90 degrees by the late afternoon. With the sun beaming down through the large, front-facing windows, Mayor Gainer lifted the clerk's pen and signed his name, marking the first true moment of Biltmore hospitality history.

The hotel was completely sold out on opening night. Lou Wallick told writers at *The Hotel World* that the Biltmore staff had to turn requests for rooms away, something entirely unprecedented in that

Providence Mayor Joseph Gainer, first official guest of the Providence Biltmore Hotel. Photo from The History of the State of Rhode Island and Providence Plantations Biographical, *1920.*

day and age for luxury hotels. To alert the public, and no doubt to showcase their tremendous success, Bowman and Wallick ran an ad in *The Providence Journal* on the morning of June 6th with the heading, "You've Been Too Good to Us." The advertisement praised the city's denizens for their incredible patronage and vowed to live up to their expectations—but regretted to inform them that there were no vacancies remaining for opening night.

It was unusual that a hotel would have a "dress rehearsal" for a dinner, but the Biltmore's opening was such an affair that a dress rehearsal is precisely what occurred the day before it opened its doors. Head Chef Charles Riedinger (who came to the Providence

Biltmore from the New York Biltmore and was called a culinary wizard by *The Hotel World*) and Maître d'Hôtel Rudolph Hoffinger barked orders at the staff of 500 servers and cooks. They inspected waiters and omnibus men, ensuring that everyone understood the run of show for opening night. No detail was left to chance. The rehearsal included a lengthy lecture by the chef and maître d'hôtel before servers were sent about setting up for the grand ball.

To celebrate the grand success of opening day, the entire hotel was illuminated from the roof to the street with 25,000 lights. *The Providence Journal* reported the following day that "the big house glittered, sparkled, tinkled, and did a number of other things that were calculated to make the nerves tingle and the senses swim. If Messrs. Bowman and Wallick set out to stage a real eye-opener, it was the opinion of their company that they had succeeded in a way that would have provided material for a thousand fables of the prodigal."

With over 1,000 guests in attendance for the tour and dinner that evening, Wallick and Bowman spared no expense. 12,000 pieces of silver were employed in the use of the ballroom dinner service, as were 25,000 pieces of china and 30,000 pieces of linen. A banquet and culinary crew of over 725 individuals were employed, including at least 50 waiters that were temporarily borrowed from the Biltmore in New York. Dinner was priced at $10 per plate (approximately $150 in 2021 value). The guests were accommodated for dinner in every restaurant area of the hotel, with the dining room and grill room on the lobby floor overflowing and the most prominent guests treated to dinner in the grand ballroom. The tables in the ballroom were set with centerpieces of roses, sweat peas, and fern. Two consolidated orchestras brought up from the New York Biltmore were in attendance, conducted by Hazay Natzy.

Securing Charles Riedinger as head chef for the Providence Biltmore was a tremendous coup in the restaurant-centric culture of 1922 hospitality. Riedenger had been chef at the Plaza in New York and the New York Biltmore, as well as the Copley-Plaza in

Boston. He was renowned for his "culinary artistry," as well as for his presidential favor. A favorite of President Wilson's, the chef was aboard the steamship George Washington that took the President to Europe to sign the Treaty of Versailles at the end of World War I. Riedinger would continue to cook at the Providence Biltmore for over a decade, even returning after a brief time in another position.

The hoteliers also cut no corners in staffing the Biltmore for opening day. *Hotel World* made note of the prominent hotel employees that were scooped up by Bowman and Wallick for their new palace in Providence. "Ernest C. Hayfield, recently affiliated with the United Hotels Company, first at the Stacy-Trent, in Trenton, N. J., and later as traveling supervising steward of the chain, has accepted the position of steward at the new Providence-Biltmore," they noted. The hotel's first manager, Daniel J. Dailey, came to Providence to manage the hotel from the Hotel Belmont, a favorite hotel of New England visitors to New York. Dailey's time with the Providence Biltmore would be short, however, as he failed to live up to the owners' expectations.

Opening day at the Biltmore was a tremendous success. Elated, well-fed, and entertained beyond their wildest dreams, guests enjoyed toast after toast through dinner and past the dessert of ices and demi-tasses, which were served well after 10 p.m. During the toasts, Arthur L. Aldred presented Bowman and Wallick with a metal box containing parchment paper upon which was written the names of all 1,800 public stockholders that had invested in the hotel to assist in its construction. Aldred declared that the box was to be placed in the cornerstone of the building and that it would remain there "as long as the building stands."

When Governor San Souci spoke, he thanked Bowman and Wallick for their visionary leadership in the development and opening of the grand hotel, but his speech also addressed the civic participation of the residents of Providence who contributed to making the construction possible. "I desire at this time to congratulate and compliment those public-spirited citizens who had faith in the future of Providence and backed their convictions with hard cash, which made the erection of this hotel a possibility." Notably, the vast majority of those individuals were not invited to be in attendance that day, but the speech was reported the following day for all to read in *The Providence Journal*.

Mayor Gainer followed the Governor, thanking all who were in attendance and speaking to the historical importance of Rhode Island:

> Historically, we go back to the beginning of the white man's history in America. No city can trace its story to a much more remote date than 1636, nor to an earlier ancestor than Roger Williams. No community can point with greater pride to a more patriotic part in the nation's building, nor in its subsequent development than these Plantations. Where in all this broad land can be found a finer galaxy of educational institutions than here in Providence, with our Brown University, our Providence College, flanked with our myriad of public and private institutions of learning. Our manufacturing industries are known all over the civilized world. Our municipal activities afford our citizens accommodations which compare favorably with those of any city in the country. Our financial credit is of the highest in the list of American municipalities. And, best of all, we have a civic standard and community spirit which I am firmly convinced few cities equal and none excel. But with all these advantages for many years we have gone on with one serious drawback. We have lacked an up-to-date, modern hotel. This was a very vital handicap, more vital in fact than many of us realized. Unable as it left us to properly care for visitors, the many valuable assets which we possessed were practically unknown to the inhabitants of the rest of the country. Large conventions with their thousands of delegates shunned us. Tourists went around our borders. Traveling men vilified us. The treasures which we held as trustees were matters of entire ignorance to a great majority of our fellow countrymen.

From now on all this will be changed. From on, Providence will take her rightful place in the first rank of leading American cities. From now on, Providence will be on the map in capital letters... the dream of years has been fulfilled. We have the finest hotel in the country right here in Providence...the great majority of stock is locally owned. The hotel is ours. We are proud of it. The cynic's sneer has vanished. The hotel is a reality. Will it succeed? Will it prosper? As I think of its history, as I realize the forces which have brought it to completion, as I look upon your faces this evening, I cannot help using the slang phrase, "I'll say it will."

PART II
THE GOLDEN YEARS

7

THE MYSTERY OF BETTY BEESWAX

As Providence prepared to unveil the country's most luxurious hotel to date, tabloids across the country were following another story of decadence and intrigue: the sweeping, nationwide manhunt for the perpetrators of the Leonard Street mail heist.

Gerald Chapman, also known as "The Count of Gramercy Park," had just become the first criminal ever to be dubbed "Public Enemy Number One" for his planning and execution of a spectacular robbery in which he and his two associates made off with $2.4 million (approximately $33 million in today's currency) in bonds, cash, and jewelry from a New York City postal service truck. This was no ordinary crime, and Chapman was no ordinary criminal. With a felonious history dating back to a stint in Sing Sing at just 14 years old, Chapman was a well-known swindler and prominent bootlegger, running operations from Chicago to New York and everywhere in between. His best friend and partner in crime, George "Dutch" Anderson, whom Gerald had met in Sing Sing, aided his operations and was both a mentor and brother figure to Gerald throughout their lifetimes. It was with Dutch that he would devise and execute the Leonard Street robbery on October 24, 1921, bewitching the public with the incredible crime and their subsequent chase across the country.

Gerald Chapman at a young age. Photo courtesy of Lewis Lawes Papers,
Lloyd Sealy Library, John Jay College of Criminal Justice/CUNY.

As this game of cops and robbers played out, a mysterious woman emerged from the background, adding even more mystery and allure to the tale. On the night of Chapman's arrest, police arrived at his posh New York townhouse on Gramercy Park to search for the bank loot and were surprised to find two striking ladies in the parlor playing cards. One of the women, a bright-eyed 20-something with a midwestern accent answered the door. Further shocking the police, she introduced herself as Betty Colwell, wife of G. Vincent Colwell, owner of the townhouse under search. Ascertaining that Colwell must be an alias of Chapman's, the police quickly apprehended the young woman and her guest, hauling them off to the same precinct where they had Chapman detained.

The police were not the only ones puzzled by the sudden appearance of Mrs. G. Vincent Colwell in the story of Gerald Chapman's life. The newspapers quickly latched on to this mysterious twist. Who was this beautiful young woman, claiming to be the wife of a man who technically did not exist? The remaining details of Chapman's mysterious lover would not surface until over a year later, when she rejoined the story of Gerald Chapman's life with a new identity herself.

Before she was Mrs. Betty Colwell, the young aspiring actress went by the name Miss Betty Bales, a soft-spoken beauty from Indianapolis. She had arrived in New York City with the hope of making it big on Broadway, as she'd heard that women could do in the post-war entertainment boom of the time. New York City in the early 1920s was everything she could have hoped for—bright lights, raucous dancing, short skirts and even shorter hair, and handsome, gregarious gentlemen at every turn who wanted to sweep her off her feet.

Dining one evening at Bertolli's, where she'd become friends with the owner's daughter, Betty was introduced to a handsome Englishman named G. Vincent Colwell. Betty was captivated with his wit and charm, impressed with how well read he was, and even more delighted at how quickly he attached himself to her. He had a deviant energy that filled her with electricity and Betty was immediately intrigued.

It is no surprise that Betty fell for Gerald. A purportedly self-made "gentleman scholar," Colwell, as he was known in New York, was respected across the Big Apple for his elite social circle and his proclivity for the finer things in life. He ran in the same circles with famous authors, playwrights, and philosophers. He drank at the swankiest clubs and donned an English accent, often telling people that he descended from royalty—thus attaining the nickname of "The Count" that was later ascribed to him. While his surname and the accent were fabrications, Gerald Chapman's intellect was very real and lent itself well to his life of disguise.

It was only a matter of time before Betty and the dashing "Englishman" were being seen everywhere, arm in arm. The two were inseparable, cavorting in the most highbrow clubs and restaurants in the city, rubbing elbows with the literati at Algonquin and the playwrights on Broadway. They socialized with Edna St. Vincent Millay and had dinner with famed actor John Barrymore. Gerald seemed to know everyone, and everyone wanted to be around Gerald. As it were, The Count had the means to keep people around. He bought

Betty the finest furs, decking her in the newest silk dresses with rhinestones and the striking fashions of the city. They frequented New York's luxury hotels often, but retained a permanent residence at No. 12 Gramercy Park together.

Gerald traveled often for "work," but he always left Betty with an ample allowance to play with while he was gone. She used the money to dine out with friends or see shows throughout the city, though sometimes she traveled back to Indianapolis to see family. Whether Betty was naive to Chapman's true source of success or she simply chose to ignore it remains a mystery. It is unlikely that they were ever legally married despite referring to themselves as betrothed. Even after detaining her in the search of the Gramercy Park home, investigators could never uncover evidence to link her to any of his crimes. What is not a mystery, however, is that Betty cared for Gerald deeply, and she in turn was his one true love. She would remain so until the day he died.

The excitement surrounding the Leonard Street mail truck robbery finally ended in July 1922, with Gerald Chapman's arrest, trial, and conviction. He and Dutch were sentenced to 25 years in Atlanta's Federal Penitentiary for the crime. As the two masterminds boarded a prison train south to serve their time, Mrs. G. Vincent Colwell was boarding another train—this one headed north, to Rhode Island.

Shortly after Gerald's conviction, Betty faded quickly from the Gramercy Park community where she and her "husband" had reigned. According to Gerald Chapman's biographer, H. Paul Jeffers, sometime in the fall of 1922, Chapman was able to get a letter to Betty from the jail in Atlanta. He pleaded with her to visit him, expressing his undying love for her. The feelings must have been mutual, because Betty agreed, making the long journey to Atlanta. It was during that visit that Betty told Gerald that she had met a Rhode Island businessman with whom she had become engaged. She told Gerald that she needed to move on with her life, despite her love for him. But she was not disappearing entirely. It was during that visit that Betty devised a plan to keep in touch with her beloved Gerald. The visit to Atlanta was brief, but it was far from the end of their story.

Chapman only remained in prison in Atlanta for a few months before a shocking escape which landed him on the run. Dodging law enforcement and crisscrossing the country under assumed names, Gerald Chapman successfully remained on the lam for nearly two years. How he stayed solvent during this time is still unknown, but rumors persisted that there was someone in the background ensuring that Chapman received funds wherever he was hiding. The identity of that person was hotly contested in the tabloids, and Chapman's Gramercy Park mistress was suspected. The papers wondered: Where would Betty have gotten the money to sustain Chapman as he eluded law enforcement? Could the funds have originated from the Leonard Street robbery? The majority of the $2.4 million loot had never been uncovered and questions arose as to whether or not Chapman's mistress had disappeared with the riches.

By October 1924, Chapman was living under an assumed name in western Massachusetts, still alluding law enforcement at every turn and devising a scheme to start a counterfeiting operation. He and a new criminal associate were traveling through New London one day when they decided to attempt a robbery of a nearby department store. The robbery went awry, resulting in Chapman shooting and killing police officer James Skelly. The newspapers went wild. Not only had Chapman resurfaced, but he had resurfaced *and* killed a cop. Outrage over the murder ensued, and Chapman was hunted by every law enforcement body in the country. "The manhunt for Chapman is fast resolving itself into one of the most intensive ever conducted in the country for a criminal," *The New Britain Herald* observed in October. The paper went on to dub Chapman a "super bandit."

The primary federal investigator on the case, Detective Edward Hickey, was on the trail of Gerald Chapman when the discovery of a stolen car, presumed to be Chapman's, led him to room C31 at the Cooley Hotel in Springfield, Massachusetts. Upon rifling through the hotel room, it was clear that its inhabitant had intended to return. Clothes hung in the closet, toiletries were strewn on the counter in the bathroom, and a deluxe volume of *Echo de Paris* lay on the bedside table. Detective Hickey inspected the desk, finding correspondence stock and an expensive fountain pen. Then, a real clue emerged. Looking down, Hickey observed a pile of torn up paper in the bottom of the wooden waste basket. Slowly and meticulously, he pieced the pages back together, revealing a series of letters between distanced lovers. The stock was clearly imprinted in each corner, and it wasn't from the Springfield hotel where he was sitting. It was another hotel, a new hotel: The Providence Biltmore Hotel. With delicate, feminine handwriting, the elusive scribe signed each letter: "With love, Beeswax."

Detective Hickey quickly phoned the post office in Providence, Rhode Island. He requested that any mail addressed to the Cooley Hotel in Springfield be held for his inspection. In addition, he ordered a stakeout of the Providence Biltmore. The detective was determined to uncover the identity of this mysterious woman who wrote lovingly to Public Enemy Number One, hoping she would lead him to America's most wanted man.

Not long after the search began, Detective Hickey received a call from the Providence post office. The stakeout of the Biltmore Hotel had been successful. Officers had intercepted a beautiful, charming woman retrieving mail under the name B. Bales at the hotel desk. Detective Hickey wasted no time. He jumped in his car and headed to Providence.

When Betty entered the Biltmore's lobby, which she did of her own accord in the company of postal service employees, Detective Hickey immediately understood what Gerald Chapman had seen in her. She was beautiful and vibrant, and she matched the description one journalist had written of her as an "especially vivid moth in the flame of Broadway." Detective Hickey and Betty Bales sat in a far corner of the hotel's lobby, near the elevators but away from the foot traffic of other guests. Hickey asked her a series of questions, including her real name, but vowed to keep her identity a secret out of respect for her new husband and her life in Providence. Hickey kept his word—Betty's new name and identity in Providence was never published or revealed. The record showed that she was the wife of a prominent and upstanding leader of the Providence business community and that she admitted that her husband knew of her previous association with Gerald Chapman. She told the investigator that when she knew Gerald, she knew him as Vincent Colwell, and that she had known nothing of his criminal activities. When asked why she continued to correspond with him once his true criminal identity had been revealed, she replied simply, "Because I still love him."

Betty answered the detective's questions but provided little that could help their investigation. She claimed that she had not seen Gerald in person since her visit to the Atlanta prison and that their letters never discussed his activities. She had told him of her new life, and he had shared stories of his travels and updates on common friends they had had in New York—including Dutch Anderson—without disclosing anything about his day-to-day movement. She told the detective flatly that should she be called to the witness stand, she would have nothing to say except that she had known Gerald in New York and that they had continued to exchange pleasantries through the post. Leaving the Biltmore that day, Detective Hickey felt frustrated. He'd hit a wall with the mysterious woman whom he'd hoped would shed light on Chapman's whereabouts and his culpability in the New London shooting. Later, when Chapman was ultimately apprehended and brought to trial, prosecutors agreed that there was no need to bring Betty Bales to testify, particularly because no one wanted to tarnish her new husband's name.

With that decision, Betty "Beeswax" Bales drifted back into anonymity. Her married name remains unknown, as the detective kept his promise to conceal her identity during the trial. Her postal box at the Biltmore Hotel was promptly closed after she was interrogated by the police, and she retreated back to her life in Rhode Island. Who Betty Beeswax was may never be known. The question of whether or not she made off with the fortune from the Leonard Street mail robbery will never be answered, and who her descendants might be can only be guessed. All that remains are rumors and conjecture in historic newspapers that will forever leave us wondering who the mysterious Betty Beeswax of the Biltmore could have been.

Gerald Chapman, however, did not escape into the shadows as his beloved had done. Gerald was captured, found guilty of murder, and executed by upright jerker in Connecticut on April 6, 1926, closing the book on one of the most intriguing criminal epics of the early 20th century.

Gerald Chapman in his jail cell, a week before his death.
Photo courtesy of the Boston Public Library, Leslie Jones Collection.

8

BOOTLEGGERS AT THE BILTMORE

"The whole world is skew-jee, awry, distorted and altogether per-
verse. Einstein has declared the law of gravitation outgrown and
decadent. Drink, consoling friend of a Perturbed World, is shut off;
and all goes merry as a dance in hell!"

—*Franklin K. Lane, US Secretary of the Interior,*
in his diary on the eve of Prohibition, January 16, 1920.

When Prohibition came to Providence in 1919, immigrants,
more than any others, felt its pressure. The Irish and Italians saw the government's intervention into customary
behaviors such as drinking and serving liquor as an infringement
on their liberty. Wine, beer, and spirits were not just beverages of
choice for Rhode Island's immigrants; they were intricately tied to
their cultural identities and provided threads of connection between
communities. From 1900 to 1920, Rhode Island had the highest
number of saloons per capita in the country and roughly 60 percent
of saloon keepers were immigrants. "The bootlegging racket was
an industry custom-made for immigrants," Daniel Okrent writes
in *Last Call: The Rise and Fall of Prohibition.* "It was a quick-turn-
over business that had no particular training, and could exploit ready

markets within the various ethnic communities before branching out into society at large." Okrent cites the "outstanding and sympathetic historian" John Higham when he says that Prohibition created "dazzling opportunities" for the children of the immigrant slums.

One immigrant family whose fate was forever sealed by the passage of Prohibition was that of Eleuterio Patriarca, a liquor store owner in Providence's primarily Italian neighborhood of Federal Hill. With the passage of the 18th Amendment, Eleuterio was forced to close his store and go to work in a jewelry shop. His young son, Raymond, was forced to leave school to help support his family. It was because of this that the Biltmore Hotel welcomed its newest bellboy, Raymond Loreda Salvatore Patriarca, when he was just the young age of 12.

At that time, the majority of bootlegging operations in New England were controlled by the Boston and Providence crime families, headed by Gaspare Messina and Frank Morelli, respectively. The two bosses ran vast, interconnected crime syndicates that controlled loan sharking, illegal gambling, and illicit alcohol trade throughout New England, and they were flourishing under the passage of the new Amendment.

Rhode Island loved rum. Rum had played an integral part in the history of Providence since its earliest days as the central port of New England's participation in the Triangle trade—the exchange of African slaves, Caribbean molasses, and rum. The trade of people and goods made many of Providence's earlier merchants exorbitantly wealthy. The booming factories, mills, and ports of Providence were built on the prosperity brought to the state by this lucrative liquid gold, and when the Temperance movement pressed for the ban of alcohol in the United States, Rhode Island took it personally.

"Rhode Island was about as Catholic as Vatican City," wrote David Krajicek in the *New York Daily News,* "Many callous-kneed papists regarded Prohibition as a Protestant connivance against the boom of immigrant Catholics, many of them Italian, Irish, and Polish." When the 18th Amendment prohibiting the sale and distribution of

Prohibition agents pour liquor into a sewer following a raid during the height of prohibition. Courtesy of the Library of Congress.

intoxicating beverages became law in December 1917, Rhode Island and Connecticut remained the only two states to refuse to ratify.

As one of the northernmost ports of the "Great Whiskey Way," Rhode Island was a key point of entry for the Prohibition smugglers who made their way from the Bahamas with cargo holds full of alcoholic goods. Bill McCoy, an infamous smuggler, noted in his autobiography that he would leave Nassau Harbor with 5,000 cases of Scotch and return with an empty hold after docking in Montauk, Block Island, or Nantucket. He noted that even after paying customs agents in the Bahamas nearly $30,000 for each shipload, he earned twice as much once he'd unloaded along the New England coast. McCoy, like other smugglers of his time, was treated like a gentleman at port. In one of his first press appearances, McCoy stated that folks in the area could "come out any time [they] want to; the law can't touch us here, and we'll be very glad to see you." When

Prohibition agents inspect a large load of smuggled liquor aboard a rumrunning ship.
Courtesy of the Library of Congress.

smugglers continued to use the inlets and coves of the Narragansett
Bay to hide their stores and smuggle illegal booze up and down the
coast, Rhode Island's law enforcement refused to intervene, in defi-
ance of the new law. In response, the federal government sent the
Coast Guard to chase down bootleggers.

As the Coast Guard doubled down on Prohibition enforcement,
rumrunners departed Rhode Island's shores by cover of darkness,
navigating stealthily around the Coast Guard's larger and more
advanced ships to dock with the liquor importers who anchored in
wait 12 miles from shore. Flags raised above the deck notified the
rumboats what liquor was being sold on each ship, and the runners
would fill their holds with whatever orders they had been prescribed
by saloonkeepers or private buyers—or they'd take what they could
get when that was not available. Dodging the chase and gunfire of

Coast Guard boats, the runners would then speed back to shore to unload their goods and hide their boats until the next run. It was in these covert operations that some of the most notorious crime bosses in New England cut their teeth, and Providence quickly became known as one of the "wettest" cities remaining in the United States. Prohibition may not have created organized crime, but it became the Petri dish in which the fungus grew, nourished by the yeast of cash from the public's mighty thirst.

Raymond Patriarca came from a poor, working class, immigrant family, not unlike many of Providence's families. It is no wonder that when the opportunity to make some real money came along, he jumped at the chance. Rumrunning and the trafficking of beer, wine, and spirits was rampant in the city when the Biltmore opened its doors, so it would be hard to say when Raymond was first exposed to the lucrative business opportunities of the criminal underworld. However, if he had any interest in the trade while he was working at the Biltmore, he did not need to look far to become connected. As a Biltmore bellboy, each day young Raymond would be positioned at the grand glass doors of the hotel's entrance, greeting its residents and guests with a smile and assisting them with their luggage and belongings. Every day, Raymond would have nodded or waved to one of the Biltmore's most well-heeled residents, Barnett C. Hart, as he came and went from his luxurious quarters upstairs. Hart was a well-known bootlegger and had moved into the hotel immediately upon its opening. While living at the Biltmore, Barnett ran bootlegging operations between Providence and New York, where he also claimed a residence on West 51st Street. His trade was no secret, and his wealth was widely known.

In the summer that the Biltmore opened, Barnett was arrested for attempting to bribe police officers in Connecticut after two truckloads, containing 7,200 bottles of illicit 5.7 percent alcohol beer, were discovered by officers in Jewett City, not far from New London. The truck's drivers, one of which was Harry Hart, Barnett's brother, were permitted one phone call. They promptly called Barnett at the Providence Biltmore Hotel. After speaking to the drivers, Barnett departed his residence at the hotel and made the two-hour drive to Jewett City. Upon meeting the prosecuting officers, Barnett removed two $100 bills from his pocket—the equivalent of approximately $3,000 in today's currency—and attempted to hand one to each of the officers, requesting that they let the shipments move along to New York.

This tactic had worked many times before, but that was not the case on this fateful day. Barnett was arrested and held in jail, pending his court appearance for bribery and bootlegging. How long he had been living at the Biltmore, or if he returned after his trial, is unknown. But it must have been exceptionally convenient for the hotel to have such a well-connected bootlegger in residence whenever the taps went dry. While Barnett "loitered in jail" in Brooklyn awaiting trial for his attempted bribery, reporters in Providence and New York mused that his "fine room at the Biltmore remained unoccupied." With their resident bootlegger away, however, hotel staff and residents did not have to look far to fill their cups. Directly behind the hotel, a speakeasy on Eddy Street prospered for many years. *The Providence Journal* reported a raid of the location in October 1924, and one man, Frank Murphy, being arrested for illegal sale and possession of liquor.

While the 18th Amendment may have forbidden the sale of alcohol, it spurred the invention of the cocktail party. New York City, notoriously "liquor-saturated," became the central axis of a country divided between law-abiding citizens and the whirlwind of social lawbreaking. As Daniel Okrent outlines in his history of the era, the cocktail party was "conceived as a gathering of men and women to drink gin cocktails, flirt, dance to the phonograph or radio, or gossip about their absent friends. For the first time, men and women were drinking together outside the home, at an event where dinner wasn't served. Even *Vanity Fair* wrote instructive articles about how to 'bait the social hook' by insinuating in party invitations that alcohol would be served, without explicitly stating it. One such suggestion included adding 'bring your corkscrew' to the bottom of the RSVP card."

Within the first month of Prohibition taking effect, hotels in New York City began to close their doors. The first in the long litany of closures was the infamous Holland House, where John McEntee Bowman had started his career under the mentorship of Gustav Baumann. And when Holland House closed, with it went its famous Bamboo Cocktail of sherry, dry vermouth, and orange bitters. Despite this vast number of hotels being lost to the new law, the Providence Biltmore was being designed with an expansive bar and grillroom, sumptuous ballrooms, and lavish dining rooms. Either the architects did not believe Prohibition would last, or they paid no mind to it as they imagined these exceptional spaces for imbibing. Perhaps it was Rhode Island's open reluctance of prohibition and its enthusiastic capital city, made up of saloon keepers, distillers,

Partygoers during Prohibition, 1920. Photo obtained on WikiCommons.

brewers, hoteliers, and other professions that thrived on the partaking of alcohol, that a hotel like the Biltmore could still have been conceptualized and pursued on the cusp of the 1920s.

There is no reason to believe that prohibition was being enforced, or even remotely acknowledged, at the Biltmore Hotel during its early days. In a *The New York Times* report from September 1922, it was stated that two of the country's most esteemed prohibition agents had gone to Providence to root out saloonkeepers and dealers only to find that Providence was quite possibly the "wettest" city still remaining in the United States. The speakeasy at 23 Eddy Street, adjacent to the hotel, provided convenient access to hotel guests and staff alike who needed to refill a flask or take a "wet" lunchbreak. Dr. Walter R. Durkin, who had paid for medical school by waiting tables at the Biltmore in its earliest years, told *The Providence Journal* years later that he frequently was sent out "to the alley" to fill up buckets with alcohol for room service orders.

Izzy Einstein, a short, heavyset man who was called a "master of disguise," was quickly dispatched to Providence as an agent of the federal Prohibition Department. Within a week, Izzy and his counterpart, Moe Smith, had made more than 50 arrests and found more than 700 places openly selling whiskey in Providence alone. *The New York Times's* report stated: "Providence is worse than New York ever was in its disregard for the prohibition law. Liquor is sold openly in all parts of the city, in the most fashionable places as well as in the cheap dives along the waterfront." Izzy himself reported, after being arrested while undercover, that "every one of the [saloonkeepers] put up a battle with the agents. In one place the saloonkeeper threw a pitcher of whisky in my face. The so-called whisky is being sold in Providence at 20 cents a drink, the price alone indicating the character of the mixture."

This kind of press must have been a boon for the Biltmore, which had recently opened its doors. What better way to draw out-of-state guests than an unsolicited advertisement from *The New York Times*

Izzy Einstein and Moe Smith, two notorious Prohibition agents who named Providence the "wettest city in America" during Prohibition. Courtesy of the Library of Congress.

on the free-flowing nature of Providence's signature whiskey, at a time when saloons and hotels in New York, Boston and elsewhere were closing down left and right? Indeed, on opening night of the Biltmore, John Bowman's speech to the hundreds of guests in the ballroom suggested that he was considering moving from New York to become a permanent resident of Rhode Island because it was, in his words, "the one place where Mr. Volstead was snubbed." The reference was to Senator Andrew Volstead, best known for being a primary author of the National Prohibition Act. One can imagine John Bowman sitting in the executive office of the hotel in the early months of the Biltmore's operation, feet up on the desk, a glass of whiskey in hand, smiling ear to ear as he read of Providence's successful and ongoing resistance to the 18th Amendment.

Prohibition did not seem to damper the spirits of merrymakers on the eve of 1923, the first of many such revelries entertained by the Biltmore Hotel. The hotel's much anticipated first New Year's party featured several hours of music and dancing, with more than 1,000 people in attendance in the main ballroom. Though the state's Prohibition agents were reportedly waiting in the hotel lobby for any suggestions of liquor law violations, they informed inquiring journalists late in the evening that not a single violation had been reported to them. It is possible that Providence was on its best behavior that night. More likely, however, was that anyone who would find it acceptable to report a pocket flask to an enforcement agent had opted to stay home or go to midnight mass instead.

While Rhode Island spurned Prohibition, saloons and taverns continued to be the domain of men throughout the majority of the 20th century. It would not be until the women's liberation movement of the 1960s and 70s that women would be legally allowed to drink "unaccompanied" in barrooms at America's hotels. The Biltmore was no exception. Writer Sascha Cohen notes: "After prohibition ended in North America, cities in both Canada and the United States attempted to 'morally engineer' public drinking, and consistently regulated female behavior more than male behavior. Unattached women at bars could be kicked out for 'intoxication,' even if they didn't have anything to drink. Some states refused to grant licenses to mixed-sex establishments, and many American cities drafted their own ordinances to outlaw women in saloons and taverns. These establishments posted signs that read 'men only' or 'no unescorted ladies will be served.' Women fraternizing outside of their race always drew extra attention and punishment from authorities. And while white women were seen as vulnerable and in need of saving from moral ruin, black women—arrested at higher rates— were targeted out of a concern that enjoying liquor and recreation would detract from their productivity as domestic workers. These deep-rooted ideas about sex and race were baked into the policies that second-wave feminists confronted decades later."

Even as Providence fought back against Prohibition, keeping up the appearance of lawfulness threatened the livelihood of thousands of individuals, and the loss of millions of dollars in profits. Opposition to the amendment came in all forms. Daniel Okrent writes that Catholic priests and Jewish rabbis were just as nefarious in the illegal alcohol trade as any speakeasy owner or bootlegger. "The leading Orthodox rabbi in Omaha, Zvi Grodzinski, complained to colleagues that other local rabbis were conducting 'a free-for-all and selling their sacramental wine to Jews and Gentiles alike.' Izzy Einstein stayed busy, busting New York rabbis operating out of tiny tenement rooms who claimed congregations in the hundreds. In Providence, the Reform rabbi Samuel Gup complained that 'local Orthodox rabbis have broken the law continuously; they sell wine for profit, they sell it to anyone, Jew or non-Jew, who is willing to pay for it.'"

The government had lost control of the situation, and savvy, sophisticated criminals stepped in to manage the chaos. Prohibition gave organized crime purpose and prosperity far beyond anything that had come before it. In bootlegging, smuggling, and selling illicit liquor and beer, the criminal syndicates in Chicago, Detroit, New York, Boston, and Providence found true purpose.

After his brief career at the hotel, Raymond Patriarca soon moved on to new endeavors. Hired to guard a shipment of illicit rum brought in from the Rhode Island coast, Raymond instead stole the liquor and sold it himself, beginning his life of crime in a double-cross. After this entree into crime, he made a name for himself on Federal Hill as a smart and dangerous young man, someone who was willing to take big risks for big profit. From that point on, Raymond Patriarca began to climb the ladder, soon rising to the top of the New England crime network. But Raymond had not lost all interest in the hotel. In a transcript of an FBI wiretap set in Patriarca's offices in the 1960s, Raymond was recorded stating that he always knew what was going on at the Biltmore, thanks to an employee at the hotel that he kept "on the payroll."

9

A LONG WINTER'S WALK

Sitting in a smoky parlor in a large Parisian home, Eleonora Sears found herself talking to a pig. The pig, quite frankly, was better company than the wildly drunk men that sat on either side of it on the settee. Cole Porter, an up-and-coming musician, was laughing so hard that his cocktail sloshed from the glass and onto the ornamental carpet. His wife, Linda, rolled her eyes from a nearby chair. Howard Sturges, owner of the pig and technically a tenant of Cole and Linda's, was loudly whispering something rather obscene in Cole's ear. Music blared from the gramophone and other party-goers swayed in various degrees of intoxication. It was another raucous evening with one of Paris's most eccentric crowds. Eleonora, visiting Paris on the invitation of Howard, was bored. Considered an eccentric back home, Eleonora's flavor of uniqueness did not quite match the boisterous company that she found herself in that evening, even though most could be called her friends.

Eleonora had grown up in incredible wealth as part of the old money, Yankee Boston, the second child and only daughter of pre-eminent businessman and shipping magnate Frederick Richard Sears. According to the New England Historical Society, "Eleonora was a model of social decorum in the mansions of the rich. On the athletic

Eleonora Sears performs a long-distance walk.
Courtesy of the Boston Public Library, Leslie Jones Collection.

field, however, she shattered the rules during the first half of the 20th century. She rode horses in pants, crashed men-only squash courts and shocked tennis spectators by playing in rolled-up sleeves. During her lifetime, she accumulated 240 trophies...She used her wealth and social standing to break down barriers for women who lacked that silver spoon at birth." This included being the first woman to play in a men's polo match, as well as smaller infractions such as smoking a cigarette in the Boston Copley Plaza hotel lobby, where only men were allowed to smoke. She was arrested for the latter.

Eleonora was engaged to Harold Vanderbilt in 1911 but was never married. Given the gossip around her failed engagement, her uncommon athleticism, and her intense feminist spirit, the rumor mill quickly swirled with gossip about Eleonora's sexual preferences. "Her sexual orientation certainly formed her character, and gave her the drive," Eleonora's biographer later told the *Windy City Times*.

"She was tremendously courageous in the way that she was willing to challenge, in a very public way, the very narrow role that woman had. She shocked the public again and again. Ministers delivered sermons against her wardrobe choice. The California Mother's Club condemned her as immodest and unbecoming, stating that 'such unconventional trousers and clothes of the masculine sex are contrary to the hard and fast customs of our ancestors,' in a statement." Eleonora challenged every barrier she encountered, on and off the playing field. In 1918, she broke a centuries-old rule of playing men on the Harvard Club's squash courts. She was the first to swim the 4 ½ miles from Bailey's Beach to First Beach in Newport, RI. And later, in 1968, she was inducted into the International Tennis Hall of Fame.

Eleonora had traveled to Paris in the autumn of 1925 to enjoy the company of the group that now filled Linda and Cole's grand parlor. Sturges, an old friend who was a native to Providence, had recently moved to Paris. It was rumored that he and Cole were having an affair, which was not a surprise to anyone who knew Cole Porter. The group of friends gathered at the Paris home were part of a well-known homosexual community that quietly lived and traveled together in the 1920s. Gay men were married to lesbian women to present a facade of heterosexuality for the outside world, but the group's proclivity toward partner swapping was widely known.

The pig was one of several of Howard's exotic pets that he kept with him in his suite of rooms at the Porters' Parisian estate. And it was to this pig that Eleonora found herself wondering out loud if Howard and Cole would ever have anything interesting to say. Drunk and taking the bait, Howard shot back, chiding Eleonora about her recent obsession with long-distance walking. After a comment about how easy it must be to break a walking record in the warm and mild sunshine of the California coast, Howard suggested that if Eleonora really wanted to prove herself, she should undertake a real challenge. Eleonora glowered at her friend, daring him to name his bet.

This is how Eleonora Sears ended up at the Providence Biltmore on December 13, 1925, prepared to win the bet she'd wagered in Paris three months prior. After two months of training for the freezing hike, she arrived at the hotel with several of her personal attendants. Checking into adjoining suites, she went straight to her room to rest while her maid and chauffeur prepared provisions for the following day.

At 12:01 a.m., Eleonora rose from her hotel bed and rang the bell for room service. After a large plate of hardboiled eggs, she dressed in extensive layers and took the elevators down to the lobby. From there, she exited the warmth of the hotel into bone-chilling winter weather, dressed in a checkered scarf, woolen stockings, ankle gauze, a long skirt, heavy shoes, and a felt hat. A private car drove her across town to Howard Sturges's Hope Street residence, where Eleonora rang the bell repeatedly to no avail. Per the stipulations of the bet, Eleonora was to leave Howard's by 1 a.m. on the dot. She had just 15 hours to walk the 44 miles to Boston in order to win their bet.

"[He] ran out on me," Eleonora complained to a reporter during her long-distance walk that day. "There was no one home there tonight, so we started from in front of the house anyway." Eleonora was not going to lose her bet, whether Sturges was there to witness it or not.

Two young college men, who had offered to "pace" her on the journey, lagged far behind Eleonora as she started up the road toward Boston. Although slowed for a time by a steady snowfall and, at one point, a squall, Eleonora did not falter. At one point, Eleonora turned to the boys behind her, grinning, and shouted into the wind, "Snap into it, boys! You offered to pace me, not to chase me! Show a little speed. If you're tired walking, run for a bit and get rested." A maid and chauffeur followed behind her in a car, carrying provisions of hot coffee, malted milk, and sandwiches.

Eleonora won the wager by a landslide. Despite bitter winds, ice, and snow, she made it from Providence to her home on Beacon

Hill in 11 hours and 5 minutes. *The Boston Globe* reported that she shocked her pacers and the crowds that had gathered to see her by jogging the final mile to her home. Then, she shocked them again by resting for just three hours before emerging from her house in evening wear. She proceeded to attend the theater and a dinner party for the remainder of the evening, "showing no signs of fatigue." Her college-aged pacers were not seen again that night. What Eleonora won in her bet against Sturges remained a secret. She told reporters that the wager included money and "something else" that she coyly would not reveal to the public. Wherever Howard Sturges was on that winter's day, he undoubtedly heard quite quickly through the grapevine that he had lost his bet.

Eleonora, eccentric as she was, was one of the greatest athletes of the 20th century. Sportswriter Grantland Rice said that "the two girls who did the most to turn the world spotlight on their sex, with the possible exception of Cleopatra, were Eleonora Sears and Babe Didrikson Zaharias." Eleonora's story, often overlooked, is a testament to the extraordinary dichotomies of the female experience in the 20th century.

10

THE SKY'S THE LIMIT

Despite the pomp and circumstance of the Biltmore's opening day, management of the hotel got off to a rocky start. Lou Wallick, for one, was unhappy with the hotel's first months of performance. Several challenges had to be addressed. First, the city's Fire Inspector took aim at the hotel for the location of their bakery, which was presented a fire hazard despite the belief that the structure was fireproof. Negotiations ensued, but it is unclear if the bakery was permanently relocated from the basement as the Inspector had requested.

Profits were also lower than expected. Under the management of Daniel Daily, overhead had far exceeded returns. After receiving reports of the numbers, Wallick came to Providence from his home in Ohio to conduct a review, quickly ousting Daily in favor of management by his 26-year-old son, Duane Wallick, who came to the Biltmore from his post as manager of the Secor Hotel in Toledo. Duane would remain manager of the hotel for nearly two decades.

Profits at the hotel suffered from the onset, even under Duane's management. In March 1923, Duane railed against a state bill which proposed a cap of working hours to 48 hours per week, stating that the law would add a considerable amount of operating expense to

*L. Duane Wallick, general manager of the Biltmore Hotel from
1922 to 1947, pictured with his chickens on the Biltmore's rooftop.
Photo courtesy of the Providence Public Library.*

the hotel's already strained budget. He further stated that this rise in expenses would have to be passed onto hotel patrons in the form of increased room and food rates. "It is my opinion," Wallick told *The Providence Journal*, "that the public considers hotel prices quite high enough at present and I doubt if it would stand for such an increase."

Perhaps in an effort to bring the overhead down, Duane quickly gained notoriety for his ingenuity and innovation at the hotel. On the roof, Duane built chicken coops, a truck garden, and floral planters to provide the hotel with a continuous supply of fresh eggs, produce, and flowers.

Duane's rooftop garden gained quick notoriety in the city, and across the country, as a cutting-edge approach to what would come to be known as farm-to-table service. However, the rooftop pro-duction line was nothing if not fraught with challenges. On one occasion, two roosters from the chicken coop began to squabble. Just as one puffed up its chest and threw back its wings in protest, a stiff breeze whipped across the roof of the hotel, lifting the rooster clear off of its perch and sending it flying across Washington Street to the roof of City Hall. After much hysteria from City Hall employees, who were notified by onlookers from the hotel, the rooster was rescued from the roof and brought back to the Biltmore. In another unfortunate turn of events, Duane brought a flock of geese to the rooftop aviary to provide both eggs and meat for the hotel's restaurants. Everything was going fine until late autumn, when the geese's migratory instincts kicked in and they took flight from their rooftop perch to head south for the winter. They never returned.

Managing a garden on the roof was a lovely pastime, but the production capacity was limited. Duane eventually gave up on his chicken coop and vegetable garden, opting to maintain a few thriving fruit trees such as apple and pear, and a small truck garden for fresh herbs. In the wake of the chicken coop failure, however, Duane invited much more exotic ideas to take roost on the Biltmore roof.

By the late 1920s, Duane had commissioned a small pond to be installed on the hotel's roof, with sunning logs adjacent. Here, he delivered a small family of snapping turtles which spent their days alternating between sunning themselves and burying themselves in the mud. From there, the habitat expanded. "The aerial garden [is] profusely surrounded in red, pink, and white rambler roses, geraniums, ferns, and a miscellany of other verdant shrubbery," reported *The Providence Journal*. But those were not the primary attraction on Duane's rooftop.

A few years into his managerial tenure of the hotel, Duane acquired two young monkeys (from where, it is not clear), which he named Maggie and Jiggs. Caged together and residing on the roof, the monkeys quickly became domesticated and a thrill for guests to visit. After Maggie and Jiggs's arrival came two four-foot alligators, who were housed in a large pond surrounded by wire caging. Then, a pair of raccoons in a wire habitat consisting of logs and platforms for climbing, playing, and resting. At one end of the rooftop "Eden," as one journalist described it, was a tropical goldfish pond with hundreds of gold and silver fish that darted back and forth among water lilies.

The cages and enclosures were connected by a winding gravel path leading from the stairwell entrance through the flowering fruit trees and serpentine grapevines, wrapping around each animal enclosure. During the day, the sweeping views of the city were breathtaking beyond the animus and intrigue of these wild creatures—virtually unknown beyond large city zoos and never before housed at a hotel in this way. At night, small lights dotted the winding path, shining upward into the vines that enmeshed the parapets.

The final addition to the grand rooftop menagerie was Cinny, a brown Cinnamon bear raised by Duane from cub to adult. As a cub, Cinny often occupied the lobby and reception area 18 stories below. The guests adored the little "ball of fur," but soon Cinny grew too big for lobby interactions. He was relegated to a rooftop habitat, where he was reported to "placidly" wander around his cage and play "slap paw" with himself, or dance for guests who ventured to the roof to see him.

Duane's zoological garden garnered him much attention from the press and created a novel experience for hotel guests. *The Providence Journal* wagered that "while other hotel men may keep pets on the roofs of their hostelries, it is believed that Mr. Wallick's is the largest of its type in New England, if not the country." And it continued to grow.

In May 1930, the front page of *The Providence Journal* ran the headline: "Stork Leaves Baby Monk at Zoo of Providence Biltmore Hotel." As it turns out, caging Maggie and Jiggs together on the isolated roof created situations even experienced hotel men weren't prepared for. The unexpected babe came to the rooftop with much media attention, with the Journal reporting that "Curator Wallick,

*L. Duane Wallick pictured with his dog and a guest atop the Biltmore in the 1920s.
Photo courtesy of the Providence Public Library.*

who has plenty to do without taking care of baby monkeys, would like to catch that stork." Baby Rosie, as she was called, quickly won the hearts of the hotel staff and their visitors. A half-page review of the zoological garden in July of that year noted how well Rosie was adjusting to her new life as the youngest member of the Biltmore family.

> "[Rosie] is every bit as demure as the name sounds. To enhance the privacy of her offspring, Maggie has a separate cage—although it is within sight and chattering distance of Jiggs, who reigns monarch of a nearby cage. Rosie is a phenomenon of modern times, one of the few born in captivity. She is a great favorite with the privileged few allowed to visit the roof. In one respect, Rosie differs a little from other babies. She sticks mighty close to mama... wherever Mama swings or ambles to, Rosie is bound to be with her.

From her snug perch, akin to that of a baby kangaroo, Rosie gazes with bright, innocent, but attentive eyes at everything which transpires. Occasionally she emits little squeaks, unintelligible to man, but which cause Maggie concern. Maggie whispers something in Rosie's ear, there is another squeak, then quiet. Mother knows best."

When the zoological garden was formerly closed, or what became of Cinny, Rosie, Maggie, Jiggs and their compatriots, is not clear. During a blizzard in January 1936, an unidentifiable fowl was found wandering the street during the snowstorm. A well-intentioned man brought it to the Biltmore thinking it had escaped from the rooftop zoo. However, when he entered the lobby with the bird he was informed that the rooftop had been closed down for several years. This is the only indication on record that the rooftop zoological garden so beloved by Duane Wallick had closed, presumably sometime right after the Depression took hold.

11

LINDY FEVER

On May 20, 1927, a relatively unknown pilot took off from Roosevelt Field in Long Island. Thirty-three-and-a-half hours later, he became an international hero. The pilot was Charles Augustus Lindbergh and, at age 25, he had just flown the first solo, nonstop, transatlantic flight. A few months later, Lindbergh-mania reached a fever pitch in Rhode Island. In its early years, the Biltmore welcomed a litany of famous and fabulous guests, from movie stars and socialites to diplomats and politicians, but none were greeted with more enthusiasm than the young pilot that was spreading his "Lindy Fever" across the nation.

Colonel Lindbergh's plane circled Providence for 10 minutes before landing at Quonset Point on the second stop of his air tour of the United States, with which he was promoting commercial aviation under the auspices of the Daniel Guggenheim Fund for the Promotion of Aeronautics. More than 300,000 "deliriously joyful" people lined the 21-mile stretch of road between Quonset and downtown Providence. It was reported in *The Boston Globe, The Providence Journal*, and *The New York Times* that Lindbergh's arrival received the most enthusiastic gathering for any visitor in the history of Rhode Island.

Charles Lindbergh, whose aero tour around America encouraged the development of commercial airfields across the nation. Photo courtesy of the Library of Congress.

Ralph Wheelock was the official event observer. Stationed atop the Turks Head Building, just a few blocks from the Biltmore, Wheelock was instructed to signal to the crowds below when Lindbergh's motorcade was approaching Exchange Place. From that signal, the crowd would produce as much noise as possible—with the aid of whistles, sirens, bells, and any other noisemakers they could get their hands on—to welcome the flyer.

So obsessed with Lindbergh were the people of Providence that when he emerged from City Hall to greet the masses, a crowd of 50,000 people pushed past the police barricade and charged toward "America's peacetime hero." Lindbergh was quickly whisked into the Mayor's office until the crowd could be gotten under control. Later in the day, Lindbergh was greeted by state officials and 75,000 additional onlookers at Roger Williams Park. Lindbergh

*A huge crowd gathered at the Biltmore Hotel for Charles Lindbergh's arrival
in Providence. Courtesy of the Providence Public Library Digital Collections,
Rhode Island Photograph Collection.*

gave a speech in front of the Benedict monument on his prediction
that, not long in the future, the United States would be served by a
network of commercial airlines. He urged Rhode Island leaders to
pursue building an airport, warning that cities that lacked adequate
airfields would be left behind in the march of American progress.

Aeronautics had already captivated Providence long before the
felicitous gathering for Charles Lindbergh. The Aero Club of Rhode
Island held its inaugural and second "Aero Ball" at the Biltmore in
1922 and 1923. At each Ball, awards were given out to pilots who
covered the most miles and those who were the fastest. The dinner
dances included both men and women and featured elaborate entertainment including cabarets and a "butterfly dance" where "glittering insects filled the room."

On the night of Lindbergh's reception, the pilot was honored at a dinner in the hotel's ballroom where 700 guests crammed into dozens of tables to hear him speak. While the guests ate, Lindbergh furthered his stance and emphasized the importance of the construction of airports all over the United States, including in Rhode Island. Under the glittering chandeliers, with the huge windows drawn open to let in the evening summer breezes, Lindbergh was gifted a silver box made in Providence as thanks for his contribution to air travel. Mayor Dunne provided a lengthy speech, expressing his gratitude to Lindbergh for making the time to stop in Rhode Island and lauded his historic flight to Paris as one of the great achievements of the century. It was "Lindy fever" that prompted the formation of the Aviation Committee of the Providence City Council and the resulting exploration of a location for a "landing strip" for Providence's future in air travel.

12

TO LIVE, TO LOVE, AND TO LABOR

Under Duane Wallick's tutelage, the Biltmore became a well-oiled machine. The most important piece of that machine, Duane knew, were its people. He encouraged a closeness among his staff, despite challenges presented by unions which rocked the labor force in the first half of the 20th century. In the hotel's early years, the Biltmore had its own baseball team, with matches against other company teams such as a Shepard Department Store's team and teams from the area's textile mills frequently being reported in the *Journal*. It was not uncommon for company management to promote recreation of this kind. Providing opportunities for employees to connect over recreational activities was seen as a preventative measure against the mounting threat of unionization across the United States. In Pawtucket, Hope Webbing Company went so far as to build a duckpin bowling alley for its workers right in the factory where they worked. The alley is now open to the public.

Workers' rights movements and labor unions have their roots in Rhode Island, as do strikes and walkouts. The first strike ever led by women in the United States took place at eight cotton mills in Pawtucket in 1824, a direct action against mill owners who increased the hours in the workday while lowering wages for the loom weavers.

The women who worked the looms revolted, walking out of the mills and, in one instance, lighting fire to mill property. The Dorr Rebellion followed suit in 1841 when Thomas Wilson Dorr organized an armed assault on Providence's arsenal building in an attempt to overthrow the local government and establish his own People's Constitution. Driving Dorr's rebellion was the disenfranchisement of mill workers, many of whom were refused the right to vote under Rhode Island law. Though the rebellion ultimately failed, it paved the way for workers' rights to remain on the ballot for the next hundred years.

Labor disputes have long been the business of hotels and the Biltmore is no exception. While constantly dealing with its own union challenges, the hotel also hosted hundreds of meetings of labor unions and workers' rights groups in its early years. It continued to be a central gathering point for the region's largest unions and associations, including the Knights of Labor, the Congress of Industrial Organizations, the International Workers of the World, and, more recently, the American Federation of Labor and Congress of Industrial Organizations. As one of the city's largest employers in the service industry, the hotel was also the site of numerous strikes and walk-outs as workers demanded more equitable treatment, better pay, and more reasonable hours. While the "red scare" and a deep fear of socialism in the United States dampened many efforts by unions during the 1940s and 50s, a resurgence in unionization occurred in the mid 1950s.

Despite on-going demands from the union, the Biltmore has managed to maintain an almost unprecedented employee retention pattern over the course of its history, beginning with the carefully hand-picked staff from the hotel's earliest years and continuing throughout the century. People who come to work at the Biltmore *stay* at the Biltmore. Barbara Johnston, whose retirement party in the 1980s was celebrated with members of the Kennedy family as well as the Cardinal of the Catholic Church, worked as a secretary under 15 general managers of the Biltmore between 1944 and her retirement. Jimmy McDonnell claimed more than 50 years at the hotel. Elizabeth Baxter, former secretary to Franklin D. Roosevelt when he was assistant secretary of the Navy, worked at the Biltmore Hotel for over 20 years. Elizabeth had come to the hotel after an impressive career in the military, serving first as a Yeoman First Class during the first World War, and then as a Volunteer Aide to the Office of Naval Intelligence during the second. While serving the country, Elizabeth also built a career in hotel administration. When the Biltmore opened in 1922, she was 35 years old and had substantial experience under her belt from her time in the navy. She was hired immediately by Duane Wallick to oversee the books of his management office. In 1925, Elizabeth moved into the Biltmore as a resident, and she continued to work and live at the hotel until her death. Countless others stayed for three, four, and even five decades before leaving or passing away. By putting its people first, the Biltmore managed to create a company culture that had staying power.

Without significant turnover, the staff of the Biltmore felt like something one could count on. Every time you went to the hotel, you were greeted by a familiar face at the door; old friends served you your meals. If the hotel was the central social gathering point of the city, its staff were the conductors of the city's social orchestra. The employees of the Biltmore may not have all been part of high society, but they were beloved by high society. They also became the subjects of city gossip. In 1930, the *Journal* reported an upcoming wedding of two Biltmore employees, noting that while the engagement party was held at the Hotel Dreyfus, it was attended by many of the Biltmore's employees and management. The orchestra for the event, furnished by Duane Wallick himself, was none other than the Biltmore's house band.

When *The Providence Journal* reported that Mr. and Mrs. John Jacob Astor had a marital dispute in the Biltmore's dining room which spilled out onto the sidewalk of the hotel, they also reported that, in an unrelated incident, one of the hotel's employees was being fined for polygamy. The staff's stories—their weddings, babies, and funerals—made the paper, and their celebrations and events were attended by important people, including the mayor. When the tragic and unexpected suicide of head waiter, Raymond Masoda—sadly slated to be married in just a week's time—took the hotel by surprise, it was reported by *The Boston Globe*. When Molly Gray, a famous dancer in Providence's cabaret scene, married William Ryan, former assistant manager of the hotel, it received a three-paragraph write-up in the *Journal*. In another article, Pastry Chef Louis Grattepanche was featured when his fiancée arrived in Providence from Aubagues, France. The article, along with a large photo of them, shared that they were married in the courthouse and would honeymoon in New York before settling into their home on Broadway in the west end. Aristide Cresto, maître d'hôtel of the Biltmore for more than 30 years, made the news when he failed to report income from tips and gratuities to the IRS. His assistant maître d'hôtel for 15 years, William Potter, was investigated and fined as well. When Gorun Gureghian, an employee of the Biltmore, developed a new method for discouraging invasive starlings from roosting on and around the hotel's roof, the *Journal* ran a half-page article on the strategy. The birds, evidently, were a nuisance for many downtown buildings. The article listed the attempts of the employees at City Hall, the State House, the central firehouse, and other notable buildings to remove and discourage the starlings from roosting. It was Gorun, however, that developed the ever-technical "stick on a rope" technique, in which he walked the perimeter of the roof each night and swung the rope along the edge of the rooftop, dragging and slapping the attached stick to the eaves. The sound startled many of the birds away, but when it didn't, a smack on their backs seemed to do the trick. Gorun reported to the *Journal* that the birds must have some degree of memory because since he'd started his rope and stick routine, the birds stopped showing up in their usual numbers.

Leveraging the celebrity of Biltmore employees and the esteem in which they were held was a common practice for businesses. One advertisement in the *Journal* in 1932 featured Paul C. Gredig, the pastry chef of the hotel, proudly holding a jar of "Formay Shortening." "Every point of excellence, at last combined in one shortening!" declared a printed quote from Gredig in large print across three quarters of a page. Every company in Providence wanted to cash in on the Biltmore's reputation for excellence.

Hotels during this era were not just spaces for accommodation and events. They were central spaces of social and political discourse, linchpins of communities all around the United States. They were so central to the community that often people went there just to stand around and see what there was to see. When one entered the Providence Biltmore's ground-floor entrance, a transformation took place. The hustle and bustle of the city outside melted away. The ring of cash registers chimed from the newsstand and hair salon. The air was filled with the scent of fresh cut flowers and warm pastries from the hotel's bakery. Ornate light fixtures and the shining golden ceiling gleamed and sparkled in the sunlight, which poured in from the cathedral-like windows on the lobby and mezzanine levels. Front and center, as guests entered from the street, was the most splendid element of all—the grand staircase, designed by Warren and Wetmore to give a sense of regal pomp and circumstance to the hotel's entrance. The grand staircase became the central meeting spot for the entire city. Politicians would meet the press at the base of the stairs, before ascending to campaign headquarters upstairs. Hollywood actresses posed for pictures, clutching the curves of the railing and smiling broadly before being whisked away to their private suites. Out-of-towners, even those who could not afford to stay at the luxuriant hotel, were frequently instructed by locals to wait by the Biltmore stairs for their hosts. In the first half of the 20th century, the Biltmore was the center of Providence's universe.

Decades later, Todd Finard of Finard Management Group would

aptly say that the Biltmore was the epitome of "a bygone era, when travel was special." A time, he said, when "you dressed up to get on a train or a plane and arrive at your hotel." The Biltmore was built to evoke a sense of pride and grandeur. Joan Stewart Hicks recalled that when she was a teenager in the 40s, it was the thrill of a lifetime to get dressed up with her friends and take the long train ride from Pennsylvania to the Biltmore in New York, just to have a meal and see what was happening in the city. Servicemen were often there, in the lobby, and Joan remembered the thrill of shaking hands with them and wishing them well before they headed out to the boats. All of Bowman's Biltmore Hotels were built with spaces exclusively for ladies, such as the Ladies Lounge and separate sitting rooms. This helped, Joan said, in convincing her father to let her go to the hotel unaccompanied.

When people needed to be found, they were very often tracked down at their favorite hotels. In the case of Russell Griswold Colt, heir to a massive rubber fortune, it was at his favorite cigar stand in the lobby of the Providence Biltmore where he was finally found by his wife, Ethel Barrymore's attorney, and served divorce papers. The Biltmore name could regularly be found in newspaper articles highlighting secret meetings, affairs, and legal proceedings. Despite the highly polarized political climate of early 20th century Rhode Island, the hotel regularly hosted concurrent election night events, with the Democrats utilizing the Ballroom while the Republicans used the Garden Room. The "X-Club," a private club of prominent Rhode Island businessmen (including several managers of the Biltmore), met in a room with a private bar at the hotel. Membership was limited to 10 people at a time and the group met regularly for lunch, cocktails, and cards.

In part due to its close proximity to Providence's courthouses, criminals were frequently held at the hotel while awaiting trial. Such was the case of John DeKay, who was extradited to the United States after apprehension by Scotland Yard. DeKay was sought on 12 indictments resulting from the failure of the Atlantic National Bank and was held on $25,000 bail. He was ordered by the court to remain in his suite at the Biltmore under armed guard as he awaited trial. When the former Governor of Rhode Island, R. Livingston Beekman, was accused of conspiracy and bribery during his campaign for the US senate, the Biltmore took center stage as the alleged scene of the crime. In the court proceedings that followed, the prosecutor was quoted in the paper asking Beekman why he had held special meetings in his apartment at the hotel. While Beekman defended his choice to hold business in his suite, the prosecutor's follow up question alluded to a common conception of the day: the people who wanted to conduct business behind closed doors at the Biltmore were the kind of people "who didn't want to be seen." They may also have been people who had fallen from grace. When *The Boston Globe* reported that Arnold C. Messler, former manufacturer from Pawtucket, was sued for $149,977 by the Equitable Trust Company of New York, his wife and he were living at the Biltmore in a four-room suite, despite claiming that they had just $40 to their names.

13

THRICE SCORNED

Luxury hotels made a substantial amount of their profit on long-term residents in the first half of the 20th century. The term "hotel" and "apartment building" were synonymous at this time, often used interchangeably. It was not uncommon for wealthy elites to maintain a rental suite at a hotel while also owning and managing other residences, such as summer estates and formal homes in the city. In the first few decades of operation, the Biltmore housed many of Rhode Island's most prominent families, often for years at a time. The public adored the stories of the Biltmore residents, and even followed news of their pets. One longtime resident amused guests and residents alike by training his dog to take the elevator down to the lobby, retrieve the newspaper, and bring it back up to his suite.

Part of the appeal of living at the hotel was that a hotel apartment required significantly less upkeep than a home. Maids and cooks and bellmen were all included in the rent, the bills were managed and paid by hotel executives, and one never needed to do any food shopping. This setup was particularly appealing to women who, due to divorce or death, found themselves single and alone later in life. Among the most fascinating of the Biltmore's widowed tenants was a wealthy recluse by the name of Henrietta Cecilia Wolf Gibson.

A wealthy, elegant woman, Henrietta lived in near solitude at the hotel for 16 years before her death. Rarely seen, the graying woman only occasionally graced the lobby long enough to pick up deliveries or to take an afternoon walk. The staff knew little of elderly woman, but rumors from the maids that cleaned her suite had spread that Henrietta had adorned her apartment with prized artwork, sculptures from Europe, porcelain vases, and ornate furnishings—a variable museum that the widow had gathered from travels around the world. Despite the impressive collection, the elusive recluse did not invite guests to see her treasures. Life had dealt Henrietta a lonely deck. Cruel gossip had eroded her spirit and broken her heart. She sealed herself off in the same manner that she had sealed up her family's grand estate, board by board, and resigned herself to a strictly private existence at the Biltmore Hotel.

It had not always been this way. Before she was Mrs. Gibson, Henrietta Cecilia Wolf had a happy life. Born on January 11, 1863, Henrietta was raised in a joyful home with two brothers, Julius and Joseph, and her sister, Alice. Emma and Benno Wolf, Henrietta's parents, were known throughout Rhode Island for their extraordinary wealth and charity. They held properties all across Providence but raised their four children in the Wolf Mansion, No. 1251 Westminster Street. The home was designed by famous architect Stanford White, who had built homes for the Vanderbilts, Astors, and, most famously, the Rosecliff Mansion in Newport, which he designed for Mrs. Hermann Oelrichs.

Benno Wolf was a self-made millionaire, most well-known as a purveyor of women's gloves and apparel. He was heralded for his shrewd business acumen and his almost prophetical investment sense. In the 1920 historical record of Rhode Island, William Bicknell writes that Benno was a man of "conservative, clear judgment, whose advice might be literally followed in business ventures." In addition, Bicknell wrote that Benno was a man of "strict honesty, the highest ethical principles, and unimpeachable integrity" as well as having a "magnetic personality," "wide intellectual attainments," and "broad sympathies." Emma and Benno "contributed lavishly to every worthy cause and movement for the betterment of conditions in the city." Benno was a Free Mason and a member of many of the Fraternal Orders in the city, and Emma sat on many charitable boards and hosted countless social engagements. By all accounts, the Wolf family was a happy and prosperous one.

The entire family shared a love of horses. Each summer, the Wolfs made the trek to Saratoga Springs to see their horses tested on one of the best tracks in the country and to enjoy the beautiful surroundings of Saratoga's Congress Hall resort. It was here where beautiful, young Henrietta and her sister Alice became royalty in the social class. While their father focused on the track, Henrietta and Alice presided over high society. In August 1892, Henrietta Wolf and her friend, Etta Rich of Boston, were crowned the "Reigning Belles" of Congress Hall, much to the delight of the newspapers' social sections.

Henrietta and Alice were inseparable. When they were not together in Providence, they were spending holidays in Narragansett or Saratoga together, or traveling together throughout Europe and the Far East. Far too interested in travel and intellectual pursuits, neither girl showed any interest in marriage, preferring to use their father's position to explore the world.

While the two Wolf boys grew up to become businessmen of their own, they often knocked heads with their father. The disputes became more pronounced as the boys grew their own businesses. Julius married, but soon after departed Providence and traveled the United States, removing himself from the family almost entirely. Joseph took over one of his father's glove stores in the city. Later in life, Benno cast light on how deep the divide had become with his sons when a codicil was added to his will a year before his death, explicitly disinheriting both sons in favor of his wife and two daughters.

The Wolfs and their daughters continued to live and travel together long after the girls had become adults. Henrietta pursued her education and explorations around the world, but managed to return with her parents to Saratoga each summer. It was during one of their Saratoga sojourns, in the spring of 1901, that 36-year-old Henrietta's life changed forever.

John McCormick Gibson was a heartbroken man. His wife, Abba, had recently died a gruesome death, throwing herself from a 14th floor window to escape a fire at the Windsor Hotel in New York. John, who had witnessed the fire, could do nothing to save his bride. The two years that followed her death were excruciating for John, as he contended with poor health and a broken heart.

Henrietta knew John and Abba from Saratoga, where the couple often summered. John was a strikingly handsome millionaire from the Midwest, where he had inherited a fortune from his family's whiskey distillery business. Soft-spoken and well-educated, with a penchant for cigars, horses, and business, he reminded Henrietta of her father in many ways. When news traveled of Abba's death, Henrietta sent her condolences to John at the Saratoga health spa where he was spending the spring. John suffered from poor health his entire life, with respiratory issues resulting from childhood battles with measles and scarlet fever. His erratic health was only exacerbated by Abba's death, so he had resigned to spend the season healing in the clear air and mineral springs of Saratoga. When he received Henrietta's kind note, he decided he would pay his friends at the Wolf estate a visit.

In his bereaved and ailing state, John seemed like a shadow of his former self. Henrietta felt saddened to see him in such pain and resolved to spend her time in Saratoga bringing him whatever cheer she could. She visited him often at his resort, escorting him on walks around town and reading to him on the porch in the evenings. Henrietta was charming and kind, and John suddenly felt the heavy cloak of sadness lifting from his troubled heart. That spring, as John regained strength and the two spent more time arm in arm, Henrietta and John began to fall in love. As the spring drew to a close, John asked Henrietta if she would marry him. The wedding was set for the following spring.

In Providence, the middle-aged Wolf daughter's betrothal to a wealthy widower was all the social buzz. Henrietta made no time to meddle in local gossip, however. She had a wedding to plan and affairs to get in order. She and John exchanged letters while she made plans to move to his home of Ohio after the wedding. He traveled twice to Providence to visit her at the Wolf's estate on Westminster Street. That summer, they met again in Saratoga for a blissful month before John returned to work and Henrietta to life in Rhode Island.

In late October, however, John's health took a downward turn yet again. Contacting his business managers and closing down work in Cincinnati, John quickly traveled to Asheville, North Carolina, famous for its crisp mountain air and world-class sanitariums. Desperate to find help for his crippling respiratory issues, John checked into the health spa on October 30, 1902. He was immediately diagnosed with aggravated tuberculosis. Within days, John's health became critical. His doctors told him the grim news: his life was coming to an end. John's thoughts were only with Henrietta, and he quickly sent word to Providence, begging her to come to his side. Henrietta all but flew to Union Station, sister Alice by her side, and boarded their father's private Pullman car to make the journey to Asheville.

Henrietta and Alice made it to John's bedside as the doctors gave him mere hours left to live. But as his beloved entered the room, something lifted John from the imminence of death and suddenly his head cleared, his fever subsided, and the air filled his lungs. The medical team was speechless. Love had seemingly saved John McCormick Gibson's life. Or at least, for the time being. John remained in critical condition, though stronger than he had been in days. Henrietta tended to him like a nurse, not leaving his bedside even to rest. Then, just two days after her arrival, John had an idea. "Marry me. Today."

Article entitled "Dr. Cupid Was No Quack" tells the remarkable tale of Henrietta and John Gibson's life-saving love affair. The World, *1902.*

A lawyer was summoned, and the local judge joined Alice as a witness. From his hospital bed, John Gibson and Henrietta Cecilia Wolf were hastily married. After the ceremony, John's doctors noted a marked improvement in his health. Newspapers across the country picked up the romantic tale, running headlines including "Wedding Saves Life," and "Dr. Cupid…Love Prescription Lifted Millionaire Gibson from His Death Bed."

After the excitement of the ceremony wound down, John set about to the business of his estate. Now married, he summoned the lawyers back to his bedside. He wanted to execute changes to his Last Will and Testament immediately, ensuring that should his health fail, his estate would be left to his new bride. A lawyer from Asheville completed the request with a stenographer present.

Henrietta and John spent five days together at the Asheville sanitarium as John regained his strength in the hopes of returning to Cincinnati with his beloved. Then, as suddenly as he had improved, just six days after Henrietta arrived, John Gibson died in his sleep.

Heartbroken and bereaved, Henrietta wept as she packed John's trunks, preparing his belongings to be returned to Ohio along with his remains. As she prepared his paperwork, however, she realized that the newly executed Will had disappeared. The sanitarium was searched, including dressers and drawers in every room, but the document was never found. Henrietta sensed foul play and immediately sent for her father. When Benno arrived, he demanded to see the lawyer who was present when John had dictated his final wishes for the new Will. Though the Will was not found, the stenographer's carbon copy notes were located. Benno and his daughter took the notes with them and accompanied Henrietta's husband's remains to his final resting site in Ohio.

Benno stayed by his daughter's side as the bereaved widow settled her new husband's affairs. But Henrietta was not met with outstretched arms in John's hometown. The Gibson family was immediately suspicious of the stranger from Rhode Island. It wasn't long before Henrietta found herself in court, defending her husband's Will and her inheritance of his multimillion-dollar estate. After much deliberation, a Ohio judge rejected the stenographer's notes as evidence of John's intentions. According to court documents, the judge ruled that the notes, which had not been signed, were void and that John Gibson's estate was to be distributed amongst his mother and siblings, with Henrietta receiving just $400,000.

Henrietta returned to the Wolf mansion on Westminster Street with a new name, a small fortune, and a broken heart. The tabloids were cruel to Henrietta, decrying her "deathbed marriage" as a scandal. Henrietta withdrew from Providence's social circles, the suspect betrothal following her like a heavy veil. She tried to travel, spending time in New York and Europe. But the world had seemed to have lost its shine. Soon she was back in Rhode Island, quietly managing the Wolf estate with her father. When Benno died three years later, Henrietta found purpose in helping to manage her mother's now extensive real estate holdings. Emma, Alice, and Henrietta became even more inseparable. They spent summers together at the Massasoit Hotel in the beach colony of Narragansett Pier, playing tennis and attending boating parties on Point Judith Pond. They lived together the balance of the year on Westminster Street. Each year, on the anniversary of Benno's death, the Wolf sisters ran a memoriam in the paper in his memory.

Then, another tabloid affair rocked the quiet, insular world of the Wolf women. Julius, Henrietta's younger brother, had been found unconscious and in critical condition in a hotel in West Virginia. From the police report taken at the scene, it appeared that Julius had taken a lethal dose of morphine while heavily intoxicated on alcohol. He died shortly thereafter. From a report in *The Providence Journal*, the Wolf women "deplored the inevitable publicity" that they expected would come from their estranged brother's death, particularly with the local gossip of Henrietta just beginning to have settled down. On the heels of their brother's death, Alice and Henrietta left for a lengthy stay in Greece, Italy, and France.

Henrietta had lost her only true love, followed in short order by her adoring father and estranged brother. Then, the unthinkable happened. In 1920, Alice died. Losing her best friend was the final straw for Henrietta, who withdrew entirely. She rarely left the Wolf house. Ceasing travel, she took to managing the family's estate from the cavernous home on Westminster Street. Now just home to herself and her mother, and without the social engagements and parties to fill the grand halls, the house became desolate and dark. On more than one occasion, the house was robbed in the middle of the night. With Prohibition weighing heavily on society, it was the Wolf's wine cellar that was the primary target. In one night, over five cases of whiskey and 30 gallons of wine were hauled off while Henrietta and her mother slept upstairs. The following year, the Providence Chamber of Commerce came knocking at the door. They wanted Mrs. Benno Wolf to invest in a new endeavor: a grand hotel for downtown Providence. Emma conferred with her daughter and the two agreed to buy stock in the new Biltmore Hotel.

Years went by, with Henrietta and Emma living a quiet existence on the outskirts of town. Then, in 1925, Emma died, too, leaving Henrietta utterly alone. A life that had begun in the warm embrace of a large, tightknit family had eroded to a cold and lonesome existence for Henrietta Wolf Gibson. When the lawyers came to present her with Emma's last Will and testament—a deed that left the entirety of the Wolf fortune to Henrietta—the despondent woman signed the documents without emotion. She knew her brother, Joseph, who had long since abandoned the family for his own fortunes, would come for his share of the inheritance. She assigned lawyers to deal with the inevitable court challenge and quietly packed her bags. And with that, Henrietta locked the front door of the Wolf mansion and instructed her driver to take her to the Biltmore Hotel.

The Biltmore was a bustling, glimmering palace at the time of Henrietta's arrival in 1925, but she was not there for the bridge tournaments or afternoon tea in the Garden Room. She wanted to be free of the endless memories that had haunted the hallways of the Wolf house. She wanted to be left alone. Duane Wallick and his staff welcomed the weary widow and respected her request for privacy. They shielded her from nosy columnists, delivered her mail directly to her room, and fielded her telegrams and other missives. For the first few months of her stay, she rarely left her suite. Her name all but disappeared from the social record. She sent out to have miscellaneous items brought to her from the mansion—a piece of art here, a trunk of clothes there. Slowly, she filled her hotel suite with her beloved possessions from happier times in her life.

One day, Henrietta decided to visit the old house. Dressing in fine clothes and an overcoat, Henrietta took the elevator down to the lobby, surprising the bellhop and the front desk clerk with her sudden, unexpected appearance. She requested a taxi be called to take her the two miles west to her family's estate. When she arrived, however, she was met with quite a surprise. Upon entering the front door of the mighty home, she found that many of the family's antiques and works of art had been burglarized. Thieves had forced their way in through a window and stolen a number of extremely valuable pieces, including a statue of Napoleon worth thousands of dollars, and a "priceless" marble bust of Mignone that she had brought home from a trip to the Mediterranean. The stolen art was just the beginning. Room by room, Henrietta found that thieves had been picking away at her belongings, slowly pillaging all she had left in the world. The invasion wounded her deeply. She immediately contacted the police and demanded that they board up the house, covering every window and door. They were to leave what remained of her valuables inside.

The Wolf mansion remained boarded up that way for many years and Henrietta resolved to forget it. She resigned herself to a life of isolation at the Biltmore, only dining occasionally with her nieces and nephews when they had the rare occasion to visit her. The front lawn of the mansion on Westminster Street was slowly encroached upon by overgrown trees and by neighboring businesses. By the 1930s, it was reported that the front lawn had been almost entirely taken over by a nearby used car dealership. The boarded-up house, set back from the road, became derelict. In 1936, the Police station had an internal memo that they need not worry about the Wolf estate anymore, as there could not possibly be anything left to steal from the boarded-up home. Hundreds of thousands of dollars of fixtures, furniture, personal effects, and structural pieces of the home had been pillaged since Henrietta had left for the safety of the Biltmore.

On September 12, 1941, Henrietta left the hotel for some fresh air. She told the front doorman that she would take lunch in her apartment after her walk and left for a stroll. When she returned only a short time later, she reported to the bellman that she was feeling under the weather. Less than an hour later, when her lunch was delivered, Henrietta was found dead in her suite. She was 78 years old.

The hotel notified Henrietta's niece of her passing. As privately as she had lived, Henrietta was quietly laid to rest in the Reservoir Cemetery, of the Congregation of the Sons of Israel and David Temple Beth-El. Shortly after her death, however, questions began to arise as to what happened to her fortune. When her surviving kin (two nieces and two nephews) gathered to hear the reading of the Last Will and Testament, they were told that Henrietta had left nearly all of her estate to one niece, Mrs. Dorothy Wolf Suddard, who resided in Edgewood. Not long after this announcement, it was revealed that a huge sum of money had been withdrawn from Henrietta's bank accounts between August and September, just days before her death. The cash was ostensibly "missing," and it was unclear where it had been spent or gifted. Either way, no one was able to locate it. The sum was the equivalent of $750,000 in present day money. Two months later, her relatives were in court, battling over the Wolf fortune. Contesting the Will were her brothers' children, Walter and Orbert Wolf, and Julius's daughter, Ruth Wolf Snyder.

This was the third time that Henrietta Gibson's fortunes were being contested in court. First, her rights as the widow of John Gibson were spurned by a suspicious mother-in-law; then, Henrietta's disinherited brother demanded to be cut in to Henrietta's inheritance, despite his father's wishes; and now, Henrietta's own final wishes were rejected in court, post-mortem. In the end, the court broke the Last Will and Testament of Henrietta Wolf Gibson, distributing her fortune amongst her nieces and nephews. Even after death, the Biltmore's recluse widow found herself scorned by the very people who were supposed to love her the most.

14

FANNING THE FLAMES

The Providence Biltmore was developing quite the penchant for fast-tracked millionaires and their glorious undoings. By the late 1920s, the Labor movement had rumbled its way through the manufacturing industry, and the booming textile mills began to see the writing on the wall. Labor was expensive. Consolidation was becoming a necessity as the country inched closer and closer to the Great Depression. In 1927, Ford Motor Company closed its factories nationwide, ending manufacturing of the Model T and retooling for the Model A. The man hit singularly hardest by this change in business was the largest and most prominent Ford dealer himself: Dutee Wilcox Flint. Flint was deeply ingrained in production and sales of the Model T and had overextended himself growing his franchise in Rhode Island and beyond. A series of poorly managed business decisions and debts had left Dutee vulnerable, and the Ford financial team latched on to this vulnerability swiftly, and without remorse.

Less than a year later, the Ford company descended on Providence in a takeover of Flint's expansive empire. Flint had little leverage to fight back. Nearly all of his financial empire was intricately tied to the Ford Motor Company. Dutee Wilcox Flint Incorporated was dismantled by board appropriation and liquidated within a matter of days. In a later interview, Dutee, who maintained that the takeover had been the workings of Ford's financial men and not Henry Ford himself, said, "They put me through the wringer. They didn't need to do that."

In reality, it had come to light that Flint owed nearly two million dollars to various banks, mostly on loans that he'd taken out and lines of credit intended to grow his franchise. When the Ford Company closed factories for retooling, there was nothing to sell, and no way for Dutee to maintain his debts in good order. While Flint had reported a sales book valuing four million dollars to Ford Motors and to his creditors, Ford auditors quickly found that the true value was less than $500,000. Dutee Flint's tremendous empire crumbled in a matter of months. Ford's men liquidated his dealerships and found buyers for his properties. They wrote off his businesses in Rhode Island, New Jersey, and New York. They also wrote off the portion of the downtown Wilcox Building that Flint had inherited from his grandfather. Dutee had reached the limits of his success.

Just when it seemed that all was lost for the Flints, a mysterious fire set ablaze their waterfront home, the very place where they had entertained John Bowman's hotel guests on the Biltmore's opening day. The flames engulfed the house in the middle of the night, burning it to the ground. Coincidentally, perhaps, the Flints had packed up a substantial amount of their personal belongings in anticipation of upcoming travel. As the ashes of their estate smoldered, Rose and Dutee Flint, along with their young teenage daughter, arrived at the lobby of the Biltmore hotel to request a long-term stay. Adding to the questionable nature of the fire was the substantial insurance claim processed on the house which provided the Flints with enough capital to sustain themselves for several years.

In the wake of Flint's financial fallout, Rose and Dutee remained residents of the Providence Biltmore for nearly two decades. Dutee maintained strong relationships in the Providence business community and the Newport social circles, despite his situation. The couple debuted their daughter, Rose, in the grand ballroom of the Biltmore on her 16th birthday. Rose's achievements in Newport Horse Shows were documented in various newspapers' social sections, and she was noted in *The New York Times* as one of the first brave swimmers to open the season at Bailey's Beach Club on June 6, 1938. Her wedding in 1945 to Lieutenant Commander John Llyod Hoen was later announced in the *Times*, listing her and her parents as residents of "Newport, Providence, and New York." The Flints maintained appearances and at least enough wealth to keep their status, despite the size of their bank account. They dined in the Garden Room and Town Room restaurants frequently, often asking to have the meals added to their running tab. All the while, Dutee continued to look for new business endeavors, including running a popular radio show from the hotel, operating as WDWF, initials chosen to match his own.

Over the years, Dutee and Rose maintained another apartment in New York City, on East 55th Street, where Dutee died on March 31, 1961. In *The New York Times's* obituary, no mention is made of the undoing of Dutee Flint at the hands of Ford Motor Company. Flint's only known biographer, Frank Comstock, maintains that Flint's ruin came well before the stock market crashed in 1929, even though the *Times* decided to blame Flint's misfortunes on being overinvested in the market. How Dutee himself would have categorized his undoing is something left to be imagined.

Just a few floors away from the Flints and the reclusive Mrs. Gibson, a foul-mouthed tabloid sensation was holed up, awaiting trial on libel charges brought by the Governor of Rhode Island himself. Walter E. O'Hara, owner of the Pawtucket horse track, Narragansett Park, had built quite a reputation—and multi-million-dollar fortune—for himself. Raised in poverty, O'Hara had risen to success in the lucrative textile industry before branching out to horse racing. Some believed he had also dabbled in bootlegging operations. Known to start drinking in the early morning and to often be thoroughly drunk by lunchtime, O'Hara was a mean and aggressive businessman as well as a shrewd money manager. He made himself, and park investors, significant profit in his days as the Park's president, largely due to his wildly unpopular payout policies at the Park.

Narragansett Park in the 1930s had become the most prosperous horse track in the country, largely due to the fact that it paid out winnings to the nearest nickel, not the nearest cent as many other parks of the day would do. Rounding down to the nearest nickel saved the park a tremendous amount in payouts (the pennies difference was called "the breaks"), resulting in more cash in the pocket for its ill-reputed owner. Another strategy employed by O'Hara to increase profit was the use of "preliminary results," or the posting of a race's winners prior to the release of the "photo finish" a few seconds later. It was in this time between the "preliminary results" and the publishing of the "photo finish results" that some bettors would find themselves tearing up a winning ticket—asserting from the preliminary listing that they had lost the race when, in fact, the photo finish showed otherwise. The paper ticket was the only proof of their bet and thus, a torn-up ticket could not be redeemed for winnings.

It was this practice that earned O'Hara the scrutiny of the Rhode Island Racing Division, who employed a steward at the racetrack to oversee operations. The Division, alerted to the discrepancies occurring between the preliminary winner posting and the photo finish, declared in October 1937 that Narragansett Park was no longer allowed to post preliminary results in the event of a photo finish taking place. O'Hara balked. He told the racetrack judges that the Division's proclamation was best ignored. Incensed, Governor Robert Quinn sent the state steward to confront O'Hara in his swanky President's apartment overlooking the racetrack. After just a few moments of heated discussion, O'Hara knocked the steward unconscious. As one journalist aptly put it, "when the state's most flamboyant businessman knocks out his principal regulator in broad daylight, word has a tendency to get around."

Walter O'Hara leaves Rhode Island Superior Court with his wife at his side.
Courtesy of the Boston Public Library, Leslie Jones Collection.

Governor Quinn hated Walter O'Hara long before O'Hara slugged one of his regulators. The two had been at odds since O'Hara had backed Quinn's rival, Mayor McCoy of Pawtucket, in the gubernatorial race of 1936, but the feud is said to have gone back much further. However, having one of his employees knocked out cold in broad daylight infuriated the Governor. He responded by having O'Hara removed as the head of the Park, pending a hearing in the Superior Court. O'Hara, however, seemed to have as much pull as the Governor in matters of justice. He called his personal friend, Superior Court Judge Charles Walsh, and convinced him to postpone the hearing and reinstate O'Hara after the end of the 1937 summer racing season.

The Governor and O'Hara continued to respond to one another's blows. O'Hara, from his suite at the Biltmore, ordered slanderous stories be run about the Governor in the newspaper that he owned,

The Providence Star-Tribune. In one such headline, the paper declared that the Governor was unwell and ill-suited for office, likely to end up in Butler Hospital—Rhode Island's largest psychiatric hospital. The headline was printed in such a way that when the paper was folded for distribution, the front page read "Governor in Butler." O'Hara was promptly sued for libel by the Governor's office.

Shortly after the opening of the track season, O'Hara and his wife were entertaining guests in their suite at the Biltmore before heading out to a private party for the evening. As the party—which included the Mayor of Pawtucket, Thomas McCoy, and the former sheriff—descended the grand staircase from the mezzanine, they were stopped by Sheriff Baird of the Providence Police Department. In the middle of the lobby, the Sheriff began to read the "writ of arrest" to O'Hara, on charges of libel. Before the Sheriff could even finish reading the writ, O'Hara was shouting loudly enough for all in the lobby to hear him, "Speak up, Sheriff, I can't hear you! Speak up! Let my wife hear you!" Mayor McCoy chimed in, questioning the validity of the writ of arrest, claiming that the signature looked like a rubber stamp. The Sheriff pleaded with the group, imploring the mayor to talk sense into O'Hara.

The feud and fighting went on for weeks. The Governor sent the National Guard to prevent the track from opening for the 1937 fall season, a major blow to the track's investors and patrons alike. O'Hara was living between his suite at the Biltmore and a lavish home where his wife resided in Pawtucket. At privately arranged press conferences, he hurled insults at the Governor, who responded with additional libel suits. Then came the final straw for investors at Narragansett Park. O'Hara was indicted for making over $100,000 in illegal campaign donations to various politicians in Pawtucket. A proxy war ensued, and the Park's investors removed O'Hara from his position at the Park. That winter, deputies of the Sheriff's office used sledgehammers to break down the door of O'Hara's Biltmore suite in a raid ordered by the Governor to confiscate all records from the racetrack that were in O'Hara's possession. "Loud booms echoed throughout the hotel corridors as the hammer fell on the mental door," reported *The Providence Journal.* "After about a dozen blows the door, badly dented, yielded."

Advertisement run by the Biltmore Hotel featuring the benefits of living at the hotel. Featured in The Providence Journal, *1938.*

The young, arrogant millionaire was depleted. He had spent hundreds of thousands of dollars battling the Governor in court and settling libel cases. His tabloid newspaper had gone under. By early 1939, his wife had left him on grounds of cruelty, taking his remaining $7,500 and the house in Pawtucket. Walter O'Hara, one-time celebrity resident of the Biltmore and tabloid superstar of the Providence elite, died penniless in a car crash on his way home from the Taunton dog racing track in 1941, at the age of 44.

The lobby of the Biltmore during the 1920s and 30s took center stage in the dramatic affairs of Providence's commercial and private interests. Millionaires flaunted their tremendous wealth throughout the hotel, hosting parties in the myriad dining rooms and taking out a multitude of adjoining rooms as private suites. Behind the scenes, however, the numbers did not add up. The facade of affluence and the trend of exceptionalism left the hotel with long running tabs and substantial debt. These diminished millionaires had become bad for business. By the late 1930s, the Biltmore was charging a minimum of $52 per week to live at the hotel, and it is clear from looking at the estate records of many of the hotel's tenants that there is no way they could afford this bill.

Walter O'Hara and Dutee Flint exemplified the rise and fall of Providence's colossal wealth, and in the wake of their downfall came mounting financial challenges for the businesses they owned and patronized. The Biltmore allowed residents to remain as lodgers on credit, often with tabs that would never be paid. As Walter and Dutee clung to what was left of their riches, Providence, too, clung to its once effervescent success. And the city's grand hotel rose and fell on the crest of the same wave.

15

ANTIDOTES FOR NATIONAL DEPRESSION

When the stock market crashed in October 1929, Rhode Island was already experiencing significant economic challenges. The state's once-booming manufacturing industry was on the decline. Mills and plants were aging, and the cost to improve them was higher than the owners were willing to spend. Southern mills were outcompeting the market with under-paid, non-unionized labor and Rhode Islanders were experiencing unemployment at unprecedented levels. Even before the market crash and the downturn of the nation's economy, the state was plunging into economic peril.

The Biltmore stepped in as an antidote to the depression. For those who escaped financial ruin, the hotel's posh Venetian Room offered solace against a darkened world. In an ad from March 23, 1930, the Biltmore promised: "Come to the enchanting Biltmore Venetian Room where you can dance and chat and sup...while the rollicking fun-makers of the Meyer Davis Orchestra hold forth. Their capers and irresistible dance music will make you feel once more that it's great to be alive!"

In 1982, Aristide Cresto, former manager of the hotel, recalled how the Venetian Room (a new name for the Garden Room) was

Garden Room matchbook from the 1930s. Courtesy of the Graduate Providence.

run by an all-male staff dressed in tuxedos. "There was no money around in those days," he said, but people came to dinner dressed to the nines, nonetheless. The room boasted an ornate parquet dance-floor and a revolving stage, where Hildegarde and Happy Felton's band performed for large crowds. In addition to the Venetian Room, the Falstaff Room opened in 1934 as a retreat for men who had enough money left to spend some on alcohol. The bar was open "for men exclusively, except for Sundays" when accompanied women were allowed to dine with their husbands. It wasn't until the 1980s that the Falstaff Room would allow women at the bar.

In the middle of this difficult decade, the Providence Biltmore

The Falstaff Bar, as photographed in the 1980s with some of the original decor.
Courtesy of the Library of Congress.

opened what would become its most famous destination: the Bacchante Lounge. The first ad, run on February 8, 1935, showcased
across a quarter page in bold text:

> Cocktails for Two in the NEW Bacchante Lounge. Beginning
> Saturday, you'll find here a new and delightful spot in which to
> enjoy the cocktail hour. Until 8 p.m. every weekday evening, the
> Bacchante has a comfortable and luxurious lounge with deep uphol-
> stered furniture, soft glowing lamps, and charming hostesses to serve
> your favorite drink. Supper dancing to Billy Lossez music every
> weekday evening until nine, no cover charge Monday through
> Friday—cover charge on Saturday evenings now only $1.00.

The Bacchante Lounge became a place to see and be seen. More
than its music or cocktail list, the most famous detail about the

Cocktails for Two

IN THE

NEW

BACCHANTE LOUNGE

Beginning Saturday, you'll find here a new and delightful spot in which to enjoy the cocktail hour. Until 8 P. M. every weekday evening, the Bacchante is a comfortable and luxurious lounge with deep upholstered furniture, soft glowing lamps and charming hostesses to serve your favorite drink.

Supper dancing to Billy Lossez music every weekday evening at nine. No cover charge Monday through Friday—cover charge Saturday evenings now only $1.00.

PROVIDENCE BILTMORE

The first advertisement for the Bacchante Lounge in 1935, as featured in The Providence Journal.

Postcard from the original Bacchante Lounge. From the author's collection.

Bacchante was its charming hostesses and their scandalous outfits. The lounge was designed to be intentionally intimate, with dimmed lights and mirrored walls. When a guest wanted to be served, they needed only to push a button on the table to summon a Bacchante Girl. Quickly she would appear, her diaphanous skirt fluttering around her, long legs exposed beneath a sheer cover. To accentuate the attire of the beautiful women, the bar area was cleverly designed with a glass floor under which twinkling pink lights cast an upward glow, intended to showcase the ladies' legs. The Biltmore took good care of their girls. Each waitress was treated to hair and nail appointments in the salon each week, and the hotel paid for their cab home each night. High heels and long legs were mandatory for the job, and no waitress was ever allowed to write down an order. Needless to say, the Bacchante Girls became the subject of much public gossip.

The Bacchante Girls' beauty would gain them their own page in Providence's history. So alluring were the waitresses that when management made a decision to redesign their uniforms and lengthen their skirts to a more conservative style, hundreds of letters poured in from disgruntled men who were aghast at the changes. Patrons

THE SHERATON-BILTMORE HOTEL
Providence, Rhode Island

Postcard featuring the famous Bacchante Girls.
Courtesy of the Graduate Providence.

demanded that the "Mother Hubbards" be allowed to return to their glamorous origins. "In the name of dear old Bacchus, give us back our nets!" one guest from northern New England wrote to the management. The return to nylon netting was celebrated by a three-page spread in *The Providence Journal*.

"We had the grandest time," former Bacchante waitress, Julie Lyons, told the *Journal* at the hotel's 75th anniversary. "New York had their bunnies and we had our Bacchante Girls. We were known around the world." While perhaps considered "PG" by today's standards, the Bacchante was as scandalous as it came in its time. Politicians, mobsters, police officers, servicemen, and businessmen

Photograph of the Bacchante Girls in 1947. Courtesy of the Graduate Providence.

alike could be found in the mirror-walled lounge night after night. Lyons's waitressing career at the Bacchante ended in 1940, however, when her husband put his foot down. No respectable wife of his would be working in *that* restaurant, it was decided.

Duncan Doolittle was in college the night he and a group of friends ventured to the Bacchante Lounge. It was 1942, and, according to Doolittle, every kid in town wanted to get into that club. The Bacchante was what put Providence on the map, as far as Doolittle was concerned. But this particular night, it was not the beautiful servers that ingrained themselves on Duncan's memory. It was a chance encounter with a little-known singer who was having a drink in the Lounge before his performance at Loews State Theatre. Duncan recalled the evening to *The Providence Journal* 30 years later: "We were at the Biltmore, in the Bacchante Room. Every college kid around Providence went to the Bacchante Room at least once, and servicemen, too. There was a group of us that evening: Franny,

Breck, Tony, Yan, and a few others besides myself. As our talk continued, Yan got up and left us. A few minutes later, he returned with a slight, skinny fellow. In those days he would have been referred to as a shrimp."

The shrimp in Duncan's story was none other than Ol' Blue Eyes, Frank Sinatra himself. The crooner had just recently left Tommy Dorsey's band to strike out on his own, but hadn't yet built the following he would have in coming years. When Frank sat down with the group, they fired off questions to him. They wanted to know if the crooner was trying to be the next Bing Crosby. Frank was jovial and down to earth. He assured the group that he didn't think he'd ever be as big as Bing.

It was during these early Bacchante years that a young Navy ensign named John Fitzgerald Kennedy began patronizing the Biltmore, sneaking away from the base in Melville with his navy pals for nights out on the town. If there was ever a barroom to match the personality, allure, and charisma of handsome JFK, the Bacchante Lounge of the 1940s was certainly it. Nights spent imbibing in the Lounge were Kennedy's first entree to the Biltmore, but he'd remain loyal to the hotel for many years to come.

A postcard from the original Bacchante Lounge. From the author's private collection.

Through the 30s and 40s, the hotel remained the only suitable accommodation for famous entertainers that passed through the city. Actors, vocalists, magicians, musicians, and athletes alike were treated to luxury service and fielded frequent requests for interviews in their well-adorned rooms at the hotel. Eva La Gallienne, a pioneering Broadway actress and founder of the repertory theater movement, resided at the Biltmore during a tour in Providence. When, in 1930, the first Broadway show to feature an all-Black cast, *The Green Pastures*, won the Pulitzer Prize for drama, the national tour brought its star actor, Richard B. Harrison, to Providence. *The Green Pastures* was run for a week at the downtown Carlton Theater, and Mr. Harrison spent that time as a resident of the hotel.

Rhode Island desperately clung to tourism as a means of revenue in the difficult decade after the stock market crash. The state relied on tourism revenue especially in the wake of the manufacturing industry's decline. The Biltmore played a central role in attracting tourism to the city during this time, as it had in the 1920s. In June 1930, the hotel held an overnight package event, courtesy of hotel management, for the American Automobile Association (AAA). "The object of the tour is to give the delegates an opportunity to gain firsthand information about New England and to see its historical points of interest," *The Providence Journal* reported. "The touring directors then are to return and explain to motorists and tourists planning vacations what is in store for them in New England." The Rhode Island portion of the tour included a stay at the hotel, a visit to Roger Williams Park, and a visit to the only lobster hatchery in the world at that time. The Biltmore was also the host of food drives and charity events that raised funds for those who were out of work and families who lacked enough income to feed their children. In January 1933, the citywide Food Drive for jobless families was launched at the Biltmore, raising more than $4000 on opening day alone.

As hotels across the United States struggled to maintain profitability during the Depression, hotel owners and operators continued

An advertisement from 1930 in Yachting Magazine, *encouraging tourists to stay at the Biltmore. Courtesy of the Graduate Providence.*

to advocate for policies and legislation that would improve financial outlooks. In 1935, the Providence City Council held an open hearing regarding proposed legislation that would limit the number of days that the Narragansett Park racetrack was open. Not a single person came forward in support of limiting the track's hours, but countless businessmen came forward against it. One pamphlet distributed at the hearing estimated that thousands of people from outside the state came to Rhode Island solely to gamble at the racetrack each day. The pamphlet furthered that to outlaw or limit legal gambling would only drive gambling underground and away from the state's ability to profit from it, citing the Prohibition era as an example of what would happen if the Council attempted to legislate people's behavior. Perhaps the most elaborate testimony given at the hearing was given by Duane Wallick himself. "In speaking for the Biltmore," he said, "I must in all fairness say that the opening of Narragansett Park was one of the outstanding boons that saved [us] from financial ruin. It is a well-known fact that the Depression years forced 84 percent of American hotels into bankruptcy. I believe all will admit that a hotel of the type of the Biltmore is an outstanding asset to Providence. The periods in which Narragansett Park operates are dull months in the hotel business and the great influx of racing enthusiasts arising in those dull times made it possible for the Biltmore to continue its first-class type of hotel operation." Wallick went on to explain that the money made at the hotel flows directly back into the city, quickly highlighting that the success of the hotel meant success for the city. The more people that came to the hotel, the more produce, sundries, and supplies would be procured from local merchants, and more maids, porters, and housemen would be hired. "In my opinion it would be an unfortunate thing for the business life of the entire community if the period of racing days were cut down." The track's hours remained unchanged thanks, in part, to Wallick's testimony.

Early in the Depression, it seemed that the Biltmore might escape the losses that other hotels were experiencing nationwide. Optimism began to fade, however, when the hotel reported losses over four subsequent years. By 1935, owner Lou Wallick began hinting at the hotel's reorganization, a move he considered proactive to save the company and allow it to become profitable in the second half of the decade.

Providence's financial decline continued throughout the 1930s. From 1923 to 1938, the total number of workers in the textile industry in Rhode Island had dropped from 34,000 to 12,000, and it was not just in textiles that the decline could be seen. All industries, trades, and white-collar jobs were affected by the Depression. The City of Providence, like cities acwross the nation, began implementing public works projects to provide jobs to unemployed citizens. Funded through state and federal loans, the Works Progress Administration (WPA) projects aimed to keep people afloat despite the desperate times. Projects included the construction of new roads, schools, public buildings, and parks improvements. While projects managed to keep people working for a time, it was not until the boom of the World War II economy that Providence would see real recovery, and even that was fleeting.

One WPA project that remains today is Pierce Memorial Stadium, in East Providence. The new stadium created jobs for local carpenters and masons, and provided a venue for community events such as baseball leagues, athletic fundraisers, and musical performances. One very special guest was welcomed at the stadium right after its completion. Newly retired, Babe Ruth came to Rhode Island in 1941 to promote his new movie, *Pride of the Yankees.* But it was not his career with the Red Sox or the Yankees that brought the crowds to the stadium. Ruth was celebrated in Rhode Island for his early career on the Providence Grays, long before he broke world records. The celebrity batter stayed overnight at the Biltmore before taking a limousine to the field for the event, where he was greeted by 4,000 fans and the Governor of Rhode Island. Three amateur pitchers were invited to pitch to the All Star, who batted five pitches out of the park that night.

Compounding the economic challenges were those of the labor force. In 1934, the United Textile Workers (UTW) union called a strike of all textile workers nationwide. It was spurred on by the desire to decrease the differential in pay between the southern and northern textile worker. Textile owners opposed the strike. The Providence Chamber of Commerce called the Wagner-Connery Bill, which

Babe Ruth with an adoring fan. Courtesy of the Library of Congress.

was designed to help unions attain collective bargaining power, "un-American" and a "direct interference with the operations of business." But the UTW supported it, pointing to the fact that southern mill owners were not following the guidelines established under Roosevelt's National Recovery Act, particularly in regard to the minimum wage. That September, 500,000 textile workers in the northern and southern mills walked out on their jobs. Union "agitators" were called "Communists" in the newspapers. The anti-communist vigilantes of the American Legion and the Ku Klux Klan vowed to "take care of" any outside agitators who came to Rhode Island.

In Rhode Island the strike was met with violence at the picket lines. Governor T. F. Green called in the National Guard. Green, a Democrat, placed the blame publicly on the millowners for refusing to bargain with the unions. With the situation escalating, President Roosevelt intervened and ended the strike on September 22nd, appointing a national arbitration board to manage negotiations. In the end, Rhode Island workers made no gains, and the union lost members.

This was not the first major strike that would send shock waves through the national labor force, and it certainly would not be the last. It was exemplary, however, of the changes in America's workforce that would continue to have permeating impacts on manufacturing and the growth of industry across sectors. The conflict between the needs and demands of the worker and the profits of the company had reached a breaking point. By the 1940s, Providence was in dire financial straits. The "manufacturing miracle" of the preceding century had finally ended, leaving in its wake a hollowed economy. While much of the country began to transition to the service industry and away from manufacturing, it would take Providence decades to make the shift in a meaningful way.

The country was suffering, and so were the hotel's books. In March 1935, Lou Wallick arrived in Providence from Ohio on the evening train. He trusted Duane's judgment in the management of the hotel, but recent financial reports had indicated that son his was in need of some help. The company's annual report showed an accumulated deficit of $763,689, as well as arrears on preferred stock dividends of more than $2,250,000 to shareholders. The deficit included tens of thousands of dollars in unpaid real estate tax and mortgage interest arrears. Lou Wallick assured the public that the Biltmore's downturn mirrored that of other hotels in the country— it was the Great Depression, after all. He exuded confidence that changes were in the works to right the ship and to "put the hotel on a paying basis." The changes began formally after a crucial meeting of the hotel's Board of Directors. Lou's intervention appeared to have a positive effect, coupled with a strengthening economy. In March 1936, the *Journal* released the hotel's profit and loss statement and declared that the Biltmore's operating loss year over year had been dramatically reduced.

Then, on March 13th, the *Journal* reported that the Providence Biltmore Hotel had entered a plea in federal court for the reorganization of the hotel under Section 77B of the National Bankruptcy Act. The intent of the reorganization was to enable the company to secure an extension of its mortgage and a reduction in the interest rate, as well as to simplify what was viewed as an overly complicated capital structure. It would also allow the company the ability to raise new funds in amounts sufficient to pay outstanding debt, including dividends in arrears to shareholders. A partial list of creditors was run in the paper on April 14, 1936, with a note that the names of all shareholders of first and second preferred stock were also submitted to the court.

During court proceedings, Arnold Jones, treasurer of the hotel company, filed a request to the federal judge presiding over the reorganization to be allowed to spend $16,000 to add air conditioning to the Bacchante Lounge and the Lunch Room, citing the steep decrease in receipts from the two eateries as soon as hot weather begins. The expenditure was approved by the court, and the hotel got its first air conditioning systems that summer.

As part of the hotel's reorganization, Metropolitan Life Insurance Co. extended the mortgage on the hotel by five years, to 1941, and lowered the interest rate from 6 percent to 4 percent. The reorganization cost the hotel corporation over $18,000 in legal fees, which had to be further approved in federal court.

It is likely that Lou Wallick and the Biltmore's Board of Directors had seen the writing on the wall. The reorganization not only simplified the hotel's books for them at the moment, but it also set up the hotel to be more attractive for potential buyers, something that would become increasingly important as the decade went on.

16

HELL AND HIGH WATER

On September 22, 1938, a thick and melancholy sky swirled over Rhode Island. As the afternoon went on, the wind began to increase, and it became clear that a storm was headed toward the coast. What came next, however, was no ordinary storm. Shortly after 4 p.m., the dark waters of the Narragansett Bay rose in a wall of sea water, charging at the coast and pummeling everything that stood in its way. In a matter of minutes, Providence found itself under 12 feet of water, with 90-mile-per-hour winds tossing trees, cars, and portions of buildings across the flooded streets.

Earlier that day, the Biltmore's banquet staff had set the ballroom for a 500-person reception scheduled for that evening. Armand DiMartino was working banquets that afternoon, finishing up the final touches in the ballroom. Engrossed in his work, at first, he did not notice the eerie silence that had fallen over the building. He turned his head, listening for other staff in the hallways. Frustrated, he headed for the door of the ballroom to call down to the kitchen. Before he could make the call, however, his eye caught the view of the east side of the city. Armand could barely believe what he saw. The Providence river was swelling high above its banks, swirling, he said, like boiling water in a pan.

Suddenly, the lights flickered on and off in the ballroom. Armand ran toward the door, wanting to get to the elevators and warn the other staff about the river. A crashing sound filled the room. Looking back, Armand saw the huge windows on the Dorrance Street side erupt into a cascade of glass. Hurricane force winds whipped through the ballroom, overturning tables and smashing flatware and glasses to the floor. Armand was sprayed with broken glass as the remaining windows cracked and shattered under the strength of the wind. He ran from the room just as the entire hotel fell into darkness. Descending 17 flights of stairs, Armand made it to the kitchen where the rest of the staff were lighting candles and waiting on news of the storm surge from those who had daringly ventured outside to brave the wind and rain in an attempt to get home to their families. Some never returned. The hotel sustained tremendous damage from the storm, with contemporary reports stating that the entire lower lobby had been destroyed. Nearly all the windows in the ballroom had to be repaired or replaced. A plaque in the lobby still marks the water line, nearly seven feet off the floor.

A postcard showing the wreckage downtown during the 1938 hurricane.
Courtesy of the Graduate Providence.

The state had almost no warning. The study of hurricanes was not new, but interest in tracking storms and being able to provide early warning was in its infancy. Just three weeks before the hurricane, the US Navy had stationed two men on a tiny remote island 150 miles off the coast of Honduras where they believed that hurricanes were "breeding." The intention was to have these Navy men remain on Swan Island and report storms as they developed by radio, which could then be relayed to Florida and up the East Coast of the United States. Unfortunately, this early prevention system had done nothing to forecast the storm that was headed for Rhode Island that day.

The National Guard was immediately deployed to clear the wreckage and stop the looting that occurred as shops were overtaken by the high water. The Red Cross worked tirelessly to assist those who were injured and to clear the bodies of the dead. As the water receded, hundreds were found drowned in the vehicles and homes across the state and hundreds more were missing, presumed swept out to sea. *The New York Times* reported estimates that put the damage in the hundreds of millions of dollars, particularly to commercial businesses, residential homes, and the industrial mills and factories throughout the state.

With *The Providence Journal* building completely underwater, a four-page paper was printed at an auxiliary printing press in Woonsocket for release the next day. In addition, more than 300 men, women, and children were imprisoned by the water in City Hall, forced to remain on the upper floors of the building until the following morning. Hundreds more found themselves trapped in the streets, with many being rescued by ropes dropped from the windows of upper floors of office buildings.

That night, Joseph and Lorraine Fogel were married at the Narragansett Hotel. When the storm took out the power downtown, the couple said their vows by candlelight. Later that night, as the flood waters receded, they were then escorted by the National Guard to the Biltmore Hotel where they were to have their honeymoon. The couple were safe and sound, but the hotel was in disarray. The elevators and power were down. In total darkness, a bellhop escorted the newlyweds up 14 flights of stairs to their honeymoon suite. At the room, however, the bellhop discovered that he had grabbed the wrong luggage and had to make the trip down and up the stairs all over again.

The newspapers followed the story in Rhode Island closely, printing long lists of names of people who were missing or pronounced dead. Entire towns had been destroyed, with hundreds of seaside homes having been carried out to sea. Stories poured in of nightmarish experiences, survivors recounting watching their loved ones be taken by the sea. A whole school bus of children was reported drowned when it was caught in the flood waters in Jamestown. In total, it was estimated that approximately 280 Rhode Islanders were killed in the storm, of the total 700 casualties. Millions of dollars of reconstruction were needed to restore the homes and businesses that had been hit by the storm. The largest single lumber operation in history originated from the need for reconstruction in New England after the storm. Two-and-a-half billion boards were felled from American forests for lumber. Although most businesses were able to return to normal operations within a few weeks, the horror and trauma of the unexpected storm would linger in the minds of Providence denizens for decades. After the hurricane, which was reported two decades later to be the most damaging hurricane in the history of the world, a dramatic increase in the US Weather Service budget was instituted, intent on increasing the ability of the federal government to track storms.

The next time the Biltmore found itself under water was on August 31, 1954. The paper's headline that day had read "Hurricane Now Losing Strength." By lunchtime, 100-mile-per-hour winds were whipping through downtown. A judge in the County Superior Court called a recess so people could go move their cars. The

Flood waters cover cars on Washington Street and surround the corner
entrance to the Biltmore Hotel. Courtesy of the Providence Public Library
Digital Collections, Rhode Island Photograph Collection.

river was rising and the torrential rains were creating floods, but business continued as usual downtown. The hurricane sirens had not gone off and people believed that the hurricane had been diminished before reaching Rhode Island's shores.

Within an hour, the Providence river completely flooded over the banks and sent cars whirling through the canal-like streets of downtown. Black, oily water poured through the lower levels of buildings. At the Biltmore, the glass doors and first floor windows were no match to the pressure of the surge. Glass shattered and the thick water filled the lobby. According to a report the next day, "Dorrance Street was an angry river, dirty gray and flecked with whitecaps and spray." While Hurricane Carol, as she was named, did not have the fatal devastation of the Hurricane of 1938, its wreckage was deeply felt across the city. Countless businesses sustained exorbitant damage. Thirty-five hundred cars were destroyed. On the heels of a second devastating hurricane in two decades, the city finally took action. An $18 million hurricane barrier was built at the entrance of the Bay. In 1991, the hurricane barrier was tested and succeeded in holding back the 10-foot swells of Hurricane Bob. Providence could finally breathe easy knowing there was protection in the face of the storm.

17

PREPARING FOR WAR

Prohibition. Depression. Hurricanes. It seemed like just as the city emerged from one crisis, another came rolling in. Sure enough, across the ocean another menace was gaining strength. Adolf Hitler was gaining power in Germany and quickly consolidating his control through violence and suppression. With the passage of the Nuremberg Laws in September 1935, Hitler had made clear his plans to rid Germany of the Jewish population. In the wake of the Great War, Americans had little appetite for battle. Hitler's advances and threats were widely viewed as a "European problem," with many Americans believing that the country would be best to stay out of it. However, not everyone had the luxury of ignoring Hitler's terrifying agenda.

At a banquet in the Biltmore ballroom in July 1936, a Jewish activist named Alter Boyman was toasting Dr. Ilie Berger, delegate from Rhode Island to the World Jewish Conference in Geneva, when he lifted his cup and saw the stamp on the bottom: *"Made in Bavaria, Germany, Expressly for the Providence Biltmore, 1935."* Boyman, the head of the Jewish Labor union, was incensed. Pointing at the dishes and addressing the crowd, Boyman heatedly assailed the "audacity" of the hotel to serve the Jewish dinner guests "on dishes made by the madman Hitler." He went on to declare that the "question of a boy-cott of German-made goods is not merely a Jewish question. The boycott of Hitler is necessary to preserve the civilized world, and I have had my banquet ruined by the fact that I had to eat from dishes made in a country where they have been stamping out civiliza-tion." The banquet descended into a storm of complaints. Boyman shouted over the din, "I hope that, when Dr. Berger returns from Geneva, we won't have to eat from dishes made in Hitler Germany!" The *Journal* reported that the banquet-goers were stunned by the revelation, and many complained directly to management about the use of the dishes.

After the attack on Pearl Harbor, the United States could ignore the war no more. The country's participation was imminent. By April 1941, the city of Providence was implementing practice "blackouts" in case a threat of aerial raids came to American shores. During one of the early tests, more than 200 spectators clamored to Prospect Terrace Park to watch their city descend into darkness. As the warning sirens blared, a dark cloak spread quickly across the city's buildings and homes. Downtown hotels had warned guests that their lights would be cut. At the Biltmore, heavy curtains were drawn in the lobby where just a few small lights were allowed to remain on. During these tests, the only lights that could be seen from the Terrace park were two spotlights that reached up toward the sky at opposite angles, forming a "V," for Victory.

Blackouts, sugar and gasoline rationing, and rubber drives served as just a few examples of how Providence, like other cities, pitched in to aid the cause. Gas rationing plans for the city were rolled out by the state's Office of Price Administration (OPA) at a meeting at the Biltmore in July 1942. The panel of speakers that day encour-aged filling station attendants to be vigilant against gas hoarding and reminded the nearly 1,000 officials and staff at the meeting that gas-oline consumption had to be cut in half, at all costs. To boost morale, the city planned free events at Roger Williams Park. In August 1942, a Biltmore vocalist, Cyrel Rodney, who normally appeared in the Garden Room show, volunteered her voice to the opening of Coast Guard Week.

The Providence Biltmore Officer's Club, which operated out of the Tower Room on the 16th floor of the hotel, hosted 16,844 officers between 1943 and 1944. The Officers were hosted by 3,432 hostesses, with 3,308 overnight hotel guests signing the register. The club boasted a weekly Saturday night dance in addition to dinners and special events to encourage optimism and boost morale amongst the Officers and their guests. The local papers covered Rhode Island's "boys at war" endlessly during those years. Article after article featured interviews with soldiers abroad, many times asking them about day-to-day life in army outposts. In one such interview, 22-year-old Rhode Islander Lt. Harvey Salk told the reporter that the weather in England was lousy; the English girls were alright; and he'd give anything to see the Hotel Biltmore in Providence just one more time.

In preparation for the war to "come home," the Army Medical Corps began a survey of hotels across the country in the fall of 1942. The intent was to identify buildings that could quickly and efficiently be converted to serve as Army hospitals should the need arise. In speaking to the paper in Providence, a spokesperson for the Medical Corps indicated that though there were no immediate plans to take over the hotel, it had been earmarked for use if need be. The hotel's "fireproof construction" was noted as a strong characteristic making it suitable for use, as well as its ability to furnish over 1,000 beds and cots in service of the Army's needs, at a moment's notice. The *Journal* also reported that the hotel's staff would continue to be employed, particularly the kitchen staff, who would be needed to serve food to medical personnel and the war-wounded. A conversion of the hotel to a hospital never came, however, as the war ended before the need arose for expanded medical facilities in the United States.

Educational institutions throughout Rhode Island began to

prepare for the possibility that their boys might face military service before they entered college. The Worcester Academy, a college prep school for boys, set up tables and held drop-in hours at the Biltmore to discuss their school with interested parents, including their new program "adapted to the needs of boys who may face war service before they finish their college work." While institutions like the Academy prepared to send our boys overseas, the Biltmore also began to welcome those who fled the plague of Nazi terror in Europe.

Long before Hollywood made them a household name, The von Trapp Family Singers were touring America, carving out a name for themselves as an endearing traveling band. The family of 12 had recently fled Nazi-occupied Austria, opting for the life of refugees over the denouncement of their Roman Catholic faith. When they arrived at the Biltmore, they were on their first tour of the US, playing auditoriums and theaters to the delight of adoring audiences.

Recounting the journey from one of their seven adjoining rooms at the Biltmore, the Baroness Maria von Trapp told a reporter at *The Providence Journal*, "'What is God's will?' we asked ourselves. This is a test to see if we have confidence in a divine Providence." When the family had first arrived in New York, she told the interviewer, they had almost nothing to their name. They immediately set about to make handicrafts, each child practicing a trade. Baron Georg von Trapp was a skilled carpenter, and the boys were silversmiths, wood carvers, and leatherworkers. The entire family pitched in to make crafts in Austrian design. Selling the crafts, the family found great success. In addition, as word spread of their talent for singing and music, they lined up concerts in which they would sing and perform on various instruments. By the time they made it to the Biltmore, they were three years into their American journey, and the von Trapps were no longer at a loss for what to do with their time or talent. In the week that they stayed at the hotel, the family performed for the Providence Community Concert Association, East

The von Trapp Family Singers on tour in the United States. Courtesy of Wikimedia Commons with the permission Bibliothèque et Archives nationales du Québec.

Senior High School in Pawtucket, and at Providence's Handicraft Club.

In *The Sound of Music,* the musical and movie that would make the family famous 15 years later, it is Maria and Georg's unexpected love affair during Austria's fall to the Third Reich that becomes the focal point of the story. In real life, however, it was the journey that they underwent *after* arriving in the United States that captivated Americans in the early years of the war. The von Trapp family and their adorable and talented children boosted morale of audiences everywhere and cemented, even further, America's conviction to fight against the terror of Nazi Germany.

18

STATE SECRETS IN SUITE 1009

With the country at war, Duane Wallick was under a lot of pressure from all sides. From food rationing and black-outs, to preparations to convert to a hospital, Wallick had more than one important task to keep him occupied while managing the busy hotel. However, the request that came on a cold February morning in 1942 was decidedly the strangest request received thus far. Wallick was told that he would be taking in a new long-term guest, and a bricklayer was going to be needed. Wallick suddenly found himself charged with protecting a life, and state secrets, for Roosevelt's War Department.

The Biltmore staff set about quickly preparing Suite 1009 for their new tenant. First, a locksmith came to change locks on the windows and doors so there could be only one key, with no master passkey like the other hotel rooms. Then, a bricklayer came. After a few hours' work, one of the suite's entrances, a doorway leading to the main hall, had been completely bricked up. Next, plaster was laid over the brick, followed by a coat of paint that only partially matched the rest of the suite. With that, only one remaining door provided access to the multi-room suite. One way in, one way out. When the workmen were done, Wallick was notified and he, in turn, called

Antoine Gazda, Swiss munitions dealer and inventor who lived under FBI surveillance at the Biltmore during WWII. Photo courtesy of Rhode Island Aviation Hall of Fame.

the contact he was given at the Federal Bureau of Investigation's Providence office. The room was ready for their special guest. The next day, a large black car pulled up to the front of the hotel. From it, agents in dark suits rounded the car and opened the door closest to the curb. Out stepped a balding, middle-aged man with a black tie and jacket, a leather briefcase held tightly in his arms. The man looked up and smiled, happy to be back in Providence.

Before coming to the United States, Antoine Gazda was a successful inventor and munitions salesman for a Swiss company that sold the Oerlikon anti-aircraft cannon. Originally designed in Germany, production and sales of the powerful weapon had been moved to Switzerland after the Treaty of Versailles banned production of ammunition and weapons of war in Germany. Rights for production of the cannon, along with many other munitions, were quickly transferred to Switzerland where German technology could continue to be produced and tested. In the 1930s, with rearmament ramping up all across Europe, trade and sales of arms became a lucrative business. Antoine Gazda was in on the ground floor, managing the Oerlikon Machine Tool Works near Zurich and overseeing sales of the Oerlikon A.A. cannon to the Germans, the Italians, the Japanese, and the English. He traveled extensively around the world with the powerful weapon, indiscriminately showcasing its powerful anti-aircraft capabilities to military leaders under the Oerlikon slogan: *"The right answer for the coming dive-bomber menace."*

The climate in Europe was changing. It was becoming clear that Germany was intent on total domination of the continent. As their military advanced, Germany cut off delivery of the many European-produced munitions to the British, including the Oerlikon. Fearful that the Germans would take him captive, Gazda used his British connections to help him secretly escape from Switzerland to the United States. With him, Gazda took one of the most prized military possessions of his day: the blueprints for the Oerlikon cannon. The British Royal Navy hoped that Gazda could set up production of the cannon in the United States, still unscathed by the war, and from there, import the gun to fight back against Hitler's air invasions. The gamble paid off.

Arriving on May 26, 1940, Gazda quickly leveraged his extensive connections in the United States government and private industry to negotiate for exclusive manufacturing rights for the cannon in the US. Upon invitation by Rhode Island's Governor, William Vanderbilt, Gazda was welcomed in Rhode Island for a demonstration of the Oerlikon at the Cranston Street Armory. The goal was to entice Rhode Island's manufacturing titans to see the merit in transitioning production from their current line to production of the Oerlikon for the war effort. In order to show off the power of the weapon, however, Gazda needed to have one on hand. Building a cannon without a manufacturing partner was impossible, so Gazda tried to import one from a contact in France. The Nazis seized his cannon in Bordeaux before it could be sent to America. Never discouraged, Gazda sent word to the British Navy to loan him a cannon for his

American demonstration. The Navy agreed, shipping an Oerlikon to Rhode Island post haste.

With the cannon set up in the Armory building, Gazda invited Rhode Island manufacturers to observe the mighty weapon. He held a multi-day visitation of the Armory where he gave talks on the profitability of munitions manufacturing and the necessity of Rhode Island's industry to the war effort. Gazda was met with some resistance in Rhode Island, particularly from those who were not sympathetic to "Britain's war with Germany," still hoping to keep America out of Europe's war. Despite pushback, Gazda was able to impress enough manufacturers and contracts for the production of the cannon soon followed. Gazda incorporated the American Oerlikon Gazda Corporation (AOG), with an office in Providence and an assembly plant in Pawtucket. Production of the Oerlikon started immediately, employing 15 other firms in Rhode Island to assist the

Aboard the HMS Rodney, *a group of officers receive instruction in the use of a 20mm Oerlikon anti-aircraft cannon. Courtesy of WikiCommons.*

manufacturing of the cannons. When larger scale production was needed, General Motors in Detroit picked up the slack and began to produce the cannon on contract with AOG. Millions of dollars in production contracts from the British Royal Navy followed. According to the Rhode Island Aviation Hall of Fame, by the end of World War II, nearly every vessel in the Allied fleet carried Gazda's anti-aircraft guns.

With a daring escape from the Third Reich, smuggling blue-prints for one of the most powerful weapons of war to the United States, and convincing the manufacturers of Rhode Island to switch gears to aid in the British and US Naval efforts, by all accounts, Antoine Gazda could have been viewed as a war hero. However, something then happened that dramatically shifted American sentiments: the Japanese attacked Pearl Harbor, thrusting the United States into the war. Immediately after the attack, and under extreme political pressure, President Roosevelt issued Presidential Proclamations 2525, 2526, and 2527 to authorize the detainment of any persons deemed potentially dangerous to the United States. These individuals were labeled "enemy aliens." In a rapid sweep, the FBI and other law enforcement agencies arrested thousands of suspected threats to the US, mostly individuals of German, Italian, or Japanese descent.

Antoine was having a quiet lunch in his suite at the Waldorf-Astoria in New York City with his friend and secretary, Baroness Lisette von Kapri of Austria, when a knock came at the door. The two Europeans were not even afforded the time to pack up their things before being promptly placed under arrest. Charged with being potentially dangerous to the United States, Gazda and the baroness were carted off to Ellis Island, where they were detained for two months pending a hearing by a citizens review board.

The Baroness von Kapri was a celebrity in her own right. According to the *New York Herald Tribune,* the Baroness learned to fly planes in Cairo in 1934 and went on to be labeled "the most beautiful woman pilot in Europe" for her well-known flights across the continent. The Baroness left Europe in 1939, interested in conferring with airplane manufacturers in the United States about the possibility of producing airplane ambulances which could serve both sides of the war on the front lines. The Baroness came under suspicion of the FBI when she went to Cuba in early 1940, where she was entertained by a prominent undercover agent for Germany and Italy, Prince Ruspoli de Colleani. Before being arrested with Gazda in New York, the Baroness had just filed for her US citizenship papers.

Gazda was incensed by the detainment, demanding to speak with President Roosevelt himself. That call never came through, but he and the baroness were released on parole to the War Department when it was deemed that his management of productions of the Oerlikon cannon were too critically important to the war effort to keep him in custody. The FBI decided that the best thing to do was to keep Gazda and his wife, Leopoldine (who had been detained elsewhere) on house arrest, allowing him to continue management of his production plant in Pawtucket. This is how Antoine Gazda, inventor and munitions dealer, came to live in Suite 1009 at the Biltmore Hotel under lock and key.

After being moved into the Biltmore, the Gazdas were monitored 24 hours a day. Antoine was allowed limited movement during his house arrest and maintained an office in the Industrial Trust Building, where American Oerlikon Gazda (AOG Corp.) was headquartered. Gazda's AOG continued production despite its founder's fate. In the weeks following Pearl Harbor, AOG secured a $26,800,000 contract with the United States Navy department to produce the Oerlikon anti-aircraft cannon for the US fleet. Within just a few months, the contract had doubled.

While housed at the Biltmore under the watchful eye of the FBI, Gazda continued his inventions. Though he maintained an interest in munitions, he did not limit himself to the war effort. While living at the hotel, Gazda secured over 280 patents for his inventions, spanning a broad range from shock-resistant handlebars for bicycles to water filters for cars to keep engines from rusting. He gained significant attention for his focus on single-person helicopters, which he called the Helicospeeder. It was his belief that, after the war ended, the helicopter would become the primary mode of aviation travel for civilians around the world.

Exactly how long Antoine Gazda remained under house arrest is unclear. We know that by 1943, the Gazdas were no longer living under the supervision of the FBI, but they continued to live at the Biltmore. Leopoldine, an experienced pilot, auto mechanic, and inventor in her own right, had added "society matron" to her long list of achievements during her time in Rhode Island. She and Antoine regularly hosted dignitaries, politicians, and wealthy philanthropists in their suite at the hotel. After the war, they bought an estate in Narragansett that they named Westlake and by the mid-40s, they were frequently tracked in the *Journal's* Society section. In 1943, the *Journal* ran a massive four-part series on Antoine's life, highlighting the incredible escapades of the inventor. By the end of the war, Antoine was celebrated for his contributions to Allied efforts, though the government never formally apologized for his treatment after Pearl Harbor.

PART III
CHASING MODERNITY

19

A NAME IN LIGHTS

D espite the economic surge caused by the second World War, the Biltmore continued to experience financial challenges. John McEntee Bowman died unexpectedly at the age of 56 after suffering complications following a gallbladder surgery. His death shocked the hotel industry, leaving the Biltmore Hotel Corp. without a leader. Lou Wallick made the announcement shortly after Bowman's death that he intended to retire, handing over management duties of the hotel to the Biltmore Board of Directors and his son, Duane. By the mid-40s, the Board began to consider their options. Inevitably, in January 1947, ownership of the Biltmore changed hands for the first time since its inception.

The new owners of the Biltmore were making quite a name for themselves throughout the country. Up and coming entrepreneurs from Massachusetts, Ernest Henderson and Robert Moore had met during undergraduate studies at Harvard. Both had been aviators in World War I and, after the war, had started their first business venture with a string of radio shops across New England. The duo then moved on to real estate, purchasing their first hotel, The Stonehaven Hotel, in Springfield, MA. Their second hotel, the Continental Hotel, was purchased in Cambridge that same year. By 1940, they had three hotels: one in Boston, one in New York, and one in Providence. Initially their venture was called the Standard Equities Corporation. However, their third hotel purchase, located in Boston, came with an expensive neon sign on its roof that carried the hotel's former name: The Sheraton Hotel. This original Sheraton had been named for Boston cabinet-maker Thomas Sheraton, and the sign was installed by previous owners. Ernest Henderson, coincidentally, had a soft spot for Thomas Sheraton's cabinetry and furniture work, having developed a love of antiques early in life. The pair decided to keep the sign, and ultimately made the decision to rebrand all of their hotels "Sheratons." The Sheraton Hotels Corporation was born. Following the formation of the Sheraton Corp., Henderson and Moore purchased the famed Copley-Plaza in Boston. By the time they purchased the Providence Biltmore in 1947, the duo had 27 hotels in their empire.

The Sheraton Hotel chain was rapidly becoming the most successful in the country, largely due to Henderson's frugality and their unique model of owning the hotels they operated, instead of simply leasing the buildings as Hilton and other chains had done. While most hotel operations frequently ran in the red, the Sheraton Corporation continued to see a profit on its assets—namely the land and buildings that their hotels occupied. Sheraton Corp. was also the pioneer of the use of technology in hotel management systems. Just one year after purchasing the Biltmore, Sheraton Corp. made history by introducing the first electronic reservation network, the telex system, which was an early forerunner to their later used Reservatron. Sheraton became the first hotel chain in the world to centralize and computerize their hotel reservation system, an innovation that would make them the most popular hotel chain in the country. Sheraton would later become the first hotel chain to implement a 1-800 number, allowing guests to manage their own reservations via telephone.

Even at its sale in 1947, 25 years after its opening, *The Providence*

Journal reported that "the [Biltmore] hotel is considered one of New England's most modern hostelries" with 600 rooms on 18 floors. The new managers of the Sheraton Biltmore advertised widely that its Falstaff Room and the Bacchante Room both featured televisions. In addition, at the time of the sale, the ground floor and lobby of the hotel still housed some of Providence's most prestigious shops. Approximately 625 individuals were employed at the hotel at its sale, and the new management told *The Providence Journal* that no changes were planned to its staff. That said, it was during the changeover to Sheraton that Duane Wallick cut ties with the hotel, marking the end of an era for the iconic landmark.

At the time of its sale, a group of prominent businessmen claimed over 70 percent ownership in the stock of the Biltmore. One of the primary owners of the hotel at the time was Malcolm Greene Chace, whose family's textile company, Berkshire Cotton Manufacturing Company, would later merge with Hathaway Manufacturing Company to become what we now know as Berkshire Hathaway. When Berkshire Hathaway was sold to Warren Buffet in 1960, the Chace family retained extensive stock in the company, making them the richest family in Rhode Island. In the Biltmore, Chace alone held over $2,000,000 in shares when it was sold to Sheraton. Chace's family would continue to hold stock in the hotel throughout its life, with descendant Arnold "Buff" Chace holding minority ownership well into the 21st century.

In addition to his family's exceptional wealth and prestige, Malcolm Greene Chace is credited with bringing the sport of hockey to the United States from Canada. While attending Brown University in 1892, Chace visited Niagara Falls with his tennis team. There, Chace witnessed the Canadian sport of ice hockey, and was intrigued. Returning to Brown, he formed a league with other students on Ivy campuses. Perhaps Malcolm Chace would be pleased to know that an ice hockey rink now sits adjacent to the Biltmore, a prominent feature in the downtown Providence of the 21st century.

Postcard of the Sheraton Biltmore Hotel photographed in the 1960s.
Photo obtained from author's private collection.

Sheraton ownership of the Biltmore was successful for two
decades. The hotel chain's diversified resources provided stability
during the economic challenges of the post-war economy, including the dip in tourism during the late 40s and early 50s. Providence's
economy was shifting and, like many urban centers in the 1950s, the
city was beginning to lose its shine. Affordable automobiles, a proliferation of infrastructure and roads, and the GI Bill that supported
extensive development of suburban housing stock encouraged families to move away from city centers. As surrounding towns grew,
downtown began to decline. Construction of new buildings slowed

to a crawl as the state and private investors focused on building where there was the most growth: outside of the city center. Even the largest industrial companies departed the city for larger tracts of land in outlying towns. American Screw Co., Nicholson File, and Brown & Sharpe left the city after decades of residency. Smaller textile companies shuttered their windows after years of decline. Providence saw a 28 percent decline in population between the years of 1950 and 1970, with the majority of individuals leaving the city for more affordable and amenable towns such as Cranston and Warwick. Local mass transit also faltered, as more and more people favored the use of individual cars over railways and buses. Downtown Providence, which once was overcrowded with commerce and trade, suddenly felt deserted.

When the Biltmore had first opened, everything needed to manage hotel operations was available in-house. The hotel print shop printed all the dinner menus, and clean linens came from the basement laundry. If a piece of furniture required repair or a room needed a fresh coat of paint, someone from the furniture refinishing or painting department took care of the task. By the middle of the century, the increase in shipping via trucking and new highway systems had dramatically altered supply chains across the country. Shortly after Sheraton bought the hotel, the print shop was closed. In 1950, the hotel laundry followed suit. For a brief period, laundry was sent out to be cleaned locally. However, local laundry companies could not compete with the larger commercial laundries now serving regional needs across New England. In short order, the hotel began to send its linens out of state to be cleaned.

The changing times required a modern management style. George Thomas Cullen was the man for the job. Cullen believed that hotels were like small cities, and when he arrived in Providence in 1955 to take over management of the Sheraton Biltmore, he intended to run it as though he was the mayor. Cullen took on his new position with gusto. His enthusiastic leadership won over the longstanding staff at the hotel, and in 1958, he was awarded the Boss of the Year award by the Providence chapter of the National Secretaries Association.

Cullen knew the Biltmore well. Long before he was manager, Cullen had been an enthusiastic patron of the hotel's Bacchante Lounge, where he had frequently shared a booth with Duane Wallick. Once, during a particularly hard-hitting night of whiskey cocktails, Cullen bet Wallick that he was too drunk to shoot straight. Of course, there were no ranges nearby where one could have safely settled this bet. But then, Wallick remembered his rooftop menagerie and declared that he would settle the score with Cullen by shooting the hens on the roof. Off the two drunk men went, picking up Wallick's Luger pistol from his 15th floor suite on the way. On the roof, highly intoxicated Wallick fired off three shots in the direction of hotel's roost. Fortunately for the fowl, Wallick missed every one. Unfortunately for Wallick, the police were there within moments to assess the situation. Since no one was harmed, and thanks to Wallick's stature in Providence, the police waived the fine. Cullen delighted in telling the story decades later, doubling over in laughter as he shared his early history with the hotel.

Cullen intended to continue the hotel's great tradition of grandeur in the city, but with more financial success. Marketing the hotel to the city's residents was a primary focus of the new manager. Among his many PR strategies was his regular column in *The Providence Journal*, entitled "Notes of a Local Innkeeper." Paid for by the hotel's advertising budget, the "column" covered myriad topics relating to trends and fads such as the "princess phone," the concept of a "compact car," and the city's event calendar. At the end of each musing, Cullen finished the column with a correlating tie to the Biltmore. For instance, one could use their new princess phone to call the Falstaff Room to make a reservation for two, for instance. The compact car, Cullen mused, was a response to the needs of the public—no different, he thought, than the way the Biltmore's staff

Advertisement for the Sheraton Biltmore's Town Room restaurant.
Courtesy of the Culinary Institute of America.

constantly responded to their guests' needs. Cullen's humorous and arrogant column entertained and persuaded, all in one.

Several annual events helped float the Biltmore's books through-out the year. One of the most consistent revenue streams was the contract with the United Jewelry Association which had been sta-tioned in the hotel since 1927. The Association leased a whole floor of the hotel for its offices and packed the hotel for trade shows in the spring and fall, completely selling out the hotel for two weeks around each show. The management of the hotel took note of this trend, and continued to seek out other conventions and trade shows to increase profits. At meetings of the Chamber of Commerce, Cullen implored the business community to do all that they could to attract more conventions to Providence. America's propensity toward, and reliance on, the automobile as a primary mode of travel was deeply ingrained by the 1960s. As a reflection of the times, the Biltmore added its multi-story garage adjacent to the hotel, allowing the hotel to accommodate parking for up to 572 cars. The garage, at that time, was connected to the hotel via a footbridge over Eddy Street.

More motorists also meant new vantage points. With potential guests coming into the city from the newly constructed Interstate 95, Sheraton took one more important measure to ensure their hotel stood out amongst competitors. The words SHERATON BILT-MORE were installed in massive red neon on the roof of the hotel, the first of the iconic neon signs that would become synonymous with the hotel itself.

20

THE WOMAN AT THE WINDOW

Author's note:

    The name of the deceased has been changed out of respect for her family. While ghost stories may be entertaining to some, their subjects are the lost loved ones of others.

The Biltmore would not be an iconic hotel without its share of ghost stories. Tour guides and storytellers revel in the tales of scandal and death at the hotel—and, when advantageous, make up their own. Some of the leading tales include the conjuring of a Satanic cult leader who supposedly invested in the construction of the hotel for his own demonic purposes. Unfortunately for the ghost tour guides, this tale has no basis in reality. Another story that gets circulated on the paranormal circuit is the ghastly undoing of a wealthy Providence financier. A typical story of "losing it all," the story goes that on the day of the stock market crash, a local banker found his way to the top of the Biltmore and, like his fortunes, plummeted to his demise below.

Despite a multitude of guest "sightings," there is no record of a suicide at the hotel in October 1929, and it is unlikely that this story is based in any fact. However, if you happen to be someone who swears to have seen the shadow of a person plummeting past your window at the Biltmore, you might not be imagining things. While it is not the ghost of a ruined businessman that you see as you open your curtains, it very well may be the tragic young Boston socialite who ended her life two decades *later,* on September 5, 1949.

As a young woman, Nancy Henry attended Madame Boissier's School in Paris. She was smart, beautiful, and of strong standing, coming from a prominent Boston family. When she married at the age of 19 to an up-and-coming investment banker and skilled yachtsman, *The Boston Globe* dubbed the wedding one of the "highlights of the society year." Nancy and her husband bought a home in the posh Chestnut Hill neighborhood where they welcomed three children in quick succession. She volunteered in the Junior League and Vincent Club, and from the outside Nancy had it all. Beneath the facade, however, Nancy was a tormented woman. While Nancy suffered in silence, keeping up appearances in the highly competitive socialite circle was taking its toll. In September of 1949, Nancy dropped her children off with relatives and left Boston for a reprieve at Butler Psychiatric Hospital in Providence. Her uncle, who lived nearby, checked in on her and picked her up after her three-day stay. Nancy did not visit with her uncle for long. Shortly after arriving, Nancy left her uncle and headed downtown to the Biltmore hotel.

The front desk clerk on duty that day, Redmond Carroll, would later tell reporters that the young woman who had checked in at 4:39 p.m. under the name of Mrs. Harry Burnham said that she was from Long Island. She was very well dressed and very quiet. She did not have a suitcase, only a small bag under her arm, and she requested a "nice, quiet room...high up." Redmond obliged and summoned a bellboy to bring Mrs. Burnham to Room #1130, on the 11th floor.

Charles Cota was just finishing work and was headed to the bar to take the edge off the day. This afternoon's drinking hour would be over, however, before it even began. Just as Charles grabbed a hold of the door handle on the corner of Washington and Eddy Streets, a

young woman's body came careening from the skies above, smashing into the pavement in front of him. Charles screamed and ran
inside to phone the police. By the time they arrived, hundreds of
people had already gathered on the corner of Washington and Eddy
Street to get a glimpse of the tragedy. Officers had to forcibly push
the crowd back to create room for a police line to be set up.

From the description provided by Carroll, the police ascertained
that the body was indeed that of the well-dressed young woman
that had checked in alone earlier that hour. Given the room number
by the clerk, police hurried to the west tower's 11th floor. The room
was locked and had to be opened by a pass key provided by the
hotel's resident manager. Upon a search of the room, police found a
woman's purse and a billfold with calling cards inside. The name on
the cards was not Mrs. Harry Burnham. The victim's true identity
came to light along with the story of her suffering, in a note they
found left on the table for her husband. Though the contents of
the note were never fully disclosed to the press, Police Lieutenant
Thomas Dunn told *The Providence Journal* that the note detailed the
young mother's wishes for the care of her three children as well as
her regrets to her husband. Pinned inside the letter with a hairpin
was Nancy's wedding ring.

Over the years, hotel staff have on more than one occasion
received a frantic call from a guest who claims that they opened the
curtains to let the light in and saw a body fall past their window. Of
course, concerned staff hurry from the front desk to the Eddy Street
side of the building to inspect the sidewalk, only to find no victim
to speak of. Whether or not there are ghosts inside the Biltmore is
unclear, but there does seem to be one *outside* the hotel. Perhaps
with a keener eye, guests would notice that it is not a banker's billowing necktie that they see fly past their window, but the flailing
arms of a young woman, her hands bare save the slight indent where
a wedding ring once was placed.

21

"MR. BILTMORE"

U nder Sheraton management, the Biltmore's role as an entertainment destination flourished. The list of performers that graced the stage at the Biltmore in the 40s, 50s and into the 60s is seemingly endless. A short list includes Louis Armstrong, Count Basie, Hildegarde, Harry James, Carmen Miranda, Sterling Hayden, Dorothy Lamour, Sophie Tucker, the Andrews Sisters, Rudy Vallee, Jack Benny, Danny Thomas, and a young Kay Thompson (who performed with the Williams Brothers before she shattered book sale records with her famous *Eloise of the Plaza* stories).

The hotel's Garden Room, in particular, was ever evolving. One evening it became an ice rink for Sonja Henie, and another it was an underwater stage (including live fish) for Esther Williams. Prize fighters fought in a ring set up in the ballroom. In the early 50s, a marquee was installed on the front of the building to advertise the talent performing at the hotel that week. In Providence, going out was synonymous with going to the Biltmore. With myriad lounges and restaurants to choose from, there were endless possibilities for entertainment at the hotel. Most days, one could choose between a big-name act performing in the Garden Room and Ballroom and a rotating cadre of local musicians playing in the restaurants. New

NOW OPEN

MEET THE
GOLLIWOG
GIRLS at the
smartest new lounge
in Providence
• GOLLIWOG LOUNGE, open
daily 'til 1:00 A.M.

• cocktails
• Entertainment every night at
the Piano Bar

THE GOLLIWOG LOUNGE
IN THE SHERATON-
BILTMORE HOTEL

*Left: Waitresses in the short-lived Golliwog Room wore their hair in ornate styles.
Right: Advertisement for the Golliwog Room at the Biltmore Hotel, 1950s.
Photos courtesy of the Graduate Providence.*

and improved venues sprung up in the hotel, including the short-lived Golliwog Room which featured waitresses with ornate hairstyles adorned with wild hats, feathers, and headbands. Columnist Martha Hurd wrote that in those 'simpler days,' outings to the hotel were informal and frequent. No matter what day it was, your phone might ring and someone on the other end of the line would say, "Whatcha doin'? Meet me at the Biltmore!"

With a never-ending event calendar in constant rotation, spaces within the hotel had to be quickly transformed. On a single day, the ballroom hosted a luncheon for then-presidential candidate Adlai E. Stevenson followed by a dinner dance for a local debutante. Another day, a visit from Vice President Richard Nixon was followed up by a private ladies' luncheon and bridge tournament. When New York Governor Nelson Rockefeller visited the Sheraton-Biltmore during his presidential run, he wooed the staff as much as ticket holding supporters. Mary Healey, who worked as a chambermaid on the 12th floor of the hotel, had her photo with the Governor make it to *The Providence Journal* the next day.

Jimmy McDonnell, dubbed "Mr. Biltmore" during his 55-year employment at the hotel, recalled that when he began his career at the hotel in high school he was fascinated by the ability of the staff to transform the various spaces within the hotel for each unique event that was held. As a teenager he worked with other employees to adorn the Garden Room and Ballroom for countless galas and balls, wheeling in self-contained fountains, potted trees, and other elaborate décor at the request of their clients. It wasn't uncommon for events to host receptions for up to 500 people, with dinner and dancing late into the evening, capped with a "midnight breakfast" before the guests departed.

Jimmy's magnetic enthusiasm was a perfect match for the Biltmore's fast-paced environment. On weekends, when the hotel would simultaneously host four or five weddings alongside a political fundraiser and a family reunion, Jimmy rolled up his sleeves and bounced effortlessly from celebration to celebration. Since he was trained by Claude Daubney (the room service captain who had once worked for the Vanderbilts in Newport), Jimmy was taught the traditional and elegant practices of the "old-school" waiter. Room service was to be as sophisticated in its delivery as table service. Table service was to be as perfect as in the highest-end restaurants in the world. Jimmy quickly rose through the ranks at the hotel, his charisma and charm making him the go-to person for customer relations. Jimmy began work at Biltmore in 1948 as a busboy and when he retired in 2003, he was the Director of Catering.

When the United Fund of Rhode Island opened its annual fund drive at the Biltmore in October 1960, it was Jimmy McDonnell who was there to greet the guest speaker—none other than America's favorite film and television actor, Ronald Reagan. The Fund aimed to raise $2,330,000 that year in support of 86 social welfare agencies across the state. That night, Reagan's speech implored Rhode Islanders to find it in their hearts to give generously to the Fund. Perhaps as an omen to his political ambitions, Reagan took the opportunity to tell the crowd of 500 that Americans ought to stay "a little bit on guard" about the expansion of social welfare services. "Do we want these problems solved in a heartless manner through some government bureau?" He asked the crowd. The answer, he forwarded, was "no."

This was not Jimmy's first time meeting the future President. In 1955, when then-actor Reagan was touring the country's GE factories as part of his hosting gig on GE's television series *GE Theater,* he checked in to the Biltmore's Presidential Suite for several days. Jimmy had just advanced from a busboy in the Town Room to a room service waiter. When the order came in for an early morning breakfast of orange juice, coffee, and a copy of *The Providence Journal,* Jimmy swiftly prepared the order and brought it upstairs. Pressing the suite's doorbell, Jimmy heard the familiar chimes playing inside the suite and the shuffle of someone coming to the door. The young man was shocked when Ronald Reagan himself answered the bell, looking like he'd just climbed out of bed. Reagan thanked Jimmy, took the tray, and signed the check, before closing the door again. Starstruck, Jimmy stood in the long corridor and beamed. When asked years later about his most memorable moments at the hotel, it was this moment Jimmy recalled fondly. "It was fantastic," he said simply, and smiled.

"Mr. Biltmore" was beloved, not only by the guests but also by management. Dick Brush, general manager of the hotel in the early 1980s, would recall that when he started working as at the hotel in

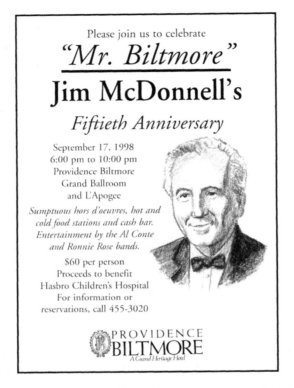

Please join us to celebrate

"Mr. Biltmore"
Jim McDonnell's
Fiftieth Anniversary

September 17, 1998
6:00 pm to 10:00 pm
Providence Biltmore
Grand Ballroom
and L'Apogee

Sumptuous hors d'oeuvres, hot and cold food stations and cash bar. Entertainment by the Al Conte and Ronnie Rose bands.

$60 per person
Proceeds to benefit
Hasbro Children's Hospital
For information or
reservations, call 455-3020

PROVIDENCE
BILTMORE
A Grand Heritage Hotel

*Invitation to Jimmy McDonnell's 50th Anniversary party at the Biltmore.
Courtesy of the Graduate Providence.*

1981, it was Jimmy who would take him by the arm and say, "I need to introduce you to someone" each time an important guest would check in. When Sammy Davis Jr. checked in for a three-night stay at the hotel in 1984, Jimmy met him at the door and personally showed him to his room. When Barbara Bush surprised the banquet staff by requesting a chicken salad sandwich over the lamb on the luncheon menu, Jimmy made sure she got it.

On the event of his 50th anniversary with the hotel, a reporter at the *Journal* asked Jimmy who his favorite guest had been. His response was Audrey Hepburn. "She was the best," he reminisced. "She was such a lady." He also mentioned that he got a real thrill from delivering food to Louis Armstrong's rooms, and rubbing

*Jimmy "Mr. Biltmore" McDonnell with Audrey Hepburn at the Biltmore Hotel.
Photo courtesy of the Graduate Providence.*

elbows with prize fighters Rocky Marciano and Sugar Ray. The celebrity guestlist was endless and Jimmy knew them all.

For Steve Lautieri, executive chef of the hotel in the 1990s, Jimmy was "the man." When you got a parking ticket, you went to Jimmy—he knew a lawyer who could get you out of it. When you needed something fixed on your house, you went to Jimmy—he knew a guy who could do quality work for cheap. When a guest was upset about something, Jimmy was called to soothe the situation. At Jimmy's events, the show always went on. There was a rumor amongst the kitchen staff that one evening, at a wedding in the ballroom, a member of the catering staff suddenly dropped dead of a heart attack while standing in the corner. So as to not ruin the event for the bride and groom, Jimmy quietly placed a table cloth over the man until he could be discreetly removed from the room.

"I doubt it happened." Steve Lautieri laughed as he recounted the tale, adding, "but if anyone would do that for the guests, it would have been Jimmy."

By the end of his tenure with the hotel, Jimmy was, without a doubt, the Biltmore's most cherished employee. After he passed away, his collection of photos (of which there were hundreds) of himself with the hotel's famous guests was donated to the Johnson and Wales University Culinary Arts Museum, where it remains part of their permanent collection.

22

PROGRESS AND PROFIT

World War II had brought destruction, death, and hardship down like a shroud across the globe. Women had entered the workforce to fill jobs left by men fighting abroad. The physical and emotional trauma of the war was brought back from the fields of Europe and Asia. American culture had been shaken to its core and that which was not yet changed, was ripe to do so. From the fertile soil of the postwar years sprouted the Civil Rights and women's liberation movements, as well as revolutions in art, music, and culture across the country.

In addition to societal changes, the postwar economy brought prosperity. The GI Bill provided veterans with opportunities to attend college, purchase homes, and buy farms. The Bill set the stage for the massive suburbanization that the 1950s became known for. However, the economic gains and optimism felt nationwide was largely relegated to white Americans. Not lost on minorities was the fact that they were continuing to be marginalized and left out of the postwar boom. Women, African Americans, and Hispanic Americans became more active in demanding their rights than they ever had been before. The Civil Rights movement that took hold at the end of WWII transformed the nation and made significant strides toward guaranteeing constitutional rights for all, regardless of color, race, or sex.

With the proliferation of automobiles across the United States in the 1940s and 50s, African Americans found a means of avoiding segregation and discrimination on public transportation. America was still a Jim Crow nation, deeply divided in terms of protections for people of color. While more and more people owned and traveled in privately owned cars, "Whites Only" policies across the nation meant that Black travelers often couldn't find safe places to eat and sleep. "Sundown Towns"—municipalities that banned Blacks after dark—were still scattered across the country. It was often unwelcoming and sometimes unsafe for Black motorists to travel outside of their own communities. *The Negro Motorist Green Book* emerged in 1936 as a response to this division, providing a detailed guide to people of color on safe institutions where they would not be refused service. *The Green Book* aimed to protect the Black traveler and allow them to travel with more confidence from town to town.

Compiled initially by Harlem-based postal worker Victor Hugo Green, the *Green Book* was organized alphabetically by state and provided motorists with key listings of hotels and gas stations where they could be assured they would be treated fairly. African Americans traveling in the US had become accustomed to being told that there were no rooms at hotels, despite the "Vacancy" signs lit outside. They were told that restaurants had "run out of food" when they could see diners eating at tables in front of them. They were informed at garages and gas stations that the mechanics could not work with the type of car they happened to be driving.

The Green Book became an essential guide for African Americans on the move. According to architectural historian Catherine Zipf, when it was first published in 1936, only three Rhode Island hotels were listed in Green's guidebook. By 1943, the number of listings dramatically increased. However, discrimination existed in Rhode Island, even if Jim Crow laws did not. Al Martin, who grew up

Please Mention the "Green Book"

Loyal, 16th & South Sts.
Tormes, 2329 Ridge Ave.
Lyons, 12th & South St.
Blue Moon, 3702 Federal St.
Butler's, 2666 Ridge Ave.
Cotton Grove, 1323 South St.
Wayside Inn, 13th & Oxford St.
Preston's, 4043 Market St.
Casbah, 59th & Fairmont St.
Last Word, Haverford & 51st St.
Postal Card, 1504 South St.
Emerson's, 15th & Bainbridge St.
Brass Rail, 2202 W. Columbia Ave.
Club 421, 5691 Wyalusing Ave.
NIGHT CLUBS
Cotton Club, 2103 Ridge Ave.
Cafe Society, 1504 W. Columbia
  Ave.
Paradise, Ridge & Jefferson
Progressive, 1415 S. 20th St.
Cotton Bowl, Master St. & 13th St.
GARAGES
Bond Motor Service, 1726 N. 8th St.
Booker Bros., 1215 So. 21st St.
SERVICE STATIONS
Witcher, 1956 No. Judson St.
DRUG STORES
Bound's, 29th & Race St.

PITTSBURGH
HOTELS
Flamingo, 1407 Wylie Ave.
Ace, 1528 Wylie Ave
Bailey's, 1577 Center Ave
Palace, 1545 Wylie Ave
Elks, 7 Reed St
TOURIST HOMES
Agnes Taylor, 6612 Center St
Birdie's Guest House, 1522 Center
  Ave
B. Williams, 1537 Howard St
Mrs. Williams, 2518 Claybourne St
RESTAURANTS
Gearling's, 492 Culver St
Vee's Dining Room, 2401 Centre
  Ave.

READING
TOURIST HOMES
C. Dawson, 441 Bottomwood St

SCRANTON
TOURIST HOMES
Mrs. Elvira R. King,
1312 Linden St.
Mrs. J. Taylor, 1415 Penn. Ave.

SELLERSVILLE
TOURIST HOMES
Mrs. Dorothy Scholtz, Forest Rd.

SHARON HILL
TAVERNS
Dixie Cafe, Hook Rd., Howard St.

WASHINGTON
TOURIST HOMES
Richardson, 140 E. Chestnut St

RESTAURANTS
W. Allen, N. Lincoln St.
Carl's, 130 Highland
M. Thomas, N. Lincoln St
BARBER SHOPS
Yancey's, E. Spruce St
NIGHT CLUBS
Thomas Grill, N. Lincoln St.

WAYNE
NIGHT CLUBS
Plantation, Gulf Rd. & Henry Ave.

WESTCHESTER
Magnolia, 390 E. Miner St.

WILLIAMSPORT
TOURIST HOMES
Mrs. Edward Randall, 719 Matle St.

WILKES BARRE
HOTELS
Shaw, 17 So. State St.

YORK
TOURIST HOMES
Mrs. I. Grayson, 32 W. Princess St

RHODE ISLAND

NEWPORT
TOURIST HOMES
Mrs. F. Jackson, 28 Hall Ave.
Mrs. L. Jackson, 25 Bath Rd.

PROVIDENCE
HOTELS
Biltmore
TOURIST HOMES
Hines, 452 North Main St.
Bellas House, 24 Camp St.
TAVERNS
Dixieland, 1012 Westminster St
BEAUTY PARLORS
F. Boyd's, 42 Camp St.
Geraldine's, 205 Thurbos Ave.

SOUTH CAROLINA

ANDERSON
RESTAURANTS
Ess-Tee, 112 E. Church St.
TOURIST HOMES
Mrs. Sallie Galloway, 450 Butler St

AIKEN
TOURIST HOMES
C. F. Holland, 1118 Richland Ave.

ATLANTIC BEACH
HOTELS
Therotha

BEAUFORD
SERVICE STATIONS
Peoples, D. Brefs, Prop.

60

Section of the Negro Motorist Green Book *that lists the Biltmore*
as a safe accommodation option for African American travelers in 1955.
Photo courtesy of the New York Public Library Schomberg Center.

in Georgia but came to Rhode Island in 1950, put it bluntly in an interview with *The Providence Journal*: "In the South, it was spelled out for you. Here, it was hush-hush. It was a smile to your face, but behind your back it was something else." Even with the diversity of immigrants in Rhode Island, African Americans still struggled to find welcoming spaces.

Zipf emphasizes that the increased number of new listings in the *Green Book* was not a reflection of a growing community, necessarily. "As the *Green Book*'s popularity grew," Zipf explains, "more businesses came forth to advertise their services. The *Green Book* reveals a community that already existed." Getting listed in the *Green Book* was less a movement than a marketing strategy. African American travelers were a new demographic to consider as businesses worked to attract customers and the *Green Book* was a critical tool for businesses that decided that profit reigned supreme over segregation. Sheraton Hotels, as one of the largest hotel chains in the country, took notice. In the 1955 edition of the *Green Book*, the Sheraton Biltmore in Providence was finally listed as a safe accommodation option for African American guests.

As the Civil Rights movement gained momentum, the Biltmore became a primary gathering place for meetings of civil rights leaders, including the NAACP. At a dinner at the hotel in 1962, Paul B. Zuber, an African American attorney who specialized in fighting school segregation cases, urged Providence's clergymen to register all Black parishioners to vote. He warned the school department that Providence had better work hard to get their own schools in order, or he would "be back in September" to sort it out himself. The dinner itself was organized in an effort to raise funds for the defense of civil rights of African Americans in Rhode Island.

Social progress was slow, but the race for modernity was moving fast. The Biltmore even hosted a conference *about* modernization in 1954, when it welcomed smaller inns and hotels from across the region to a two-day showcase by the American Hotel Association. At the event a new "package guest room" was unveiled by L.B. Herbst Corporation of Chicago featuring a low-cost "yet stylish" furniture set that would help older hotels modernize at a fraction of the cost. The Herbst package cost approximately $570 and included every-thing from the wallpaper to the ashtrays, everything a hotel owner needed to outfit each guest room. The Hotel Association hoped that by modernizing more hotels across the state, Rhode Island could hope to attract more tourists.

The Sheraton Biltmore continued to purge the old to make room for the new. In one of the old sample rooms, an office suite was set up for Trans World Airlines (TWA) to operate a travel agency and recruitment office for pilots and airline stewardesses. The hotel's restaurants were also transformed. The Falstaff Room was renamed The Town Room. A small cocktail bar adjacent was opened under the moniker The Jewel Box. Perhaps most shocking to the public, however, was the announcement of August 13, 1960, that the Bac-chante Lounge was closing for good. In an advertisement placed in the *Journal* alerting the public, the Sheraton's management declared:

"Wars, hurricanes, torrential floods, depressions couldn't do it—but progress has! The Sheraton-Biltmore's famed Bacchante Room is in its convivial final week! This affectionate eating place goes the way of all outmoded eating places forever more. Remember the world-renowned diaphanous skirts? After Saturday night, only memories will linger on."

The restaurant was renovated and reopened as The Mansion House, a more upscale, less risqué establishment that catered more toward family dinners than the after-hours crowds. Despite the push to modernize the hotel, the Mansion House name harkened back to an 18th century inn that had stood at the corner of Meeting and Benefit Streets. Constructed in 1798, it reportedly housed George Washington, John Adams, and Thomas Jefferson in its time. The

Postcard of The Mansion House restaurant. From the author's collection.

Providence Preservation Society heralded the opening of the new eatery as a celebration of the historic importance of Providence.

While Sheraton boasted a modern approach to management, some antiquated practices remained in place. Notably, the oak-lined Falstaff Room on the first floor, recently renamed The Town Room, continued the practice of only serving men. While women were allowed in the bar with their husbands, it was generally frowned upon. Unescorted women (i.e. women without a male chaperone) were refused service outright. Despite society's slow move away from the practice of gender-segregated bars, a Rhode Island law remained in place through the 1970s that prohibited the serving of alcohol to unescorted women in any establishment holding a Class C liquor license. The bar refused service to women for its first 52 years in operation.

This law was not uncommon and was not without controversy. Taverns and saloons had long been considered a male domain, dominated by rough talk and unfiltered jokes, and they were (perhaps most notoriously) the only place where men could interact with commercial escorts and sex workers without the knowledge of their wives and neighbors. The barrooms of America's hotels, considered the most upscale establishments for post-Prohibition indulgences, carried the torch of gender discrimination throughout the 20th century. Because of their elite reputations, hotels were the focus of many protests during the feminist movement of the 1960s and became obvious targets for gender integration efforts.

Perhaps the most famous action in the barroom integration movement came in February 1969 when feminist protestors staged a sit-in at the tony male-only Oak Room of New York's Plaza Hotel. The Plaza, by rule, had excluded women during weekday lunch hours, citing the need to provide a distraction-free environment for businessmen to conduct deals. Despite the sit-in, the female protestors were refused service and the tables they sat at were silently removed

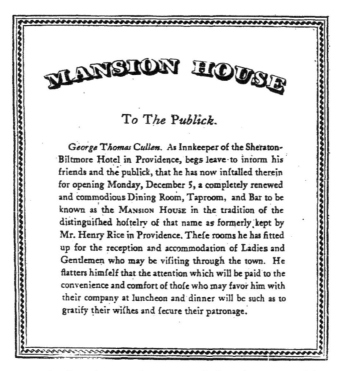

MANSION HOUSE

To The Publick.

George Thomas Cullen. As Innkeeper of the Sheraton-Biltmore Hotel in Providence, begs leave to inform his friends and the publick, that he has now inſtalled therein for opening Monday, December 5, a completely renewed and commodious Dining Room, Taproom, and Bar to be known as the MANSION HOUSE in the tradition of the distinguiſhed hoſtelry of that name as formerly kept by Mr. Henry Rice in Providence. Theſe rooms he has fitted up for the reception and accommodation of Ladies and Gentlemen who may be viſiting through the town. He flatters himſelf that the attention which will be paid to the convenience and comfort of thoſe who may favor him with their company at luncheon and dinner will be such as to gratify their wiſhes and ſecure their patronage.

Advertisement placed in The Providence Journal *about the opening of the Mansion House restaurant. Photo obtained from* The Providence Journal *historic archives.*

from in front of them by the staff. The Plaza won the battle, but ultimately lost the war. After a barrage of negative media coverage, four
months after the sit-in, the hotel overturned their 60-year policy
and allowed women to drink in the Oak Room.

The Oak Room sit-in was part of a nationwide effort by the
National Organization for Women (NOW) and marked the first
coordinated action against the legal and social tradition of gender
exclusion in barrooms. Of the movement, reporter Sascha Cohen
wrote that, "feminists framed the issue of male-only accommodations as a civil rights violation, akin to racial segregation. African
American NOW member Pauli Murray referred to gender discrimination as 'Jane Crow.' Exclusion from the sites of commercial
and political power-broking, feminists argued, contributed to their
status as second-class citizens...Those against the feminist campaign
were armed with an array of reasons for denying women equal
access to accommodations. Some suggested that women lacked the
ability to calculate the check and tip correctly; that bar crowds were
too 'rough' and boisterous for them; or that male-only spaces were
sacred respites for politics and sports talk, where men could share
'lewd stories' or 'have a quiet beer and tell a few jokes.' The manager
of Biltmore Hotel in Manhattan insisted that businessmen's conversations were simply 'not for women'."

In 1971, the movement made it to Providence. On the heels
of the NOW actions across the US, a group of Brown University
faculty and graduate students formed to tackle the issue of gender
discrimination in the city. Donna Hoffmeister was a student at the
time and helped organize the action. As part of the effort, Hoffmeister and her colleagues issued a press release damning Doorley's Tap
(formerly the Falstaff Room) at the Biltmore Hotel for its discrimination against women. A call for volunteers went out and a group
of women gathered at the barroom to request a drink. The sit-in
attracted media attention and local television crews descended on
the bar. Not surprisingly, they were refused service. The local papers

had a field day with the coverage, sparking an intense public debate about the discriminatory law.

Hoffmeister and her group responded to the hotel's discrimination by filing a class action suit against the Biltmore and Doorley's Tap. With the help of a pro-bono attorney, the Brown group won the suit, leading to the reversal of the law that prevented women from being served. In an interview, Hoffmeister stated that the suit was about principles, not practice. She, for one, had no plans to exercise her newfound right, she told the paper. Recalling the case years later, Hoffmeister stated, "As I recall, we won our suit around the time that Nixon released the Watergate tapes. I [went on] talk radio about winning our suit and the men calling into the radio station focused totally on me. It was all negative. Callers claimed I must be a prostitute, for why else would a woman want access to a bar. It was a circus."

Even after the Class-C liquor license law was reversed in 1974, men across the state retaliated. "The first time a woman comes in here," said the bartender at the downtown Dorrance Bar, "I'm going out and joining the YWCA, just for the heck of it. If they can come into a man's bar, then I can join one of their clubs." The bartender furthered that he objected to women drinking in the bar because of the language used by male patrons. "Besides," he expanded, "where would you put a ladies' room in this place?"

Bartenders and managers across the state shared the sentiment. In Warren, Ronald Chauvin of Andy's Bar stated that most of their customers went to Andy's Bar "because we don't have a phone and we don't have women." Bruno Maromelli at Duffey's Tavern in Pawtucket told *The Providence Journal* that "a man doesn't have a shot in the world today. They ought to give the men a break and let them be themselves for change." In Warwick, Joseph Vanasse of Mac's Bar stated: "I think it's terrible." He told reporters that if women came into his bar, he would still refuse to serve them despite the ruling. "Let them go get the police."

Despite being the center of the media firestorm, the manager of the Biltmore bar told the paper that he didn't think women actually wanted to come into the bar. Dismissing it as frivolous, he assured the *Journal* reporters that the case would be forgotten just as soon as it was out of the headlines. "It was just a few women who wanted to say they can drink anywhere," he asserted.

Doorley's Tap would close permanently just a few months later.

23

THE GOLDEN TICKET

When the Biltmore first opened, owners John Bowman and Lou Wallick knew that the only way to ensure its success was to attain excellence in the kitchen. Bowman hired Chef Emile Durand to create menus of rotating, assorted cuisine to impress the finely tuned palates of the Biltmore's guests. Durand was no stranger to fine dining. He had a reputation worldwide and had supervised kitchens in London and Paris, including the preparation for the coronation of King Edward VII in 1903. *The Providence Journal* ran ads on a weekly basis that highlighted the various eateries within the hotel and featured their current menus. The Mayor of Boston was so impressed by the food at the Biltmore that he gave one chef a key to the city of Boston.

As the Sheraton-Biltmore, the kitchen did not break stride. The Biltmore's grand kitchen spanned the length of the hotel, with large sun-drenched windows and meticulously maintained stations. It was something of a dream job for up-and-coming chefs and became the preeminent training ground for cooks, linemen, pastry chefs, and executive chefs. To work in the Biltmore kitchen was to have arrived at culinary greatness. The kitchen staff was also a family. Before each dinner shift, the banquet waiters would set a long table in the kitchen, fully adorned with white linens, matching china, and polished silver. Then, before the restaurant patrons and hotel guests began putting in orders, the cooks would sit down and share a meal together. This nightly ritual was cherished by the kitchen staff and set the wheels in motion each night for another busy shift of round-the-clock orders, prep, and presentation.

As was popular in its day, chefs from the Sheraton-Biltmore competed in competitions around the region. In 1954, executive chef Angelo Marchitelli won the top prize at the New England Hotel and Restaurant Show in Boston for his edible sculpture entitled "The Progress of Women in America." *The Providence Journal* article highlighting his win noted that he'd been trained in Rome and Venice and that *tallow sculpture,* or sculptures made from mutton fat and paraffin, were one of his specialties. For the Hotel and Restaurant Show, Marchitelli had worked in seclusion for weeks in a top floor suite of the hotel, meticulously constructing his sculpture. The women in the diorama were made from wooden puppets that were then slathered in layers of tallow to make them appear 3D and lifelike. The sculpture won numerous awards in the show that year. *Bon appetite!*

Competitions aside, it was the unmatched quality that came from the Biltmore kitchens that gained it the reputation as the leading kitchen in New England. Following in the footsteps of Duane Wallick's rooftop henhouse and gardens, the hotel sourced only the freshest foods, local fish and meat, and finest imported delicacies. When Adolf Schrott was recruited to the kitchen in 1959, *The Providence Journal* asked him what he thought the difference between a good hotel and great hotel was. Always to the point, Adolf answered simply, "Food." And food they served. "In the course of a day," the chef wrote in his autobiography, "we would use 75 pounds of hamburger, 65 pounds of pork chops, 462 chickens, 132 pounds of sirloin steaks, 50 pounds of veal cutlets, 120 pounds of rump steak, 930 pounds of roast beef, 21 pounds of lamb chops, 50 pounds of shrimp, 800 pounds of potatoes, 200 pounds of bread flour, 200 pounds of pastry flour, 120 dozen eggs, 120 heads of lettuce, 100 pounds of tomatoes, 194 pounds of sugar, and 50 pounds of salt. On an average day, we served 2,500 customers."

Born in Austria in 1925, Adolf pursued culinary arts from an early age. Breadmaking was one of his earliest childhood chores. At the age of 14, Adolf left Austria for Bavaria where he was to take an apprenticeship at a baker's shop. However, the trajectory of his

Bacchante Room
Supper Menu

APPETIZERS

Fresh Shrimp Cocktail .. 1.10   Lobster Cocktail 1.45
Crabmeat Cocktail .... 1.15   Assorted Hors d'oeuvres 1.25
Fresh Fruit Cocktail .... .65

French Onion Soup .... .45

SEAFOOD AND A LA CARTE SPECIALS

Lobster Newburg 3.95
Fried Fantail Shrimp 2.75
Fried Cape Scallops 2.50
New York Cut Sirloin Steak 4.95
(Mixed Green Salad or Cole Slaw and French Fried Potatoes
Served with Above Orders)
Welsh Rarebit on Toast ...... 1.25   Golden Buck 1.50

SANDWICH SUGGESTIONS

Minute Steak 3.75
Sheraton-Biltmore Club 1.35
Chopped Sirloin Steak, Sliced Onion 1.50
Lobster Salad 1.65
Hot Chicken Sandwich with Gravy 1.35
Cold Roast Prime Beef 1.75
(Above orders garnished with Potato Chips and Dill Pickle)

DESSERTS

Your Selection from the Sheraton-Biltmore
French Pastry Tray .... .50
Your Selection from the Cheese and Cracker Board .... .60
Pies or Cakes du Jour .. .40   Your choice of Ice Cream
Frozen Eclair .... .60   or Sherbet .... .40
Cherries Jubilee 1.35

BEVERAGE

Individual Milk, Sanka, Postum .... .30
Coffee (pot) .... .45   Tea (pot) .... .30
SUPPER SERVED FROM 9:30 - 12:30 A. M.

Sheraton-Biltmore
11-59   **Providence, Rhode Island**

The menu from the Bacchante Room in the early 1950s.
Courtesy of the Graduate Providence.

future took a dramatic turn when, on September 1, 1939, Germany invaded Poland. "During the first three years of [the war], I continued with my apprenticeship. My dream was that after the war ended, I would be able to use my trade and sign up with the Merchant Marines and travel the world on a ship as a baker or cook," Adolf wrote in his autobiography.

Adolf would travel, but it would not be as he'd imagined. In June 1942, he was conscripted into the German Navy. After being trained in Holland and shipped off to the German border near Denmark, Adolf was transferred to Corfu, Greece, where he was to serve as an anti-aircraft gunner. It was there that he was taken as a prisoner of war by the British army. Adolf spent two-and-a-half years in a POW camp in Alexandria, Egypt. Calling his time in Africa "the murder of his youth," Adolf recounted that life in the camp was marked by extreme heat, dehydration, and most of all, hunger. The former bread-maker dreamed of life outside of the camp, writing that "there were many times I said to myself that I wished I just had enough bread and water for one day."

With the defeat of Hitler's armies, Adolf was freed to return to Austria. Before going home, he took an opportunity to work for a short time in the British military's bakery, finally able to return to the trade he had loved so dearly. When he did go back to Austria, he was frustrated to find that there was no work to be had in the war-torn country. Scraping together a meager savings, Adolf emigrated to Canada, searching for a more prosperous life. Adolf's resilience and determination paid off. After a stint in a Jewish bakery, he landed a job with the Canadian Pacific Railroad Hotel System and then as a vegetable cook at the Chateau Frontenac in Quebec City. Adolf worked for three years without a vacation, saving every penny he made.

In the first half of the 20th century, European cooking was considered the most sophisticated culinary tradition in the world. Restaurants across the United States and Canada boasted menus with French, German, Swiss, and Italian dishes. "American cuisine" was not yet defined, and immigrants trained in the culinary traditions of their homelands were highly sought-after in hotel kitchens across the country. Adolf's experience and mastery of German, French, and Austrian cuisine gained him an immediate foothold in North America. In 1956, Adolf was granted a visa to emigrate to the United States where his career took him to California. In Hollywood, while working at the Ambassador Hotel, Adolf cooked for Elizabeth Taylor on her 25th birthday, and for Frank Sinatra, who once was so drunk that he had to be carried through Adolf's kitchen in a chair. Adolf met celebrity guests including Harry Belafonte, Lena Horne, and many others who entertained at the hotel. It was during this time that Adolf wrote to Helga, his sweetheart back in Austria, asking her to marry him. Helga joined him in the United States shortly thereafter, and with his family growing, Adolf knew it was time to take the next step in his career.

The newly launched Sheraton Corporation was growing rapidly across the country and the people working in the hotel industry were taking note of its success. When Adolf learned about Sheraton from another chef at the Ambassador, he immediately reached out to the company to inquire about opportunities. Adolf's reputation preceded him and within a short time, he had accepted a job in faraway Rhode Island as a chef at the Sheraton-Biltmore. Adolf was quickly put in charge of the Biltmore's three kitchens, four restaurants, 48 chefs, and 2,500 meals a day. He started at $140 a week and worked most nights and weekends, and often holidays.

For Adolf, working for Sheraton was a tremendous opportunity. Like the countless other immigrants that made up the lifeblood of the Biltmore hotel, being employed at the grandest hotel in Rhode Island was tangible proof of the American dream. One cook who worked under Adolf credited the diversity of the kitchen staff with the hotel's culinary success. "We were like the League of Nations," the cook shared in an interview. "There were people from everywhere and they all brought their unique specialties and their different talents."

Kitchen staff of the Sheraton Biltmore Hotel in 1960. Adolf Schrott pictured in the front row, fourth from left. Photo courtesy of the Schrott Family.

Just shy of 10 years after leaving his beloved Austria, Adolf became a US citizen. "This country has been very good to me," Adolf wrote in his memoir. It was one of his proudest moments.

Shortly after Adolf took over the kitchen at the Biltmore, the Narragansett Hotel down the street from the Biltmore closed its doors after 88 years on Dorrance Street. In short order, the Crown Hotel followed. The hotel industry was floundering in Providence, but Sheraton's massive nationwide infrastructure, bolstered by its state-of-the-art automated reservation system, was able to keep the Biltmore afloat. However, even with Sheraton's innovative systems and their competitive rates, maintaining profit and decreasing costs were a constant obsession of hotel management.

Adolf worked closely with General Manager George Cullen to ensure a minimal cost of food per day, largely dependent on Adolf's scrutiny of food purchasing orders. Cullen was obsessed with the cost of food. "I was one of the first people, as we were emerging from the Depression," Cullen later told reporter James Kaull, "who subscribed to the new theory that any hotel's food department must make money." During Prohibition, he said, "we had to do without liquor. All we had to do was eliminate food waste and update menus to the tempo of the times." Under Cullen's watchful eye, the Sheraton Bilt-more began to see its restaurants cranking out profits. By the early 1960s, the restaurants were exceeding $1,500,000 in annual sales, with rooms generating just $1,000,000. For a rare moment in time, the hotel restaurants were profitable—something generally unheard of in most hotels, then and now. George Cullen was so personally invested in the excellence of the Biltmore's restaurants that he was known to "check the quality" of the prime rib himself, several times a week.

As Executive Chef, Adolf took it upon himself to ensure that quality remained high even while costs remained low. Quality was everything to Adolf and he instilled this in everyone that worked below him in the kitchen. When the job needed to be done perfectly, Adolf stepped in and did it himself. That is why it was Adolf who made breakfast on the morning of November 7, 1960—fruit, bacon, and eggs—for soon-to-be President John F. Kennedy before his famous speech on the steps of City Hall. Under the watchful eye of a slew of Secret Service agents, Adolf Schrott fried the Presidential candidate a half pound of bacon and carefully arranged it on a plate before sending it upstairs.

That was the same year that 13-year-old Jimi Pugliese came home from school to be told by his mother, "You're going to work. You got a job." With that, she put him in the car and dropped him off at the Biltmore. Jimi's uncle worked at the hotel and had secured him a gig in the kitchen. The new Johnston High School had just opened, and they had a tailored schedule for working teens, allow-ing Jimi to go to school from 7 a.m. to 11:30 a.m. and then straight to the hotel. To go to school and work full time, young Jimi had to work 10 hours on Friday and 10 hours on Saturday just to make his required 40 hours. Being under the legal working age of 14, Jimi was told by his uncle not to mention his age when he was at work.

On his first day, Jimi's was instructed to "find the kitchen and report to Adolf." He was excited, albeit a little bit scared. The enormous hotel felt like a labyrinth. When he finally found the main kitchen, the towering Austrian with a heavy accent introduced himself with a stern handshake and pointed Jimi in the direction of a massive steel sink. "Pots and pans," Adolf said. So that is what Jimi set about to do.

The second person Jimi met in the kitchen was a pastry chef named Jack Roundtree. Jack stood out to Jimi not only because he was tall, strong, and wearing a massive white hat. He was also the first Black person that Jimi had ever seen. Jimi had grown up in a completely Italian neighborhood, with Italian parents and Italian neighbors. In Jimi's neighborhood, adults rarely even spoke English. Jimi, the skinny little Italian kid from Johnston, stared at Jack Roundtree with amazement. But the novelty of Jack's appearance only lasted for a moment because something else—something much more enticing—had caught Jimi's eye.

In front of Jack's pastry station, filling cooling rack after cooling rack, were the most perfect, mouthwatering pastries Jimi had ever laid eyes on. Oversize sterling silver trays with ornate handles overflowed with every treat you could imagine: everything from decadent napoleons to whipped cream swans, from giant eclairs to fresh fruit tarts overflowing with raspberries, cherries, strawberries, and blueberries. Next to the serving trays was a massive vat where 50 gallons of eclair custard was rolling at a slow boil. But Jimi's eyes were soon fixed on the grandest creations of them all: Jack Roundtree's famous cheesecakes. These were the most beautiful cheesecakes Jimi had ever seen. His mouth watered and his stomach growled. Towering over the scrawny youngster, Jack crossed his arms and observed the teenager gawking at the cakes. After a moment, Jack spoke. "You want a piece?"

Jimi hadn't eaten all day. His eyes darted from the cheesecake to the huge man in front of him. Gregarious as he was, Jimi tested the waters. "Can I have *two* pieces?"

Jack let out a billowing laugh. "Jimi," Jack said, clapping flour off of his hands and onto his apron. "You work at the Biltmore. You can eat all you want. As much as you want. Of whatever you want. Any time you want it." Jimi's eyes bulged in disbelief.

"Seriously?" he squeaked, "If I wanted to eat that whole cheese-cake, I could?" Jack laughed and nodded, pounding Jimi on the back with the side of his flour-filled fist. He turned back to his station and began rolling out the dough in front of him.

Jimi could not believe it. He glanced around the kitchen to see if he was being made the punchline of a practical joke. But everyone around him was focused on their work. No one seemed to notice or care what the new kid was doing at the pastry station. Worried that Jack might change his mind, Jimi quickly reached up to the shelf and took an entire cheesecake down with both hands. Heart leaping in his chest, he took the cake back to the corner dishwashing station and placed it proudly, like a trophy, on the shelf over the sink. From the drying rack, Jimi picked up a silver spoon with the letter "B" engraved on the handle. Triumphantly he plunged the spoon into the cake and set about helping himself to as much cheesecake as he wanted, any time he wanted it, for the entirety of his shift.

Melvin J. Roundtree, or "Jack" as he was known around the kitchen, stood at the pastry station of the Sheraton Biltmore for 22 years. He was a Navy veteran of World War II and had come to the Sheraton shortly after his time in the service. Dedicated to and meticulous in his craft, Jack had a profound impact on the kitchen staff at the Biltmore during his two decades of time there. Most of the guests never heard his name, but nearly all of them marveled at his mastery of sugar, dough, and flour. In an interview in 2022, Jimi remembered Jack with a smile. And according to Jimi, no one since has ever made as good a cheesecake as Jack Roundtree.

Learning how to cook in the Biltmore kitchen was an invalu-able experience. There was no kitchen training anywhere in New England that compared to it. Sitting in his log cabin in Johnston in 2021, Jimi reflected on his time at the hotel with as much wonder as he had that first day he entered the kitchens. "Working in the Bilt-more Hotel, that was the golden ticket," he smiled, his eyes closed in memory. "There was never a job I applied for that I couldn't get.

Melvin "Jack" Roundtree, pastry chef of the Sheraton Biltmore.
Photo courtesy of the Schrott Family.

Once they saw where I'd worked, where I had been trained, that was it. It was all I ever needed. The Biltmore was the golden ticket."

It certainly has seemed like the golden ticket for many chefs. Jasper White, the preeminent expert on New England cooking, got his start at the Biltmore in the late 70s, and still considers it his early training ground. From the Biltmore, White went on to the Copley Plaza, then opened his own restaurant, Jasper's, on the Boston waterfront. Later, he was a leading consultant to Legal Seafood. Steve Lautieri, Executive Chef at the hotel many years after Jimi's time, agreed with his sentiments. "The Biltmore was the greatest kitchen of all time," Steve lamented. "It was classy. It was the last great kitchen in Rhode Island." Adolf Schrott, after leaving the Biltmore, went on to found the local chapter of the American Culinary Federation, and then work as an Executive Chef for the state of Rhode Island. He retired in 1989 after more than five decades in a kitchen. In 1990, he was honored by the Federation with a Lifetime Achievement Award.

24

BREAKFAST AT THE BILTMORE

Perhaps no technological advancement of the 20th century had a more permeating effect on day-to-day culture than the home television set. Prior to 1948, very few households boasted a TV. The majority of broadcast viewing occurred at appliance stores that sold TVs, or at local bars and taverns. When Sheraton bought the hotel, the Falstaff Room had at least one television set, a feature that set it apart from its contemporaries in the city.

In the early period of television broadcasting, an at-home TV set cost a small fortune. As demand went up and the benefit of television advertising became apparent to business owners, the price of individual sets was driven down. By 1956, nearly 70 percent of homes in America had a TV, a trend spurred on by early television stars such as Lucille Ball and Milton Berle. Until then, radio was king and many radio stars of the day were reluctant to transition to this risky new medium. Bob Hope, Gracie Allen, and George Burns, for example, held successful radio careers that they were hesitant to put on the line for the newest fad. Clearly, they quickly came around.

As television's popularity took off like wildfire, local broadcasting stations were quickly established to compete for broadcasting

Children tune in to early television programming, 1950.
Courtesy of the Library of Congress.

hours. Providence's largest downtown department store, The Outlet
Co., established Rhode Island's first television station in 1949. WJAR
carried broadcasts from all four of the country's national networks
of the time: NBC, ABC, DuMont, and CBS. In these early days of
television, videotape recordings had not yet been formally introduced, so it was live broadcasts that drew the public into the new
entertainment medium.

As Americans tuned in to view live variety acts, news reports,
and talk shows, Providence was tuning in to see who was dining
at the Biltmore's esteemed Garden Room restaurant. *Breakfast at
the Biltmore*, WJAR's live morning talk show, began airing in 1954
out of the hotel's most popular restaurant. In a book written later
about the Outlet Co., *Breakfast at the Biltmore* (also sometimes listed
as *Breakfast at the Sheraton*) was noted for being the "first regularly
produced daily remote" on local television. It was the only daily live

remote in New England in the mid–50s, and featured live music, an emcee conducting interviews, and information on new products.

Breakfast at the Biltmore featured 100 guests enjoying breakfast and participating in the show live every weekday morning, five days per week. Each day, viewers could tune in to watch emcee Johnny King (a well-known radio host) and leading lady Nancy Dixon interview Providence denizens dining on omelets and toast about their opinions on local issues of the day. Dixon's tremendous charisma stole the show. The beautiful blonde hostess swept through the ballroom, soliciting live feedback from breakfast diners about a rotating list of topics. Her gregariousness was contagious. The crowd adored her, and the show's ratings followed. In a *The Providence Journal* profile of the local star, Dixon emphasized the level of dedication it took to host a show of that caliber each day. She wowed reporters with her commitment to success, sharing that she had to get up at 5 a.m. every day to catch the train to Providence from her home in Boston. During an era where women were often still seen as homemakers and housewives, Dixon was a poster girl for the modern, professional woman. She prepped for the show by reading hours' worth of newspapers on the train into the city each day. "An hour-a-day show," Nancy groaned, "is so grueling that I am ready to go to bed by 7 o'clock every night."

Serving as a handsome counterpart to Dixon's bold personality, Johnny King also drew in the crowds. King was already popular before joining WJAR's show, having cut his teeth in musical cabaret throughout New England and the Midwest. From there he had gone on to host shows in several Detroit ballrooms and was among the first emcees to perform on network TV in Detroit. King's good looks gained him celebrity status in Providence, and he was regularly asked questions by reporters about his diet, exercise regime, and how he was able to maintain such a successfully healthy head of hair. (He massaged his scalp every day to prevent baldness, he told inquiring minds at the *Journal*.) Having the show airing live in the Garden

Room excited the hotel staff, as well. Waiters would often try to lean into the view of the cameras with the hopes of having their face on TV. Jimmy McDonnell recalled years later, with a laugh, that this was considered a great way to impress girls in those days.

Dick Brush was just a small boy when his father, Robert Brush, took over as general manager of the Sheraton Biltmore. In one of his earliest childhood memories, Dick recalls the excitement of his father taking him into the Garden Room and sitting him down at one of the tables. Suddenly, cameramen and bright lights surrounded him, and little Dicky was on live TV for the world to see. The excitement of being a momentary star at the Biltmore never seemed to wear off. Thirty years later, Dick Brush would follow in his father's footsteps and become the general manager of the hotel when it reopened in 1980.

Breakfast at the Biltmore was a perfect testament to the times, leveraging a winning combination of the modern television craze with the grandeur of the city's most expensive eatery. For those who could not afford a $2 omelet, the show let people feel as though they were there in the Garden Room each morning. For those who *could* afford it, the gimmick of dining on live TV was too tempting to pass up. Reservations for breakfast in the Garden Room skyrocketed, alongside viewership for WJAR's most popular morning show.

25

(I CAN'T GET NO) SATISFACTION,

GUARANTEED

In 1964, the American music scene was exploding with what became known as the "British Invasion." The Beatles, the beloved, quirky pop group from England, tore into the American music scene, a much-needed diversion from the gloom that hung over America after President Kennedy's assassination. On February 9, 1964, 73 million Americans gathered in front of their TV sets to catch a glimpse of the first live Beatles performance on US soil on the popular *Ed Sullivan Show.* Despite the viewership, the reviews all but buried the Fab Four, with *Newsweek* reporting: "Visually, they are a nightmare: tight, dandified, Edwardian/Beatnik suits and great pudding bowls of hair. Musically, they are a near-disaster: guitars and drums slamming out a merciless beat that does away with secondary rhythms, harmony, and melody. Their lyrics are a catastrophe, a preposterous farrago of Valentine-card romantic sentiments." The article ended with the following prediction: "...the odds are they will fade away, as most adults confidently predict."

Thankfully for music history, the Beatles did not fade away, and the British Invasion continued. A new group was entering the scene, only this one was wild, edgy and, to some, threatening. The headlines in US papers said it all. When they arrived in the United States for their second tour in November 1964, the headlines read: "Would You Let Your Daughter Marry a Rolling Stone?"

The Rolling Stones didn't wait to have a hit single in the US before embarking on their first American tour. Stones bassist Bill Wyman remembered the tour as "a disaster." "When we arrived," he later recalled, "we didn't have a hit record or anything going for us." The band played a quick 11 concerts, then headed back to England to regroup. Returning to US soil in October, the band went straight to the source for the American market: *The Ed Sullivan Show*. The Stones' *Ed Sullivan* debut solidified their reputation as Britain's sexiest and edgiest rock group. When Mick Jagger danced across the stage during "Time Is On My Side," screams from the crowd were so loud that Jagger's voice could barely be heard above them.

First with the Beatles, then with the Stones, the crowd of infatuated youth had taken over the orderly live audience setting and incited chaos in the studio. Ed Sullivan had had enough of the Brits. "I promise you they'll never be back on our show," Ed declared to the press after the show. "It took me 17 years to build this show and I'm not going to have it destroyed in a matter of weeks." According to *The Ed Sullivan Show's* historic archives, when the band's manager called Sullivan's bookers to try and change their mind, Ed sent the managers a note reading: "We were deluged with mail protesting the untidy appearance—clothes and hair of your Rolling Stones. Before even discussing the possibility of a contract, I would like to learn from you whether your young men have reformed in the matter of dress and shampoo." Whether or not a suitable reply came back from the band's managers is unknown, but it seems Ed came around. The Stones were back on his show just a few months later. The *Ed Sullivan* appearance propelled the Stones to new heights of popularity in the United States. The band's management had vastly underestimated the power of the show to boost ticket sales, and the theaters and auditoriums that the band had already booked were suddenly woefully inadequate for the crowds expected.

On November 4, 1964, Providence's Loews Theater was bursting at the seams with throngs of screaming fans. Tickets, at the price of just $2.50, had quickly sold out after the group's *Ed Sullivan* debut. Even before the Stones took the stage, the crowd had descended into chaos, with teenagers clamoring on top of each other in the aisles and standing on the armrests of the theater seats to get a better view of the stage. The opener, Georgie Porgie and the Cry Babies—a local band from Attleboro—played over the noise for half an hour. When Mick Jagger took the stage, however, the theater fell into hysterics. The Stones opened with "Not Fade Away," trying desperately to play over the chaos. They made it through "Walking the Dog" and "If You Need Me," but were cut short in the middle of "Carol" by the concert's promoters. The pandemonium in the theater was deemed too dangerous to continue, with the promoters fearing lawsuits if they let the show go on. The entire concert lasted only 20 minutes before the band was whisked out of the theater and into their van before the masses could reach them.

A lot changed for The Rolling Stones between October 1964 and November 1965, when they returned to Rhode Island for their second appearance in the state. Almost a year to the date, the Stones this time performed at Rhode Island Auditorium on North Main Street, a 5,000-seat arena and the largest in the state at the time. Everything about this show was doubled from the 1964 performance, including the number of seats in the arena and the ticket prices. One thing hadn't changed, however: the chaos. In Rochester the night before, the crowd hurled garbage and food at the police in protest, and the concert was halted after only six songs. Back in Providence, however, the show played through.

The Stones had built a massive fanbase in the year since their first *Ed Sullivan* gig, and they had made a pretty penny on album sales

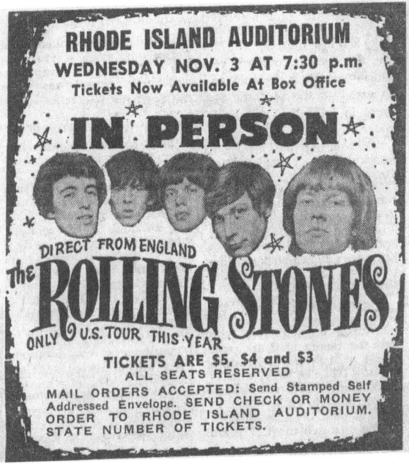

Advertisement from the newspaper for The Rolling Stones' concert. The band stayed at the Biltmore after the show. Photo obtained from RI Rocks.

from their newest release, *Out of Our Heads*. With their newfound fame and cash in the pocket, the band graduated from sleeping in their tour vans and cheap roadside hotels. This time, in Providence, they checked in to the Biltmore.

Rumors were circulating that the Stones would be staying at the hotel days before their RI Auditorium gig. The kitchen staff at the hotel were placing bets on what the wild boys from Britain would eat during their stay. Management was doing everything they could to keep the band's visit under wraps. If the chaos and destruction at Loews Theater the year before had taught them anything, it was that The Rolling Stones could be both good *and* bad for business.

That night, the Stones closed out their show with "(I Can't Get No) Satisfaction," bringing down the house. Once again, they hurriedly ran from the venue with the press in close pursuit. Moments later, their van pulled up to the front of the Biltmore and Mick, Keith, Brian, Bill, and Charlie were rushed through the lobby, up the stairs, and into the elevators. The hotel staff scrambled for a glimpse of the larger-than-life rockstars before the door to their suite slammed shut for the night.

Down in the kitchens, 17-year-old Jimi Pugliese and the rest of the staff were buzzing with energy over the infamous rockers upstairs. While the band's manager was not about to let the British rockers out of his sight that night, the Biltmore staff had a front row seat for the post-show party. Stories about the noise in the suite reverberated throughout the hotel, the gossip quickly spreading from the front-desk clerks and bellhops to the engineers and housekeepers. In the kitchen, every time the band placed a room service order, whoops and shouts broke out amongst the cooks. Over the course of the night, the band called down multiple times with elaborate requests, course after course from each of the room service menus. But what caused the most cheering from the kitchen was the wine orders: nearly two dozen bottles of the hotel's most expensive vintage, tallying up hundreds of dollars in orders that were placed well into the early hours of the morning. When the band left for New Haven the next morning, their hotel suite was a tornado of plates, glasses, and empty bottles.

26

THE KENNEDYS' HOTEL OF CHOICE

Of all the famous guests to grace the halls of the Biltmore, Rhode Island's adopted son, John F. Kennedy, is perhaps the most well-known. Handsome and spirited, Jack had a soft spot for Rhode Island and the feelings were mutual. In his early years, the President-to-be was a central figure in Newport's social circle, rubbing elbows with the upper crust of the summer colony families throughout the 1930s. In the 40s, Kennedy spent weekends away from the Motor Torpedo Boat Squadrons Training Center in Melville to entertain friends at the Biltmore's famed Bacchante Lounge. After their marriage, he and Jackie would return to Rhode Island many times, famously for their wedding in 1953 and often to what became dubbed as the "summer White House," Jackie's child-hood home of Hammersmith Farm.

The Providence Journal, like all of New England, followed Kennedy's rise up the political ladder with bated breath. When he announced his bid for presidency, Rhode Islanders were overjoyed. Kennedy toured the country relentlessly during his campaign, criss-crossing the nation to rally support for his presidential bid. The last stop on his tour was symbolic for Kennedy, a return to his second home and a hotel that he loved dearly. On the very last night of his whirlwind campaign, at 2 a.m. on November 7, 1960, John F. Kennedy's tour bus pulled up to the Sheraton Biltmore. Arriving with the presidential hopeful was a staff of 67 aides; Kennedy's sisters, Mrs. Peter Lawford and Mrs. Eunice Shriver; his sister-in-law, Mrs. Robert Kennedy; and his grandmother, Mrs. Edward Fitzgerald.

Hundreds of well-wishers had crammed into the Biltmore's lobby to extend their support of the senator on the eve of the election. Many had waited for hours to greet him, and excitement was in the air. One hundred and thirty young girls, dubbed the "Kennedy Golden Girls," waited to meet their candidate in one of the hotel's parlor rooms, while dozens of boys donned plate-sized Kennedy campaign buttons and packed the corridors, hoping to catch a glimpse of their hero. Exhausted from the trip, however, the senator

Senator John F. Kennedy greets well-wishers outside the Biltmore Hotel on election day, 1963. He would be elected President later that day. Photo courtesy of the Providence Public Library.

told his team he needed to go right to sleep despite the crowd that eagerly awaited his arrival. With little more than a wave, Kennedy was whisked past the crowd by his security team, into the central elevator, and upstairs to his suite. When he awoke a few hours later, Kennedy was disappointed to see on the front page of the *Journal* critiques, that he'd let his crowd of supporters down.

Sitting in his underwear at the edge of his bed, Kennedy turned to Marvin Holland, a Providence member of his advance team. Shaking his head, he remarked: "Here you [guys] make one decision in this campaign, and the newspaper calls *me* on it." Marvin knew the Senator was joking—Kennedy didn't really blame the advance team for his choice to go to bed—but still, Marvin remembered the jab years later. After a hearty breakfast prepared by Adolf Schrott himself, Kennedy dressed and checked out of the hotel before emerging onto Exchange Place. Waving and smiling broadly, he greeted more than 25,000 enthusiastic Rhode Islanders who packed the square, thanking them for their support. That day, voters gave Kennedy almost 64 percent of the vote from Rhode Island, his highest percentage victory from any state in the Union.

After JFK's assassination, Exchange Place was renamed Kennedy Plaza in honor of that day and in memory of Rhode Island's beloved adopted son.

27

MOTOR INN, MONEY OUT

As the 1960s neared a close, a massive shift at Sheraton Corporation caused the fortunes of the Providence Biltmore to take a downward turn. Ernest Henderson, Sheraton's founder, died in 1967, leaving his son to manage the corporation. With Ernest's death, Sheraton immediately went up for sale and was quickly acquired by the International Telephone and Telegraph Company (ITT), an international telecom company that was currently leading the trend of national corporate mergers. ITT was not interested in hotels for the sake of hotels—they were interested in profits. Any hotel in the Sheraton chain that was not turning a profit was quickly repackaged and sold to the highest bidder.

Eighteen of Sheraton's holdings were sold immediately after ITT took control of the company, including the Sheraton Biltmore. The buyer was a little-known real estate investment company called Wellington Associates, made up of Sol Goldman and Alex DiLorenzo of New York City. The investor duo established Gotham Hotels Ltd. to manage the acquisition of the Sheraton Properties and, after the purchase, immediately leased the hotels to other operators for management.

Most of the hotels acquired by Gotham went out of business

shortly after the acquisition. Many of these hotels, like the Biltmore, were historically significant properties. The Hotel Belvedere in Baltimore, for instance, had been a Biltmore contemporary in the early part of the 20th century. In an article in *Baltimore Magazine* about the history of the hotel, the sale to Gotham is cited as its downfall: "When the Sheraton Corporation was sold to ITT in 1968, the Belvedere began a rapid downward spiral. Less than three months later, the Belvedere itself was sold by its new parents in an 18-hotel package deal to Wellington Associates...who ran it into the ground and closed it." Other hotels in the sale followed suit: the Warrior Hotel in Sioux City, Iowa; the Hotel Fontenelle in Omaha, Nebraska; and the Hotel McAlpin in New York City all quickly folded under the leasing and management arrangements of Gotham Hotels Ltd.

To attract motor tourists, Sheraton changed the hotel's name to the Biltmore Hotel and Motor Inn. Photo courtesy of the Graduate Providence.

Shortly before the sale to Gotham, Sheraton had repackaged the hotel as the Biltmore Hotel and Motor Inn. The name change was a sign of the times. The 1960s had seen a significant increase in automobile travel for families across the country. In addition, more regular and affordable air travel had boosted the hotel industry's occupancies during the decade. Motor hotels, or motor "lodges," or, eventually, "motels," were often known for being the easiest, most accessible accommodation option for car travelers. In addition, motels—more so than their "hotel" counterparts—were gaining popularity for their gimmicks and attractions, such as vibrating beds, color TVs, and outdoor pools. Guidebooks printed for American motorists listed all of the motels around the country. Larger and more established hotels quickly jumped on the bandwagon, rebranding themselves as motor lodges, motels, or, in the case of the Biltmore, *motor inns.* The hope was to attract automobile tourists to the hotel by packaging the stay as part of the new and improved "motel experience." Unfortunately, the Biltmore needed more than a new name to stay afloat.

By the early 1970s it was clear that Gotham's Providence holding was not going to be able to sustain itself, no matter how many advertisements were placed in AAA Magazine. The city was experiencing rapid decline and the Biltmore's business was going down with it. A final blow to the hotel was the departure of the bi-annual jewelry show, once its most reliable source of business each fall and spring. The show moved to the Holiday Inn around the corner from the Biltmore in 1972 due to better facilities and more competitive rates. Beloved Rhode Island native, actor Van Johnson, summed up the state of the Biltmore in a 1974 interview: "My father used to take me to the Biltmore to eat," he told a reporter over dinner one evening at Pot Au Feu. "The waiters dressed in black ties and the place had a lot of charm. I won't even look at it today."

Discussions began on what to do with the failing hotel. One idea was to convert the Biltmore into luxury apartments; however, the

Catering menu for the Biltmore Hotel and Motor Inn, shortly before the sale to Gotham Hotels. Courtesy of the Graduate Providence.

owners quickly found that there was no market in downtown Providence for expensive accommodations. In 1974, in an effort to revitalize downtown, the city launched a study under the Department of Planning and Urban Development to measure the feasibility of restoring the Biltmore to its original grandeur as a luxury hotel. The study, part of a larger downtown revitalization project called *Interface: Providence,* was undertaken in partnership with Rhode Island School of Design as an attempt to reimagine the decaying urban center. As part of the effort, a group of downtown business owners called the 21st Providence Group began to look at the prominent buildings in the city's center and evaluate their ongoing value to Providence. The Biltmore was at the top of their list.

It was not just the management of Gotham Hotels that were to blame for the Biltmore Hotel and Motor Inn's short lifespan. The beginning of the 1970s was a bleak time in Providence.

The flight away from city centers, often called the "suburban boom," that occurred post-WWII had driven the population of Providence down from 248,000 to 179,000 by the beginning of the 70s. Federal funding provided from President Johnson's urban-renewal program had dried up. The giant department stores that had once been the pulse of downtown started to close their doors, replaced by suburban malls and shopping centers that were located closer to where people lived. "The cynics said that Providence was beyond salvation," wrote the Pulitzer-Prize-winning journalist, Mike Stanton. Business owners and city administrators worried that the reduction in residents, compounded by an aging and less-affluent population, would have dire outcomes for the city's coffers. Once majestic, the historic downtown was beginning to look decrepit.

Not only had Providence run out of money, and residents, but it had been run into the ground by the thugs and thieves that had moved in when the "respectable" folks had moved out. For more than 30 years, the criminal underbelly of Providence had grown and thrived under the iron fist of its notorious leader, none other than the Biltmore's 1922 bellboy, Raymond L.S. Patriarca. The young bellhop had grown up, and from the back room of his Coin-o-Matic vending machine storefront, Patriarca had built a multimillion-dollar criminal empire.

According to Stanton, Patriarca "owned Connecticut, vowed to declare martial law to end an Irish-Italian gang war in Massachusetts, and arbitrated disputes among the Five Families in New York. He owned part of the Dunes Hotel and Casino in Las Vegas, had dealings with Jimmy Hoffa and Meyer Lansky, and was a silent partner in a Massachusetts horse track with Frank Sinatra and Dean Martin." In 1950, the Kefauver Committee in Washington DC reported that Patriarca was the "king of the rackets." In 1955, a bank robber in Boston stated during trial that he had robbed the bank because he owed Patriarca money, and called Patriarca "the mayor of Providence." In 1959, Bobby Kennedy brought Patriarca into the US Senate to interrogate him about his criminal background during a rackets committee hearing. By the 1960s, the former bellhop was known around the world as an integral part of the global criminal network.

Back home in Providence, however, Patriarca's legacy was more complex. To some, he was heralded as the grandfather of Federal

Raymond Patriarca leaving court with his attorneys.
Courtesy of the Boston Public Library, Leslie Jones Collection.

Hill. His network of lieutenants maintained order amongst the various criminal groups in the city. Some said that Patriarca actually kept the streets safe, at least for those who were not involved in organized crime. If someone lost something, Patriarca's guys found it. If a kid needed money to go to college, Patriarca found them scholarship money. He handed out candy bars in the street. He maintained law and order in the neighborhoods, despite questionable means. Much like all powerful men in Rhode Island, he had a loyal cult following—as well as a group of people who wanted to bring him down. "Patriarca reigned over a world of floating crap games, bookie parlors, and brassy nightclubs," Stanton wrote in *Prince of Providence*. However, "by the late 1960s, a growing number of citizens felt that things had gotten out of control. They were tired of reading about gangland slayings and shootings in broad daylight…[and] the police became jaded by the violence."

The Biltmore continued to play a part in Patriarca's story. In 1969, jurors in a Superior Court loansharking trial against Patriarca were sequestered in the hotel. The new TVs that had been installed in each room were removed. The daily newspaper deliveries to the rooms were suspended. The trial included testimony from undercover FBI agents who had infiltrated Federal Hill's underbelly, revealing an extensive network of illegal activity. In one testimony, Robert Yakubec, a federal agent, testified that Angelo DiPalma, an associate of Patriarca's, once told him that he had to turn over 50 percent of his loan shark "juice" to Patriarca and that Patriarca's lieutenant, Rudolph Sciarra, would take care of anyone who didn't comply. The judge was aware of the kind of city Providence had become. He ordered that the jurors not to leave their rooms at the Biltmore between trial dates. For that reason, the court took the unusual step of holding Saturday court sessions in an effort to shorten the length of the trial itself and allow the "release" of the jurors sooner than later.

This was the version of Providence that witnessed the Biltmore Hotel and Motor Inn's final hours: a dangerous, seedy town that had become overrun with criminals and thugs. This was not a place where cheery motorists wanted to stop on their way to Cape Cod. This was not a town that could host large out-of-state conventions and trade shows. The Biltmore's long corridors were suddenly filled with echoes, its restaurants left barren. It was 1974, and it seemed like the end of the road for the Biltmore.

28

"SELL AND GET OUT"

On January 14, 1975, Providence Gas Co. filed a suit in Rhode Island Superior Court to sue the management of the Biltmore Hotel for over $29,000 in unpaid bills. Promptly after the filing, the gas company shut off service to the entire hotel. The 10 remaining residents of the hotel frantically demanded to know why they had no heat. The hotel managers had no answer. They picked up the phone and called the utilities company. While they waited for an explanation from the gas company, staff were instructed by management to shut down the water system to avoid frozen pipes. The water was never turned back on.

A regular at the Biltmore's ground-level bar, Doorley's Tap, recalled that he was sitting in the bar that day when he asked the barkeep for some water. "He took the glass over to the tap and turned the water on, and no water came out. He picked up the phone to tell the maintenance man, and found out the place had just gone out of business."

The meager attempts by Gotham to save the hotel had failed. *The Providence Journal* ran the headline on the front page the following day: "DEBT-RIDDEN BILTMORE CLOSES." The article cited $29,000 in outstanding gas bills, $30,000 in unpaid water bills, and over $117,000 in unpaid taxes as the reason for the closure. A few weeks later, Narragansett Electric would follow with their own suit, suing Gotham for over $18,000 in unpaid electric bills. The hotel had been operating at less than 20 percent occupancy for many months, and, on its final nights, even the lights had been used sparingly. Within 24 hours of utilities being turned off, heavy steel grates were pulled down over the main entrances.

Despite knowing for months that the hotel could not pay its bills, Gotham management decided not to inform the long-term tenants of the hotel of the inevitable closure. The 11 remaining commercial businesses who had offices in the hotel frantically ran ads in the paper notifying the public of their relocation. One commercial tenant, Ralph Stuart Music, Inc. would follow up from the closure by suing Gotham Hotels for $50,000, stating that the abrupt closure caused the company to lose a great deal of business. Many of the hotel's staff had been let go over the preceding months, though the remaining staff were just as shocked at the sudden closure as the tenants. Raymond Wilbur, at 62 years old, had been working as a doorman at the hotel for 36 years. Fired two days before Christmas, Raymond continued to work the hotel door without pay. "At 62, where could I get a job?" Raymond told the paper. He continued to show up every day and work only for tips until the hotel officially closed in January.

The hotel was still home to several long-term residents at that time, and the surprise closure left them furious. Suddenly without heat or water, they were forced to find emergency accommodations. After 29 years of living in a suite of rooms on the hotel's 14th floor, Lewis Gilmore, a 70-year-old, retired lawyer, was irate. Referring to Gotham, Gilmore called the managers of the hotel "ruthless" and "unethical." When asked where he would go or what he would do, Gilmore was bewildered. He was the longest standing tenant of the hotel, having moved in right before it was bought by Sheraton. He told the paper that he would probably stay the night in his suite, despite the lack of heat or water. "I'm all mixed up," he said. "Probably tomorrow I will think more lucidly. I will probably move into another hotel, but it won't be as convenient."

Samuel Leviten, Board chairman of Big G Food Stores, had resided at the hotel for 22 years. He was relaxing in his five-room suite on the 15th floor when he heard that the hotel had abruptly closed. Leviten, however, seemed less shocked than his neighbor. He told *The Providence Journal* in an interview the following day that the hotel had been gradually declining for years. He had even installed his own air conditioning in his suite two years prior after the hotel told him that they would not foot the bill. Leviten said that someone had tipped him off at noon that day that the gas was to be shut off, but even having had warning he fought back emotions as he remembered the hotel he had moved into in the early 50s.

"This was a landmark," he told Doane Hulick of the Journal, "This was one of the best hotels in the country. They don't build them like this anymore." Leviten had decided he would purchase a home after being ousted from the hotel, but he shared concern that the other tenants might not be able to find new homes as quickly. With little remorse and much public outcry, the Biltmore officially closed its doors to the public on January 15th, 1974.

Joe Doorley, Providence's mayor, tried to toe a hard line with Gotham Hotels about the Biltmore's fate. He sent a warning to the hotel's owners that the clock was ticking—they either needed to fork over the $150,000 due in back taxes and water bills, or find a buyer for the hotel that would pick up the bill. If they failed to do so, the mayor declared that the city would move to foreclose on the hotel. Gotham's management in New York replied to the mayor that they had no interest in losing any more money on the deal. They wanted only to "sell and get out," and that this had been their only interest in the hotel for many years.

Providence's Chamber of Commerce told the mayor that they were perplexed by Gotham's response. According to the Chamber, they had approached Gotham's owners more than once about estab-lishing a group of prospective buyers for the hotel in an effort to avoid the situation that the hotel presently found itself in. Why Gotham had failed to follow up on these efforts was unknown. What was known, however, was that the hotel was quickly going into dereliction. Without the loving attention of its adoring staff, many who had been suddenly laid off after decades of employment at the hotel, the Biltmore soon found itself shuttered and suffering under a thick layer of neglect.

29

THE 21ˢᵀ PROVIDENCE GROUP

Vincent Albert Cianci Jr., or "Buddy" for short, grew up in the Silver Lake section of Cranston, the son of first-generation Italian Americans. A lonely and bullied child, Buddy developed a thick skin, with resentment in his blood. To bridge the divide between himself and his classmates at the elite Moses Brown School, Buddy developed an exceptional sense of humor and a magnetic charisma that he wielded like a sword and shield.

From Moses Brown, Buddy went on to college and then law school, followed by a short stint in the Army. Returning to Providence in 1969, Buddy set up a law practice in his father's old doctor's office and was then hired as an Assistant to Attorney General by Herb DiSimone. Buddy's entree into Providence politics was as a volunteer on DiSimone's campaign, and Buddy was quickly hooked. In his Pulitzer-Prize-winning book, *Prince of Providence*, Mike Stanton called Buddy a "political junkie." He spent countless hours plotting strategy with DiSimone during his unsuccessful gubernatorial campaigns in 1970 and 1972, all the while building his own reputation as a hardline prosecutor. In addition to his penchant for politics, Buddy had it out for Raymond Patriarca and the Providence mob, who he viewed as giving Italians everywhere a bad name.

Buddy was still relatively unknown when he started to frequent Doorley's Tap, the ground floor bar of the Biltmore, during the first half of the 1970s. He liked Doorley's, if not for any other reason than the fact that a lot of politicians hung out there, specifically the Mayor. Joe Doorley, Providence's mayor from 1965 to 1975, could often found at his namesake bar (owned and operated by his brother), or in his private hotel suite upstairs where he often entertained friends until the early hours of the morning. Toward the end of his time as Mayor, it was easier to find Doorley on a barstool than in the Mayor's office. In 1973, when Doorley's new civic center project faced rumors of corruption, the case was brought against him and tried by none other than Buddy Cianci, bringing the two Biltmore regulars head-to-head in the courtroom. The trial helped Buddy develop his reputation as the "anti-corruption candidate" when he became inspired to run for mayor in 1974.

Campaign poster for Buddy Cianci's 1974 mayoral campaign, running under the slogan "The Anti Corruption Candidate." Photo obtained on WikiCommons.

Having grown up in Providence during the Biltmore's Sheraton years, Buddy believed the Biltmore was the central axis of downtown. In April 1974, it was at a rally at the Biltmore that Buddy, a little-known Republican challenger to a longstanding mayor, announced his campaign. After winning the election, Buddy operated out of a 12th-floor suite at the hotel while waiting for Doorley to vacate City Hall. However, when Buddy took the oath of office in January 1975, the Biltmore had just closed its doors due to Gotham's mismanagement. Standing on the steps of City Hall on a cold January morning, Buddy watched with a heavy heart as a grand piano was wheeled away from the front doors of the iconic hotel.

Mayor Cianci's time in City Hall was fraught with scandal, corruption, crime, and tabloid exploits that even fiction writers couldn't make up. In *Prince of Providence*, Mike Stanton details the unprecedented rise of the unlikely mayor and his stunning downfall amidst a Grand Jury indictment and federal corruption investigations: "Not since Babe Ruth was slugging for the Providence Grays had the city seen someone with such star power…In national Republican circles, Cianci was a curiosity—an ethnic, urban mayor—and the party cultivated him like a rare orchid." Flipping the longtime Democratic city of Providence on its Republican head seemed like a feat only a master politician could have pulled off. It drew attention all the way to the top. Cianci was invited to the White House and courted throughout the country. But back in Providence, Cianci had his hands full. The school system was in shambles. The economy was dismal. Crime was rampant. If the "anti-corruption candidate" thought that winning the campaign was the prize, he soon realized the work had barely even begun.

Cianci's early years as mayor included never-ending scandal and turmoil, including an accusation of rape stemming from his college years and rumors that he had pressured a police chief so intensely that it resulted in the chief's suicide. Despite the scandals, Buddy plowed forward, brushing off the rumor mill and reporters and keeping himself busy with an overhaul of downtown Providence. The boarded-up Biltmore hotel was an eyesore in the middle of town, and Buddy took it personally. Several groups approached Cianci with requests for use of the building, including a group from Central Falls that submitted a proposal to have the Biltmore turned into housing for the elderly. Buddy wouldn't entertain it. He was committed to reinstating the hotel as a luxury accommodation in Providence, against all odds. During an event at the hotel years later, Buddy would lament that the reason he couldn't let the hotel go was because, for him, the Biltmore was synonymous with Providence. "When you see Providence, you say Biltmore," Buddy concluded matter-of-factly.

Providence's business community was slowly making a comeback under Cianci leadership. The city had invested in upgrading the harbor and port, cleaning up the dilapidated waterfront and building a new marine terminal. Manufacturing had mostly departed from Providence, but a strong service industry was beginning to replace it, as well as the rapidly growing healthcare sector. Retail and financial services were also on the rise. With the diversification of Providence's economy, the city began to slowly pull itself out of a 20-year decline. It was on the wave of this reinvigorated downtown that the leaders of Providence's commercial sector banded together to invest in the historic gems of Providence's past, including its grand old hotel.

Even with the economic comeback that the city was making, Providence was facing a facilities issue. The Chamber of Commerce had been turning away out-of-state companies and conventions for years, citing the lack of rental space available for offices and a deficit of large meeting space. The Providence Foundation released a report in 1975 that showed that out-of-state businesses had not been courted well enough by the Chamber and that the City needed to offer tax and financing incentives to developers if they hoped to bring in outside interests. In addition, the report mentioned that if

Vincent "Buddy" Cianci's official portrait in City Hall.
Courtesy of the Providence City Hall Collection.

the Biltmore invested in renovating its meeting spaces and rooms, it could become an attractive alternative to the Holiday Inn around the corner. Instead, the Biltmore remained boarded up and abandoned by the city. The report strongly urged Providence's business community to turn this around.

Heroes come in all forms, and the Biltmore's heroes came dressed in suits. A group of business owners, operating under the name of the 21st Providence Group, responded to the need for a reinvigoration of downtown by turning their sights toward the historic hotel. The group was made up of some of Rhode Island's hardest hitting executives: Bruce Sundlun of the Outlet Company, John Henderson of Textron, G. William Miller of Textron, Michael Metcalf of *The Providence Journal*, and Jim Winoker and Dominic Zinni of B.B. Greenberg Company, as well as several other companies.

Bruce Sundlun, President of the Outlet Co., and one of the leading businessmen
in saving the Biltmore. Photo obtained on WikiCommons.

The first challenge they had to undertake was to unearth the
Biltmore from the mountain of debt accumulated by its negligent
owners. Leading negotiations between Gotham Hotels and the
group was Henderson, a senior Vice President at Textron and the
head of the 21st Providence Group. Talks between the group and
Gotham began in June 1975. Alongside the 21st Providence Group,
a little-known hotel management company called Hotels of Distinction was rumored to be part of the deal. Their impact on the
hotel would far outlive their contract.

Negotiations dragged on between Gotham and 21st Providence
Group, with Gotham dropping its asking price several times. At one
point, the *Journal* quoted Gotham's legal representative stating that
Gotham's owners were "desperate" to get rid of the hotel, but that
they had not decided to whom they would sell it. In the end, 21st
Providence won out, purchasing the hotel for a meager $925,000,

despite the original asking price of $3.6 million. They would spend more than $15 million on its renovation, which included a new roof, sprinkler systems, and renovated kitchens—big-ticket items that were required to modernize the hotel and to bring it up to code.

Securing the deal on the Biltmore was a coordinated effort for the city of Providence. The 21st Providence Group leveraged every resource available to them to make the project go through. US Senator John O. Pastore, Democrat from Rhode Island and the first Italian American ever elected to the Senate, advocated for the project to the Economic Development Administration. As chairman of the Senate appropriations subcommittee for the Department of State, Justice, Commerce, and the Judiciary, Pastore used his influence to push several Rhode Island projects into the appropriations bill. The 21st Providence Group, with Pastore's support, applied for a $2.5 million, long-term, low-interest loan from the EDA to finance the renovations on the hotel. Buddy Cianci even headed to Washington that year to encourage the decision. He returned to Providence confident, touting that he had received assurances from President Ford's staff that the administration would work with Providence officials to secure funds for his projects. When asked directly about the Biltmore, however, Cianci balked. He had not received specific assurances on any project in particular, though he wanted his constituents to believe he had. He smiled broadly at the press at T.F. Green airport and assured the residents of Providence that he had the President's ear. Whether or not Cianci played a role is unclear, but the EDA approved the loan to the 21st Providence Group to help finance the renovations. Momentum increased dramatically by July 1976, when the City Council voted strongly in favor of providing a 10-year tax break for the Biltmore Hotel.

The Journal published numerous articles leading up to the City Council vote, one of which was an editorial supporting the measure and stating that the tax break for the Biltmore would benefit "all of Providence." *The Journal*, whose owners were part of the

21st Providence Group, was slammed the following week by several "Letters to the Editor" which decried the conflict of interest in the paper publishing support for the project from which they would financially benefit. Ultimately, the complaints were published but seemed to have little sway. The Council voted in favor of the tax break by a large margin.

The tax structure, strongly endorsed by Cianci, called for the owners of the hotel to pay a fixed annual tax ranging from $25,000 in 1977 to $100,000 in 1986 regardless of any changes in the city's tax rates or the hotel's profits. The tax break was seen as a major political win for Cianci since nine Democratic councilmen voted to approve the measure despite regularly voting against the Republican mayor's wishes. Cianci touted the decision as a great day for the city, stating that the Council had "put Providence ahead of politics."

At the meeting where the tax break was approved, John Henderson outlined 21st Providence's plans for the shuttered hotel and the tremendous boost it would provide for the downtown area. In a two-page article featured in the *Journal*, Henderson stated that the group had received an "oral commitment" from the federal Economic Development Agency that they would be receiving $2.5 million in loans to renovate the hotel. The group still needed $1 million more, which they aimed to raise from smaller businesses in Providence. The goal was to encourage investments between $25,000 and $50,000 from local businesses in return for becoming part owners in the project.

Once more, the people of Providence were being called on to invest their private capital to open (or in this case, reopen) the Biltmore. Similar to efforts in 1922, the city's most prominent businessmen appealed to the public on the grounds of civic duty. The newly renovated and reopened Biltmore would reinvigorate pride in the city, Henderson assured City Council. City residents would benefit from the hotel's new and modern amenities, and optimism would radiate out from the grand hotel's doors. The beautiful destination would attract investment in the city, of that Henderson was confident. Not to mention more than 300 jobs being brought back to downtown, he reminded the Council members.

At this City Council meeting, an unknown hotel group named Hotels of Distinction was mentioned as the leading management company being considered for the project. Some of the renovation ideas were shared for the first time, including the addition of a glass elevator to be added to the outside wall of the hotel. Alan Tremain, the head of Hotels of Distinction, cruised into Providence in a Bentley and told the Council that he aimed to turn the hotel into a "fun place" where businessmen and tourists could experience the elegance of a historic building but in a comfortable, modern environment. He suggested that the average room rate would be $30 per night. Tremain, however, did not stay the night. He hurriedly headed back to Boston before the meeting was even concluded.

After more than a year of intense negotiations between Gotham Hotels and the 21st Providence Group—and with loans secured, a new mortgage signed, and a tax break on the horizon—the sale of the hotel was finalized on September 2, 1976. Reopening was scheduled optimistically for January 1978. In a show of continued support for the project from City Hall, the City applied in April 1977 to have the Biltmore added to the National Historic Register. This effort allowed Mayor Cianci access to federal historic preservation tax credits, supporting the new owners as they began the pricey rehabilitation of the hotel.

Renovations on the hotel began almost immediately. In January 1977, the *Journal* ran an article with the headline, "Old Biltmore fixtures go on sale tomorrow," notifying the public of the items headed to auction from the boarded-up building. Three hundred TV sets priced at $30 a piece, a thousand bed sets at $40 to $80, 700 wool blankets at $5 a pop, and hundreds of pieces of glassware at just 50 cents to a dollar—all were headed out the door to help pay off the hotel's debts. Other items that were auctioned off during the two-day lobby sale included desks, dressers, lamps, china, silverplates,

Advertisement for a Flash Sale at the Biltmore, 1977.
Photo obtained from The Providence Journal *historic archives.*

commercial stoves, sinks, and marble slabs. Porcelain sinks dating back to 1922, down to their original brass faucets, were wheeled swiftly through the front doors and into wholesaler's moving vans. The public was encouraged to negotiate prices because everything had to go. After the initial auction, people were invited to make appointments to visit the hotel and purchase items on multiple floors. The full sale lasted nearly 60 days, overlapping with work being done in the building by Sturges, Daughn, and Salisbury, the architectural firm hired to work up drawings for the renovation.

The Biltmore renovation was repeatedly packaged for the public as part and parcel to the larger revitalization of downtown Providence, part of a larger vision that included the restoration of Union Station and a rehab of Exchange Place. At a meeting at the Providence Art Club, William Miller of Textron told the city's upper crust that the plans laid out by 21st Providence Group were not just about revitalization; they were about "the destiny of the city." With a nod to statements already made by Buddy Cianci, Miller ended by saying that the city of Providence "can be among the best in the world, if we want it to be."

30

THE BILTMORE REIMAGINED

The 21st Providence Group had no interest in managing and running the Biltmore Hotel. Their interest was in the restoration of a vibrant downtown, one where their businesses could be proudly headquartered and where restored commerce would breathe life back into the cobblestone and brick of the historic city center. Once the sale was assured, the Group immediately brought in management firms to discuss renovations and future management of the hotel.

The Providence Journal covered the debate about management companies for the newly purchased hotel with as much interest and fervor as they had in 1921 before the Bowman Hotel Corp. was awarded the management contract by the Chamber of Commerce. Just as E.M. Statler and John McEntee Bowman had two entirely different visions and two entirely different track records, so did the two frontrunners eyed to renovate and manage the Biltmore. Hotels of Distinction, a flashy management company headed by an equally flashy executive, was making waves with the Copley Plaza in Boston and presented a modern take on how the hotel should be managed. Dunfey Group, a more well-known and conservative management group, showed interest in restoring the hotel to its distinguished New England charm. In the end, the sensational Copley model outshined Dunfey's longer track record of success. Hotels of Distinction was awarded the management contract and went about redesigning the hotel from the inside out.

Hotels of Distinction had recently been established by the former general manager of Sheraton Plaza in Boston, Allen Tremain. Tremain had recently made waves when he broke from Sheraton and formed his own company. His intention was to take over the Copley Plaza, which was, at that time, owned by John Hancock Life Insurance Co. The risky move had worked, and the insurance company had ended their contract with Sheraton to award management of the hotel to Tremain's newly formed company. Tremain was credited with having stopped the historic Copley from going under, directing major renovations of the hotel, and attracting a higher-end clientele to its pricey rooms and meeting facilities. This limited but impressive track record was just what the 21st Providence Group executives wanted to see happen again at the Biltmore Hotel. Under this new management group, the Biltmore reopened in 1979 and was renamed the Biltmore Plaza, a nod to Tremain's Copley Plaza in Boston.

Alan Tremain was as eccentric as he was savvy. An Englishman with a handlebar mustache who had a pet parrot named Clyde, Tremain left an indelible mark on the people he met and the hotels he worked in. Tremain had come to hotel work as a result, he proclaimed, of Adolf Hitler's campaign of terror. During the second World War, Tremain evacuated from his home in Somerset, England to a small town of Bognor Regis where his aunt owned an inn. It was there that Tremain was introduced to hotel work and where his love of hospitality blossomed. In an interview in The Palm Beach Post, Tremain declared his life of travel as delightfully exotic, having climbed the career ladder in far-flung places such as New Delhi, Hong Kong, Auckland, and Canada. It was there that Tremain began driving a Rolls Royce—a point he was fond of making—and he'd driven nothing but luxury ever since.

Tremain held on to cars, but not to partners. He had four wives and five marriages in his lifetime, telling the *Post* that "the [hotel] business is hard on your home life. I learned the hard way that women don't like an environment where they can't be casual, where they have to dress up as soon as they walk out the door."

Tremain saw himself as a curator of his guests' experiences, especially the wealthiest of guests. "Running [a hotel] is like producing a play. The lobby and the public rooms are the stage sets, and the staff are the actors. Most hotel people have a touch of the theater—the flash of the napkin as it's laid in your lap, for instance." He greatly enjoyed the celebrity status afforded him as the manager of high-end hotels. In taking over the Copley Plaza in Boston, Tremain frequently comped celebrity guests' rooms and made sure it was widely known that they were staying at the Copley, nudging local news outlets to highlight their stays in the paper. He called this tactic "cheap advertising."

"Celebrities like to hide in their rooms," Tremain said in an interview. "I would take them to my apartment for dinner. Luciano Pavarotti didn't want to eat in the dining room because he was afraid he would be pestered. Of course, after a couple of drinks, he started singing to my wife. A great ham, but a nice man." Tremain was so enamored with his own celebrity circuit that he ended up self-publishing a book about his hotel encounters entitled "Without Reservations." Despite the grandiosity and gravitas of showmanship, Tremain was reputed to be a successful hotelier. He was revered in Boston for his turnaround of the Copley Plaza and called "creative and honest" by many of the people who worked for him.

Contracted to save the Biltmore, Tremain brought on Jean-Claude Mathieu to run day-to-day operations of the hotel. Mathieu's most notable imprint on the hotel would be in the redevelopment of the penthouse restaurant, a buttoned-up French eatery he named L'Apogee. It was intended, at the time, to be the most exquisite restaurant in Rhode Island. In addition to L'Apogee, Hotels of Distinction opened a second restaurant in the hotel, Goddards, named after the

prominent Rhode Island textile industrialist, Robert Hale Ives Goddard. The famed Garden Room—which had welcomed hundreds of
international performers in the 1940s and 50s—and John F. Kennedy's
beloved Bacchante Room were redesigned as conference rooms.

It was Tremain who recommended that the renovations include
a reduction in the number of rooms in the hotel, substantially cutting the number from 500 to 350 in an effort to create larger, more
"first-class" rooms for more well-heeled guests. Tremain initially
pushed for the grand ballroom to be converted into a nightclub and
bar, but this idea was ultimately shot down by the hotel's owners.
In addition to opening L'Apogee on the top floor, Tremain pushed
for the purchase of the adjacent parking garage, which had by then
been sold to the city. In his vision, Tremain hoped that the top floor
of the garage would be converted into tennis courts for the hotel
guests to use. This vision never came to fruition.

The most controversial change implemented by Hotels of Distinction, and the change felt most deeply by those loyal to the hotel,
was the decision to tear out the hotel's marble grand staircase. No
longer could someone say, "meet me at the Biltmore stairs," as had
been said so many thousands of times before.

The removal of the grand staircase was undertaken to make room
for the installation of the most ostentatious part of the renovation:
a glass elevator that would take guests from the ground floor all
the way to the Ballroom. The elevator, reminiscent of the Wonka-
vator in *Charlie and the Chocolate Factory*, was designed to be both
modern and ornate. The hulking glass shaft extends from the inside
of the hotel's three-story lobby, outward and upward, climbing the
remaining 15 floors on the outside of the hotel's facade. The see-
through shaft and carriage affords anyone inside the elevator a full
view of downtown and, as the elevator goes higher, across the east
side of Providence. In clear weather, a full view of the city could be
seen from the top. While fantastic in theory, in practice the elevator
was fraught with challenges. With the staircase removed, there was

no way for guests to access the second floor of the lobby, and the three-story atrium that connects the lobby to the mezzanine was suddenly cut off from the hotel's entrance. Guests had to ride the elevator up to the mezzanine and then take the side staircase down to the second floor if they needed to visit an office on the main lobby floor. The elevator, ironically, removed access to a large portion of the public space of the hotel. Despite the design flaws, the gimmick of the glass elevator had sticking power. When the hotel reopened, people from across the Ocean State hurried to take a ride on the newly installed amusement ride.

Perhaps the most lasting change to the hotel made during the renovations was a change to the neon sign on the roof, which had once read Sheraton-Biltmore. With no small amount of effort, the sign was retooled to simply say "BILTMORE," creating a symbol for Providence that, to this day, is celebrated as a staple of the downtown aesthetic.

In the end, Hotels of Distinction was not a good fit for the Biltmore or for Providence. The hotel lost millions in its first year of reopening, losses that had to be subsidized by its owners at Textron, Outlet Co., and the *Journal*. Occupancy rates were down to less than 55 percent, substantially lower than industry averages at that time and shockingly low compared to the feasibility study conducted by the owners prior to opening. Adding insult to injury, the downtown Marriott had just added an additional 100 rooms to its operation. The renovation of the Biltmore encountered delays, pushing the opening later than anticipated. Inflationary prices caused costs to exceed original estimates. In addition, the hotel had been hit by an 11-week employees' strike in late 1979, further damaging profits. A recession in the early 80s was the final straw. Even with hotel profits slowly starting to rise, Hotels of Distinction lost their management contract of the hotel after just two years at the helm. Allen Tremain packed up his Bentley and headed back to Boston with little to show for his time in Rhode Island.

31

RESTORATION FOR THE PEOPLE

Dunfey Hotel Group was brought on board in October 1981 to reimagine the Biltmore. The first thing the new management company noted was that the hotel seemed alienated from the community in which it was situated. The Dunfey brothers' first move was to fire the Boston-based PR firm utilized by Hotels of Distinction and to replace it with Duffy & Shanley, a Providence agency that was already managing other historic Rhode Island clients, such as the Arcade building around the corner from the hotel.

In an interview about the PR efforts with *The Providence Journal*, W. Robert McIntosh, Dunfey's vice president and director of operations, stated that, in talking with the locals about the hotel, they had found "a genuine disappointment that the hotel hadn't been a success, a sense that the people were counting on the Biltmore and had been let down." He furthered that under Hotels of Distinction's management, Rhode Islanders felt that they were being looked down upon by the Biltmore, patronized by its management and owners. "A community of any kind doesn't like to be talked down to. We're told that this is the way people felt."

To introduce the new management team to the community and to help break down the barriers that had existed under Hotels

The Dunfey Brothers photographed in the 1980s.
Courtesy of the Southern New England University Shapiro Library.

of Distinction, the 21st Providence team threw an elaborate 300-person cocktail party in the ballroom of the hotel. Featured on the menu were bündnerfleisch (a costly, Swiss, cured beef), "slipper tails" (Scandinavian baby lobsters), venison pate, Russian caviar, and pheasant galantine. During the party, the brothers Dunfey—namely Jack, Bill, Walter, Jerry, and Bob—greeted Rhode Island mayors, business community board members and chairmen, important publishers, bank presidents, legislators, and other luminaries of the community. The event was a sort of speed dating for hotel business contracts. The sooner the Dunfey brothers could get in cahoots with the business and political networks of Rhode Island, the sooner the hotel could start making money again.

The Dunfey group had its roots in New England, and they understood how to play the game in Providence. Having started with a 32-room inn in Hampton, New Hampshire, the family-run business was famed for its clam shacks as well as its inn. When Dick Brush was a teenager, he worked in what was fondly referred to as

Number 13, a clam shack in New Hampshire owned by the Dunfeys, who were then just his childhood friends. "Then in 1980, I got a call from them, asking if I wanted to come up and run a new hotel they had acquired in Providence," Dick recounted. "They had no idea my dad had been the manager there in the 40s. They didn't know anything about my connection to it." Dick was thrilled by the opportunity to return to the Biltmore and swiftly resigned his position at a hotel in Atlanta to move back to Rhode Island, becoming the Biltmore's General Manager under the Dunfey Group in 1981.

When Dick arrived at the Biltmore Hotel with his wife, daughter, and infant son, downtown Providence was not what he remembered. "I think we were the only family living downtown," Dick recalled in a 2021 interview. "*No one* lived downtown. It wasn't that kind of place." Despite Buddy's efforts, the city's commercial center had not yet bounced back. Dick was charged with fixing that. For the next several years, the Dunfey group and Dick Brush worked tirelessly to restore business to the Biltmore Hotel. They focused on conventions, traveling tours, and corporate groups to cover the bulk of reservations at the hotel. With the reinvigoration of the hotel came at least one guaranteed business boon from the past: the annual jewelry show. The United Jewelry Show which had packed the Biltmore for two weeks twice a year for many decades returned in 1981 to the restored hotel with over 300 vendors in attendance.

Under Dick's management, and with the support of the Dunfey brothers, the hotel set about rebranding itself as the hotel of the people once more. L'Apogee, which had been opened as an exclusive, elegant black-tie eatery targeting the creme-de-la-creme of society, quickly dropped its prices. Early in 1982, advertisements were run inviting people to come to the restaurant for a $9.95 brunch. The headline of the ad was, "Brunch like a Millionaire for just $9.95!" The menu featured champagne mimosas, a buffet of eggs, seafood Newburg, roast beef, veal, shrimp salad, pastries, cakes, and dessert crepes, all set against the backdrop of live piano accompaniment. In

Biltmore general manager Dick Brush photographed alongside Buddy Cianci and George H.W. Bush at the hotel in 1982. Photo courtesy of Dick Brush.

addition to L'Apogee, the hotel boasted a restored Falstaff Room, Goddards restaurant and bar, the Garden Room ballroom, and a newly renovated and reopened Bacchante Lounge.

The new approach doubled down on local patronage. Management set up new programs such as the Executive Service Program, which had been successful at other Dunfey hotels. The crux of the program was that members would receive VIP treatment at the hotel and guaranteed reservations up until 5 p.m. on the day of arrival. The program was advertised locally and intended to drum up business from Rhode Islanders, not just people coming and going from T.F. Green airport. Jack Dunfey stated in one interview with the *Journal* that the hotel's style "is to sell to the local community. It's the local community that generally directs incoming visitors about where to stay…The travel agencies, the executive secretaries, the marketing managers—we sell locally; we don't sell to the person coming on the plane from Chicago." The Dunfey group wanted to reestablish the Biltmore as the hotel built by and for the people, and by all accounts, they succeeded. The hotel also welcomed numerous political figures during the Dunfey years. George H. W. Bush frequented the hotel on the campaign trail. As Vice President, he spent hours side by side with Mayor Cianci during a fundraiser for Secretary of State Susan Farmer's bid for Lieutenant Governor.

It wasn't all business at the Biltmore under the new management. Continuing an event that began under Jean-Claude Mathieu, Dunfey Hotels hosted the annual Bastille Day Race, an event sponsored by the hotel as a fundraiser for local charities. Waiters from the hotel competed in the 50-yard dash down Dorrance Street, clad in tuxedos and tennis shoes. Participants were required to balance a tray of wine glasses as they ran past hundreds of spectators lining the sidewalks. According to coverage of the event, the competition had its roots in France, where waiters traditionally raced through the streets of Paris each July 14 in celebration of the day the French rose against the government of Louis XVI and stormed the Bastille. Similar competitions are held throughout the US each summer, and there is even a national championship race. The Biltmore would continue the crowd-pleasing event for nearly two decades.

32

DINING OUT OF ORBIT

The word *apogee*, according to the Merriam Webster Dictionary, means "the point in the orbit which is farthest from the earth." Hotels of Distinction's leading Frenchman, Jean-Claude Mathieu, was likely going with the more literal description of "the highest point" when he decided to name the penthouse restaurant L'Apogee. But over time, the restaurant would take on the personality of a goliath, towering over the city and providing a backdrop for events that would have to be recounted in court as sworn testimony. It was, indeed, an eatery at the farthest reaches of Providence's orbit.

To begin with, L'Apogee was the finest dining that could be found in Providence and for that reason, it attracted all the stars that came through the city. Though one might not expect to find the blood-spitting, fire-breathing likes of Gene Simmons, front man of rock band Kiss, dining on white tablecloths, L'Apogee was just the place Simmons liked to go after raucous shows in Providence. After removing his signature black-and-white make up and cleaning any remaining fake blood off of his costume, Simmons enjoyed the panoramic views from the top floor eatery while quietly nibbling baguettes and fielding questions from some of his biggest fans. Karen Lesniewski, editor of a Kiss fan newsletter, fondly recalled dinner with Simmons in the restaurant where she interviewed him for the newsletter after the show. Despite their often disturbing performances, Lesniewski staunchly defends Simmons and the band as ordinary, down-to-earth guys. Unlike their show, Kiss's dinner at L'Apogee was so uneventful that it wasn't reported in the paper until a decade later.

The 17th floor of the hotel also claims another intriguing rock and roll milestone from this era. Frank Black, best known as the lead vocalist of the alternative rock group, Pixies, gave his first ever public performance in the Biltmore's ballroom, not long after its reopening. Black, then in high school, had recently moved from Los Angeles to Massachusetts with his family. One spring evening, he attended a prom at the Biltmore where he was persuaded by his classmates to get up on the microphone. Belting out Wilson Pickett's "In the Midnight Hour," Black recalled the thrill the microphone gave him. It was so memorable that he cited it as his first public rock performance when interviewed by the *Journal* 15 years later.

L'Apogee also emerged as a restaurant of choice for the Kennedys, bringing the presidential family back to the hotel two decades after JFK's memorable stay at the hotel at the end of his campaign trail. This time, however, it was John Jr. who was in the spotlight. Attending Brown University as an undergraduate, Kennedy's only son enjoyed a rare moment of relative normalcy in his life, joining the Phi Kappa Psi fraternity, acting in college theater, playing rugby, and studying history. During these years, the Biltmore provided the Kennedy family with a welcoming and discreet homebase for visits with John. The newspapers kept their distance, and the University and hotel worked together to provide privacy for Jackie Onassis and her family. Jackie loved the historic charm of the Biltmore and appreciated the hotel's respectful discretion of her visits.

Dick Brush, General Manager of the hotel during John's time at Brown, shared that Jackie did not have a specific room or any detailed requests when she came to town. She stayed in various

Jacqueline Kennedy Onassis, photographed here in 1978, spent many nights at the Biltmore when her son was attending Brown University. Courtesy of The Library of Congress.

suites at the hotel during John's time at Brown. Her only request to the management was that one particular table was reserved on the second floor coffeeshop each morning, just a stone's throw from where her husband had once entertained his navy friends in the Bacchante Lounge. However, while handsome, confident JFK would have had a table front and center in the Lounge, Jackie's preferred place at the Biltmore was tucked away in a corner of the mezzanine cafe. Dick recalled her visits with a smile, remembering the special understanding between them. "She would always take the table facing the window, with her back to the room. She could enjoy her morning coffee in peace. No one ever even knew she was there." When John graduated from Brown in 1983, Jackie phoned the hotel to make a larger than usual request. She reserved seven rooms on the 14th floor, and the Kennedy family held an intimate party for the graduate, dining at L'Apogee on prime rib while the press was held at bay by hotel staff outside.

John's graduation dinner would not be the last Kennedy event at the Biltmore. In 1988, at the young age of 21, John's cousin, Patrick Kennedy, became the youngest member of the family to hold elected office when he won a seat in Rhode Island's House of Representatives. He was only a Junior at Providence College. Patrick celebrated the win at the Biltmore, following in the footsteps of his uncle, aunt, and cousin as he enjoyed the grand ballroom and restaurants on the campaign trail and victory night.

More than any other person during this era, however, it was Buddy Cianci whose fingerprint could be seen everywhere in the city, especially at the Biltmore. "[Buddy] was the can-do mayor of the comeback city, the energetic urban philosopher who could cut through red tape and bring home the bacon," wrote Mike Stanton. Buddy successfully brought "fifty million dollars in downtown investment since taking office in 1975, supported by another 10 million in city and federal funds." Buddy leveraged every tool available to him, including historic preservation, to secure the funds he needed to refurbish downtown. By personally taking on the restoration and preservation of the Biltmore Hotel, as well as the rejuvenation of Federal Hill and the construction of new office buildings, Buddy created an energy of progress that instilled excitement throughout the city. These projects successfully masked, at least for a time, the dark underbelly of Buddy's work that would ultimately lead to his political demise.

During his few years as manager of the hotel, Dick Brush and his family "lived in," a practice that had begun to dwindle in hotel management over the years. Living at the hotel afforded Dick the opportunity to keep an eye on things at all times, and with clientele like the Federal Hill boys and Buddy Cianci, this was more than necessary. To ensure the hotel didn't fall into chaos, Dick made it his business to head down to Goddards restaurant each day around 5 p.m., "just to see who was around." It wasn't uncommon to see Buddy and his associates drinking and smoking at the bar, Buddy waving his cigarettes so wildly that ash would inevitably end up all around his barstool. Even today, Dick remains close-lipped about much of what he saw and heard during those years, though he shares that Buddy wasn't someone who appreciated being confronted about his behavior, especially in what Buddy considered to be "his hotel."

One evening, Dick was summoned to deal with an issue that was irking the staff. The expensive Egyptian linens adorning the tables in L'Apogee were being defaced. Unfortunately, the perpetrator was none other than the city's venerable mayor, and no one wanted to deal with it. Sitting in L'Apogee with his assistant, pen in hand, Buddy had scribbled notes on the tablecloth as he espoused a frantic campaign strategy. Diagrams, arrows, and incoherent letters seeped into the linens. L'Apogee's head waiters looked on in dismay. Dick was summoned from his apartment downstairs and as he entered the restaurant, he observed the mayor slam down his cocktail and strike a line through something he'd written on the tablecloth. Dick approached the table with reserve, catching the mayor's eye.

"These are really expensive linens, Buddy," he said in a whisper. Buddy looked up at him with vitriol.

"You fucking kidding me?" he laughed, looking around. He waved a hand of dismissal at Dick and went back to his conversation.

Recounting the event, Dick laughed. "That was just the way Buddy was. He just didn't care what the rules were." That sentiment could not have been more true, whether it referred to the rules of the hotel or federal law. Buddy picked and chose what applied to him and what he would ultimately ignore.

In a particularly Machiavellian fashion, L'Apogee once again became the backdrop for a confrontation between the mayor and an unwitting victim of his mania. This time, it was in March 1983. The mayor had just been indicted by a Grand Jury for the kidnapping and assault of Raymond DeLeo, a local contractor that he accused of sleeping with his wife, Sheila. Even though Sheila and Buddy were separated and headed toward divorce, rumors of her affair enraged him. One night, Buddy called DeLeo and told him to come to his house on Power Street for an important meeting. When DeLeo arrived, Buddy had an off-duty Providence patrolman frisk DeLeo, and then lead him into the living room.

For several hours, Buddy proceeded to interrogate DeLeo about his affair with Sheila. All the while, DeLeo denied that the affair had happened. As the clock ticked, Buddy became more enraged, attacking DeLeo, pulling his hair, punching him, and slapping him. Buddy's lawyer sat in silence on the other side of the room, as did the police officer. At one point, Buddy grabbed a burning log from the fireplace and charged at DeLeo, but the others in the room intervened before DeLeo was burned. The abuse and rage went on late into the night, with DeLeo telling a jury later that he felt like Buddy's prisoner. Eventually, Buddy let the battered and bleeding DeLeo go, on the promise that DeLeo would pony up $500,000 to the mayor, in exchange for the mayor's forgiveness. DeLeo never paid Buddy. Instead, he went to the Feds.

The FBI immediate launched an investigation based on DeLeo's story, charging Buddy with kidnapping, assault, torture, and extortion. Buddy was desperate to find someone to corroborate the story that Sheila had been cheating on him and he believed that person could be Lenore Steinberg. Lenore was a wealthy widow, previously married to a successful lace manufacturer from Central Falls who had tragically taken his own life a few years prior. Lenore had become friends with Sheila Cianci during the early days of Buddy's campaign and had contributed to his campaign war chest. After her husband committed suicide, however, Lenore had remarried and relocated to West Palm Beach.

A few days after his attack on DeLeo, Buddy called Lenore. She was packing for a trip to Providence where she was taking care of some family business. Buddy told her matter-of-factly that he had found out about Raymond and Sheila. Lenore was shocked, telling Buddy that she didn't know anything about it. Buddy wasn't having it. He demanded she give him information about the affair, anything to corroborate his belief that Sheila and DeLeo were intimately involved. Lenore denied knowing anything about the affair but agreed to meet Buddy when she was in Providence later that week.

When Lenore arrived at the Biltmore Hotel, Buddy was in the lobby waiting for her. By his side was a uniformed police officer. Lenore was immediately on guard. Buddy smiled wryly and said, "I came to welcome you back to Providence." He gruffly told the front desk clerk to check Mrs. Steinberg in and said that they would be heading to L'Apogee for a late dinner. Lenore allowed the mayor to lead her to the elevator with the police officer in tow.

The two sat down at a secluded table overlooking the Providence skyline. L'Apogee was quiet that evening, and a feeling of desolation swept over Lenore. Buddy immediately dug in. He demanded that Lenore tell him about the affair. She continued to deny any knowledge of it, further fanning Buddy's rage. Buddy went on to tell her in detail what he had done to DeLeo, embellishing the story and adding that he had "almost killed DeLeo." He then threatened Lenore, insisting that if she didn't corroborate his story of the affair for the upcoming trial, he would launch his own investigation into Lenore's husband's suicide. In his rage, he charged that he would tell the world that Lenore had played a role in her husband's death if she didn't acquiesce to his demands for information about Sheila and Ray's affair.

Mortified, Lenore told Buddy that she was disgusted by his behavior and that she wanted no part in his ludicrous story. She rose from the table and hurriedly left the restaurant without finishing her meal. Safely in her room, she called for room service. However, her fear that Buddy would arrive with the food kept her from answering the door when room service rang. For the remaining days in Providence, Lenore would not go anywhere alone. She walked on eggshells, convinced Buddy would emerge at any moment to accost her. She was so scared of him that she called a mutual friend, a police officer, and asked for a police escort to take her back to the airport at the end of her trip. A month later, when Buddy was charged with kidnapping, assault, and attempted extortion of Ray DeLeo, Lenore would be subpoenaed to appear in court and testify about the encounter in L'Apogee.

In the end, L'Apogee lived up to expectations as the premiere setting for Providence's dinner scene, but perhaps got more than it bargained for when it ended up being treated as the mayor's private dining room. In 1984, a grand jury found Buddy guilty in the assault of Ray DeLeo. Buddy was forced to resign his post as mayor, though he would not serve any jail time. It was the first time that Buddy had to step down from his mayorship on criminal charges, but it would not be the last.

33

THE CURIOUS CASE OF

CLAUS VON BULOW

B
y the 1980s, the Biltmore had made somewhat of a tradition of providing refuge for the down and out. From Dutee Flint to Frank O'Hara, from Antoine Gazda to Henrietta Wolf Gibson—and not to mention the refugee von Trapp singers—the hotel has opened its doors and rooms to accommodate countless victims of fate. Keeping to this tradition, the Biltmore welcomed a particularly peculiar guest in 1985. Whether he was a victim of fate or ruthless killer, the world was waiting to find out.

By all accounts, this looked like the end of the line for Claus von Bulow. All that sat before him was a likely sentence of 30 years in the Rhode Island Adult Correctional Institution, unless he won his final appeal in the Rhode Island Supreme Court. Five years prior, on December 22, 1980, the wealthy Danish aristocrat had stood over the body of his unresponsive wife, who lay crumpled in her night-gown on the marble floor of their Newport mansion. What was going through his mind would be the focus debate for two separate juries over the course of a three-year trial. Had Claus truly stumbled upon his unconscious wife, Sunny von Bulow, that morning at Clarendon Court? Or had he tried to murder her? In a case that would be later called the most "sensational social drama" of the 1980s by *The New York Times*, the story had everything the media circus needed. "It has money, sex, drugs; it has Newport, New York and Europe; it has nobility; it has maids, butlers, a gardener," a prosecutor on the case would go on to state proudly to the press.

The case would also make Alan M. Derschowitz, Claus's defense attorney, famous. Derschowitz went on to write a book about the case, which was then turned into an Academy Award winning film *Reversal of Fortune.* In addition to his writing, Derschowitz would continue to make a name for himself on high profile cases. From O.J. Simpson to Harvey Weinstein and Donald Trump, Derschowitz would cut a career out of the defense of the indefensible.

The Claus von Bulow trials were prime time sensations. The story followed Sunny and Claus, two New York and Newport socialites who shared a tumultuous and drama-filled marriage. Sunny was known for her drinking and drug-use, once being dubbed by Truman Capote as "an expert at injections." Claus was portrayed as a gold-digging adulterer, frequently abandoning his wealthy but unstable wife for the arms of other women.

Sunny von Bulow was born Martha Sharp Crawford on September 1, 1932 on her father's personal train car en route from Virginia to New York. The only child of utilities magnate George Crawford and his wife, Annie-Laurie Warmack, Sunny inherited more than $100 million upon her father's death when she was only three. Sunny spent her life bouncing between the elite social circles of New York, Newport, and Europe. In 1957, she married her tennis instructor from a Swiss resort, Prince Alfred Eduard Friedrich Vincenz Martin Maria von Auersperg, with whom she had two children. The marriage ended in divorce and Sunny remarried Claus von Bulow in 1966.

Claus Borberg was born in Denmark in 1926, son of a Danish playwright and theater critic who was later accused of being a Nazi sympathizer. Due to the Nazi association, Claus opted to go by his mother's maiden name of Bulow instead of his father's. Notably, Claus added the "von" to his name himself, which typically denotes royalty, after he moved to the United States.

Claus attended Cambridge, graduating with a degree in law and going on to work in banking and then as an administrative assistant to J. Paul Getty, founder of Getty Oil Company and American's richest man. It was through his association with Getty that Claus met Sunny at a social event in 1965. They were married in 1966 and had a daughter together, Cosima. The couple settled in New York, purchasing a palatial 5th avenue apartment before buying Clarendon Court, the spectacular Newport mansion where the dramatic events of December 1980 would unfold.

Things started to get suspicious when, the day after Christmas in 1979, Sunny was found unconscious in her bedroom at Clarendon Court. Doctors determined the coma was the result of low blood sugar and diagnosed Sunny with hypoglycemia. They advised her to avoid sweets and the couple returned home to the Newport estate. Sunny had another incident in April, where she was again hospitalized for what was reported as reactive hypoglycemia. The following winter, Sunny was discovered unconscious on the bathroom floor of her and Claus's bedroom at Clarendon Court. Sunny was rushed to the hospital, where she was determined to have suffered a brain injury as a result of a drug overdose. She remained in a coma, while her two children from her first marriage began to suspect that something had gone awry. With the help of their grandmother, the teens hired a private investigator to find evidence that Claus had caused their mother's health crisis. After months of evidence gathering, prosecutors presented the case to a grand jury who returned an indictment. In July 1981, Claus von Bulow was charged with two counts of attempted murder, accused of using insulin injections to try to murder his wife.

After the first conviction, Claus hired Harvard law professor Alan

Dershowitz to represent him on appeal. The appeal focused on a small black bag that had been allegedly found in Claus von Bulow's closet and contained vials, yellow paste, and a needle with insulin crusted to its tip. It was these items that the private investigation had focused on and presented as evidence that Claus possessed the murder weapons. Fueled by controversial testimony by Sunny von Bulow's maid, as well as the estate's gardener and a host of other characters, the jury in Newport had found Claus guilty. Dershowitz assembled a team to overturn the conviction.

The appeal was held in the Rhode Island Supreme Court in Providence, mere blocks from the Biltmore. When the appeal was announced, all the area hotels began to vie for a cut of the business. Not only did hotels compete to house the jurors, but they aimed to target room rentals to the news outlets that were flocking to Providence from all across the country, as well. "We've contacted all the networks," said Bruce A. Marks, manager of the Biltmore Plaza. "We're not just talking about NBC, CBS, ABC…There's the Cable News Network, Independent News Network…We're looking at AP, UPI, Time, Life, Newsweek. We have a list of about 45 potential outlets. We haven't captured all of the market, but it's our feeling at this point that we're talking about somewhere around 40 to 50 rooms a night, which is substantial business… Being concerned about democracy, my first concern as a citizen is that there be a fair trial. Now my business sense—if more business is coming into town, I want my fair share of it."

Marks could not have been more overjoyed, then, when he found out that he'd be getting the most important guest of them all: Claus himself, and his mistress Andrea Reynolds. The pair arrived in Andrea's station wagon, brimming with case notes and files, as well as suitcases and boxes. Patiently seated on the backseat was the third member of their party: Claus's golden retriever, Tiger Lily. The bizarre trio would spend nine weeks living at the Biltmore while Claus awaited fate.

Claus von Bulow and Tiger Lily, photographed after living at the Biltmore during his appeal. Photo obtained on WikiCommons.

The press followed Andrea almost as much as they followed the legal proceedings of the appeal. When Andrea went to Radioshack to buy a cassette player, *The Providence Journal* reported on it. When she had her hair set in the Biltmore's salon, the *Journal* noted it the next day. When she sent back her steak in L'Apogee, the waiters whispered the news into phone receivers.

In her self-published memoir, Andrea speaks highly of her time at the Biltmore during the trial. She even compliments L'Apogee's menu, mentioning specifically the superb lobster dinners that she enjoyed with Claus while they went over the details from court that day. Andrea accuses an anonymous villain of breaking into her suite at the hotel and stealing clothes and other items from her room (notably, a Pointer Sisters tape), but then goes on to say she never reported it to police because she did not want to upset Claus during his trial. Somehow, perhaps not too mysteriously, however, *The*

Providence Journal picked up that tip as well. Despite both she and Claus having substantial wealth, the paper made a spectacle of the fact that the pair traveled to and from New York in Andrea's aging station wagon.

Claus's appeal was followed by millions of Americans. It was *the* celebrity court drama to watch. Opinions over the case divided the social fabric of Newport. When Claus won the appeal and was found innocent, flowers arrived by the truckful from supporters across the globe. In Claus and Andrea's 14th-floor suite, champagne was popped and reporters kept at bay. But in the lobby, representatives from CBS Morning News, NCB's Today Show, and ABC's Good Morning America all clamored to lock down interviews. Claus vowed not to go on any of the major networks until after his scheduled interview with Barbara Walters.

After nearly two months at the hotel, Claus von Bulow was a free man. He and Andrea packed up their suitcases and departed through the back entrance of the hotel, where the station wagon was waiting on Eddy Street. Claus eventually moved to London, where he wrote occasional reviews of art shows and operas and went into general obscurity. Andrea went on to marry her fourth husband and live in upstate New York. Sunny von Bulow spent 28 years in a persistent vegetative state before her death in 2008 at the Mary Manning Walsh Nursing Home in New York City. Her two eldest children still believe that Claus is responsible for their mother's death.

34

OMNI HOTELS

Around the corner from the Biltmore Hotel is a small granite building in the Greek Revival style that could easily be overlooked by the average pedestrian. As America's oldest extant shopping mall, the Providence Arcade Building originally housed 78 tiny storefronts, as well as providing a pedestrian route between Weybosset and Westminster Streets, two of Providence's most important downtown thoroughfares. The Arcade has repeatedly gone the way of historic city properties—losing occupants and being threatened with extinction. However, City Hall's commitment to preserving its historical buildings in the 1970s saved the Arcade from assured demolition. In 1976, it was added to the National Register of Historic Places and in 1980 it was renovated and reopened for public use.

Shortly after the Arcade reopened, a small bookshop called Cornerstone Books leased a storefront in the sun-drenched corridor. The store, owned and operated by Robb Dimmick and Ray Rickman, specialized in rare African American books and was marketing itself by hosting a lecture series of African American authors around the city. It was thanks to Cornerstone's lecture series that the Biltmore Hotel welcomed one of its most esteemed guests in 1984, acclaimed poet, storyteller, activist, and autobiographer, Maya Angelou.

Before a public reading at Hope High School's auditorium, Angelou invited Cornerstone's owners to tea with her in her suite at the hotel. Sitting on the brand-new upholstered chairs adorning the modernized suite, Angelou commanded the room, "her handsome brown face all-knowing with beatific smile, searching eyes, and regal bearing, making a throne of her chair," as Dickman wrote in a piece commemorating the evening. Her talk that night was sold out, with over 750 people attending in the overcrowded auditorium. After the event, she returned to Cornerstone to sign book copies. At the end of the evening, Angelou packed up her things and strolled out onto Westminster Street, turning right down Dorrance to the Biltmore. She greeted the front desk staff warmly before retiring for the night.

Unlike Angelou, Providence was struggling to find its identity. Like many post-industrial cities, the small capital held a massive void left by the mills and manufacturers when Reagan's deregulation moved jobs overseas. Small businesses, in particular, felt the strain. In Providence, the consortium owners of the Biltmore knew that in order to keep the hotel afloat, they needed more than standard hotel rooms—they needed incentives.

Reorganized into the Providence Hotel Associate, consortium members Bruce Sundlun, James Winoker, Domenic Zinni, and *The Providence Journal* bought out the partners from Textron and Outlet. With new, consolidated ownership, the hotel approached the city council to assist with a new fundraising scheme to help bolster the hotel's bottom line. With the city's help, Providence Hotel Associates was able to secure funding through an Urban Development Action grant, under the Department of Housing and Urban Development. Without Buddy in office to sugarcoat the deal for the public, the Associate's connection to the federal funds became a hotly contested issue in that year's mayoral race. One candidate, Keven McKenna, told the *Journal* that he believed that the private group seeking a Federal loan "had a bad odor about it." "It seems like this is the same old gang back at work again, trying to protect downtown investors in a questionable enterprise," he said. George Goulart, who said he was speaking for the Taxpayers Alliance of Providence, denounced the grant as "welfare for the rich."

In addition to the HUD grant, the new consortium of owners sought $9.5 million in a low-interest loan from the RI Industrial Facilities Corp., an affiliate of the Rhode Island Port Authority, to assist them in refurbishing 329 rooms to make the hotel more profitable. Ultimately, HUD granted the group $1.4 million for the renovations. The application stated that the loan was to be used to "convert 80 of the hotel's 329 rooms to 40 larger, more luxurious rooms, buy new furniture, refinish the lobby and corridors, and change the décor of L'Apogee, the rooftop restaurant." The City of Providence was to receive the loan on behalf of the owners, who agreed to repay the loan plus interest over 15 years. While not everyone on the City Council agreed with the plan, by 1985 the funding was secured.

The Biltmore's refurbished lobby became the one of the city's most visited sites for Christmas photos and celebrations during this time. The annual Giving Tree, established when the hotel reopened in 1979 in partnership with the Providence-based toy company Hasbro, brought Christmas cheer to the city each December. In 1984, the hotel received 30,039 handmade ornaments from various organizations throughout the state to adorn the massive 18-foot tree. Donors included local nursery, elementary, and high school students, along with Cub Scout, Boy Scout, Girl Scout, and senior citizen groups. The tree itself was donated by Hank and Judy's Homestead. The purpose of the Giving Tree, beyond becoming a beautiful backdrop for family photos, was to raise funds to distribute Christmas gifts to children in foster care in the state. Hasbro donated one toy for every ornament made, gifting tens of thousands of presents to children and families in need each year.

The glass elevator that had been the crown jewel of the renovations in 1979 continuously caused problems for hotel management.

The Omni Biltmore's Christmas card from the late 1980s, featuring the Giving Tree.
Courtesy of the Graduate Providence.

In one distressing incident, a couple got stuck in the elevator for over an hour when it jammed, and then had to be rescued by an elaborate set of ladders which provided passage for them to safety. One woman was trapped in the elevator for three hours, hanging precariously in the shaft on the outside edge of the hotel, until she was rescued by firefighters. To reach the trapped passenger, members of the Special Hazards Unit of the fire department had to use the emergency access door on the seventh floor and lower an aluminum ladder down the shaft about 20 feet to the top of the elevator. A second ladder was lowered into the elevator from the small door at the top of the elevator. The fire department guided the shaking and sobbing woman up the ladder until she reached the seventh-floor entrance.

After subsequent jams over the years, the glass elevator was eventually shut down permanently. It now remains simply as a reminder of more glamorous, and harrowing, times at the hotel. In recent days a sign has been added that states "For Time Travel Only." It is unclear if that is a time that anyone would want to go back to.

Shortly after taking over management of the Biltmore Plaza, the Dunfey Hotels group was purchased and was reorganized into Omni Hotels. As part of the reorganization, the hotel was renamed once again, this time as the Omni Biltmore Hotel. "Although its ownership will not change, the Biltmore Plaza will get a new name and a new image when it joins the Omni hotel group. The 64-year-old hotel will be called the Omni Biltmore, and will join the likes of the Atlanti Omni and the Omni Park Central in Manhattan," said Jacques V. Hopkins, lawyer for the owners.

In 1986, Omni embarked on a $7.5 million renovation of the Biltmore under General Manager Reinhard J. Heermann's direction. The early stage of the renovation took six months, at which time the hotel was closed for extensive construction in the lobby. When the doors reopened to the public, a familiar sight was there to greet guests and patrons: a newly rebuilt grand staircase. Heermann proudly unveiled the changes, stating in one interview, "When I think of the number of wedding parties and senior proms that must have taken place on the old staircase, I wonder why they took it down, or at least why they didn't replace it once they were done installing the elevator. I have a feeling that people are really going to enjoy having it back."

Heermann specifically went for a 1930s renovation design, working with a Warwick based company to oversee the changes. Among the work was a total makeover of the 287 guest rooms—each room was painted, received new carpets, wallpaper, fixtures, furnishings, and drapes—and a redesign of 40 new two-room suites. In addition, Heermann directed that the gaudy fountain that had been installed during the 1979 renovation be removed from the lobby. He also had the lobby walls repainted to reverse the darkness of the early construction. Heermann noted in the paper that the previous rehab of the hotel had created "a really gloomy atmosphere," and that now "everything that was dark is now light, like a photographic negative." Perhaps the most notable change was the removal of Goddards restaurants on the first floor and L'Apogee from the top of the hotel. In just six years, the storied restaurant had played host to countless scenes of drama and intrigue, and just as quickly as it had gained its reputation, it was closed for good. The restaurant was disassembled and converted into a multi-function rental room, leveraging the beautiful views of the city for higher-price private events.

To replace Goddard's, Heermaan and his design team opened a new and improved restaurant concept. Conceived to be five spaces in one, Stanford's American Bar and Grille was designed with the elegance of the big band era in mind, but with a modern twist. Included in the space was an expansive bar, a main dining room, a courtyard, a bistro, a refurbished Falstaff Room, and two private dining rooms. The idea was that someone could go to Stanford's for lunch and then return for dinner, feeling as though they were in an entirely different restaurant. The restaurant was met with glowing reviews in the press, with the *Journal* highlighting its diverse menu and noting that Heermann's German background, coupled with Food and Beverage Manager Jerome Gerrese's Belgium upbringing, lent themselves to exciting European menu options.

The return of the Falstaff Room was a celebrated change, as well. The historic watering hole with its dark-paneled oak bar and Shakespearean wall coverings was reopened under Omni management, welcoming patrons back to experience the bar's "Old World charm." When the hotel was photographed for the Historic American Buildings Survey in 1986, several photos were taken to document the unique and historic Falstaff decor. The photos can now be seen in the archives at the Library of Congress.

Despite efforts to restore the hotel to earlier glory, the Biltmore continued to contend with the modern-day challenges facing downtown Providence. Crime in the city was rampant and trends from the street seeped into the hotel. In February 1987, a $100,000 bottle of champagne which was on display in a glass case in the Biltmore lobby as part of a 13-city tour of the rare bottle, was stolen right out from under the security guard's nose. Designed in Paris by a world-renowned jeweler, the bottle was bedecked in gold and diamonds and contained a 1976 vintage of Champagne *Rare*, produced by French champagne vintner, Piper-Heidsieck. The theft was no easy feat. The glass-paneled case that held the bottle was attached to a pedestal by thick wire, which had to be cut with wire cutters to be removed. The police reported that the case had to weigh at least 100 pounds, making the theft even more perplexing given that security was reportedly on duty at all times. The Providence police did not have much to say about the theft, except that they found the situation "very strange."

Very strange was an apt way to describe much of what happened at the Biltmore in the early Omni days. Aside from the run-of-the-mill arrests and instances of petty crimes, downtown Providence was having a bit of a problem with prostitution. In one such incident, hotel management called the police when a fully naked woman burst from the elevator and ran straight through the hotel lobby, leaping into a cab outside. The woman, it turned out, was a sex worker who had just gotten into a dispute over the last line of cocaine with her patron. The dispute had turned violent, and the prostitute fled without her clothes. In a more harrowing scenario, a fugitive was arrested at the hotel after fleeing the scene of his crime in Newport, where he had broken into a house on Bellevue Avenue, held eight people captive, raped a woman, and made off with more than $1 million in cash and jewelry before taking a taxi to the Biltmore and checking in.

This was not the kind of press that the Omni wanted for its hotel, and the events staff were charged with doing everything they could to boost the good name of the Biltmore brand. Determined to impress, the Biltmore catering staff went above and beyond to impress guests at a dinner for Astronaut Sherwood "Woody" Spring, upon his return to his native Rhode Island. The NASA celebrity was toasted at a formal dinner at the Biltmore where Governor Edward DiPrete and Admiral Gary C. Schuler of the Rhode Island Commodores entertained a black-tie crowd. Lauded for being the state's first man in space, Woody had even taken the Rhode Island flag with him for his voyage into orbit. Knowing that the hotel's reputation had taken a few serious blows of late, the executive chef prepared a veritable feast for the astronaut's party. The menu included salmon mousseline, champagne sorbet, beef tenderloin, endive and watercress salad, strawberries, and petit fours.

The hotel's marketing team also saw an opportunity for more positive reviews in the paper when the smash Broadway hit, *Cats*, came to Providence's Performing Arts Center. Transforming the ballroom into a glamorous junkyard, complete with old tires, graffiti, auto parts, trash cans, and props from the show, the event staff even added an element of satire when they poked fun at PPAC's Board through whimsical messages spray-painted in stage graffiti. The 800-guest extravaganza was a showstopper, with ice sculptures, exotic foliage, and sumptuous buffets adorning the Garden Room and ballrooms for sponsors and guests of the show.

Cheap thrills were not below the hotel management during the Omni era. When SeaWorld was amping up efforts to increase visitorship, the Biltmore jumped in feet first. Welcoming the hotel's *tiniest* guests to date, the general manager himself greeted Pete and Penny when they arrived with the media in hot pursuit. The duo, adorned in their natural tuxedos, quickly became the talk of the town when hotel management greeted them at the door, even attempting a handshake. The two Magellanic penguins were on tour as goodwill ambassadors for SeaWorld and had arrived in a limo from Hartford, descending to a red carpet laid out by Biltmore staff. Bob James, the managing director, and Sam Schorr, the resident manager, knelt in front of the wobbly little ambassadors to pose for the press before the feathered guests were hoisted atop the check in counter and told of all the hotel amenities by the front desk clerk. They were then guided at a slow waddle to the elevators that led to their suite. Perhaps Duane Wallick, with his proclivity toward the exotic, would have nodded approval at these winged guests and their celebrity treatment. The zookeepers at the Roger Williams Park Zoo, however, did not. Voicing their disapproval to the *Journal*, they made a point to differentiate between "novelty" animals that were desensitized to human interaction and animals that were kept for conservation purposes at the Zoo. Either way, the hotel staff and other visitors had a ball with their new Arctic friends. "I've cooked a lot of birds," said chef Alymer Given, who prepared a platter of iced Atlantic herring on silver trays for the guests, "But I've never cooked *for* a bird." If the Biltmore was good at anything, it was good at being flexible.

Needless to say, the Biltmore was not the pillar of elegance that had been when it opened its doors in 1922, but, despite its myriad transformations, the hotel still maintained a solid footing in the hearts and minds of many Providence natives. When Michael Fournier moved to Providence in the 90s, he was surprised to learn how important the hotel was to one longtime resident, in particular. Michael was new to the city and in an effort to get to know some of the locals, he had begun to have lunch at the Down City Diner on Weybosset Street each day. The diner was close to his work, and he appreciated the local vibe at the casual eatery. The head waitress during lunch hour was Merry, and she and Michael became fast friends. One day, Merry introduced Michael to a charming older woman sitting alone in one of the diner's booths. Dorothy, 87 at the time, impressed Michael with her vintage charm—including the care she took to always have her red lipstick on, her rotating cadre of fashionable hats, and the great pride she took in her appearance despite it being obvious that she did not have much money to her name. Michael soon found out that Dorothy was widowed, left alone and unsupported after the death of her husband who had squandered the couple's savings before death. Merry made sure that Dorothy had a free lunch each day, and Dorothy had become a loyal patron of the Down City Diner.

Nothing about Dorothy's situation had dampened her spirit. She regularly regaled Michael with tales of the glorious parties, dances, and celebrations that she and her husband had attended at the Biltmore in its glory days. Dorothy deeply loved the hotel and regarded it as the pinnacle of class and extravagance in the city. One day over lunch, she told Michael that her only dying wish was to have her ashes thrown from the top of the grand hotel.

When Dorothy died a few years later, Michael made up his mind to ensure Dorothy got her wish. Rallying Merry to help him, Michael set about figuring a way to get Dorothy to the top of the Biltmore. Despite his commitment, there were a few challenges to seeing the plan through. For one, there was no longer roof access for guests at the hotel. Secondly, Michael and Merry were not guests, and could not gain access to the upper floors.

Merry's connections through the diner proved valuable. After a few phone calls, Merry, was able to convince a hotel employee to grant them access to a room on the 15th floor. It wasn't the roof, but it would do. Michael and Merry rode the elevator in silence and quietly slipped into the unoccupied room. Inside, a much bigger problem presented itself. During renovations, all windows on the highest floors had been sealed. There was no way to open the window and release Dorothy out into the ether. Michael and Merry, standing in the carefully made-up room, stared blankly at the small box in Michael's hands.

A few moments later, having conceded defeat, the pair rode the elevator back to the lobby. It was hard not to feel that they had let their friend down. As they left the hotel, they decided that if

Dorothy could not have her wish to be thrown to the wind from the roof of the Biltmore, then she'd have to settle for resting in its shadow. Keeping an eye out for any inquisitive onlookers, Michael and Merry discreetly sprinkled Dorothy's ashes in Burnside Park, in an area where they felt she could still see and feel the presence of the great hotel that she had loved so dearly.

35

HOLLYWOOD AT THE BILTMORE

The Biltmore Hotel has no shortage of red carpet. Under several of its owners, the entire lobby was adorned with it. Perhaps the rotating cast of celebrities that have chosen the hotel for their Rhode Island stays made the carpet choice an easy one. No need to roll anything out—just invite them inside. From its earliest days, stars of vaudeville, silent movies, the live stage, and even circus productions have come to the Biltmore to wine, dine, and unwind after performances. Movie stars were also not new to the Biltmore, though Providence's reputation as a city down on its luck had deterred visits from some stars in the 1970s and 80s, most of which found they had no reason to come to Providence on their way from Boston to New York.

As was his approach to many things in the city, Mayor Cianci wanted to change that. After laying low in the years following his Grand Jury indictment, Cianci had recently been reelected to serve as Mayor of the city in 1991. Reinstated, Cianci continued to push the "renaissance" of the city that had begun under his first administration. Part of his vision was bringing Hollywood to Providence. By offering incentives to production companies, Cianci embarked on a campaign to bring on-location filming to the city. Unlike similar efforts made in other turnaround cities, Providence failed to attract much attention from the silver screen. However, the projects that did come to the Ocean State made some big headlines.

The 1990s were a time of lewd comedy, renewed interest in horror, and record-setting sensational dramas. Hollywood was churning out seemingly endless numbers of explosive and expensive blockbusters, to the tune of *Titanic, Jurassic Park, Independence Day, Scream, Forrest Gump, Toy Story,* and *Men in Black.* Some of the most beloved comedies of the millennial era came out at that time: *Tommy Boy, Mrs. Doubtfire, Dumb and Dumber, True Lies, Sister Act, Ace Ventura, The Big Lebowski,* and the list goes on. When Tommy Chong, of Cheech and Chong, stayed at the Biltmore in 1990 during promotion of his film *Far Out Man,* he followed in the footsteps of many celebrities before him—keeping a low profile, ordering room service, and allowing a few in-suite interviews. The interview he gave to the *Journal* from his room focused on his recent split from longtime comedy partner, Cheech Marin. He told the *Journal* he felt like he was "starting over." Arguably the inventors of "stoner comedy," the Cheech and Chong films paved the way for many of the comedies that followed in the 90s.

If Cheech and Chong had set the stage for "anything goes," then the 1990s followed up with total reckless comedic abandon. It was a decade of unpredictable and shocking content, and perhaps no film shocked the general public quite as much as the Rhode Island-based romantic comedy, *There's Something About Mary.* Roger Ebert's review of the film called it "an unalloyed exercise in bad taste." The film's directors, Rhode Island natives Peter and Bobby Farrelly, had already proven their comedic genius with their hit film *Dumb and Dumber* and the follow up, *Kingpin. There's Something About Mary* became an instant hit with its highly intentional shock value, climbing the charts in record time. Portions of the film had been shot in Providence, thanks to Mayor Cianci's incentive structures and the Farrelly brothers' love for their home state. When the brothers had initially set their sights on the city, Mayor Cianci had assured them that he'd take care of anything they needed to ensure success of the shoot. He made good on his promise. Over the four-day shoot, Cianci had 25,000 fliers handed out to commuters letting them know that temporary bus stops would be added to make up for closures along routes that would then be within the parameters of the film location. He also personally stopped by the film set each day just to make sure everything was going well, or at least to get a quick photo with the film's stars.

Always true to their roots, the Farrelly brothers hosted their east coast premiere of *There's Something About Mary* in Woonsocket, Rhode Island, at a theater they had frequented in their youth. Most of the cast and crew attended, including Ben Stiller, his sister, and his parents. An extravagant premiere party followed in the Biltmore's ballroom. Nine hundred guests packed the 17th floor of the hotel, including Stiller and his co-star, Matt Dillon. Much to the delight of the press, an exhausted Dillon showed up early and signed autographs in the hotel lobby. The premiere made headlines, but it was not the Farrelly brothers' first time at the Biltmore. Before going on location with *There's Something About Mary,* the brothers had holed up for several days in a suite on the 14th floor with writer and director Michael Corrente to polish the script for *Outside Providence,* a movie based on a book by Peter Farrelly. That film, starring Alec Baldwin and Shawn Hatosy, was shot at the Cranston Street Armory at the same time that the Farrellys were filming *There's Something About Mary.*

Their love of the Biltmore spanned their careers and the Farrelly brothers continued to bring Hollywood to the hotel. In 2003, during the east coast premiere of the brothers' newest film, *Stuck on You,* Cher stayed at the Biltmore before being escorted to the Woonsocket auditorium. She celebrated the film's success at an intimate post-premiere party at the hotel later that evening, alongside Johnny Knoxville, the Farrellys, and a host of friends and colleagues.

The Farrelly Brothers, photographed at the Tribeca Film Festival.
Photo obtained on WikiCommons.

Mayor Cianci continued to try to lure Hollywood to Providence through festivals and award shows. At one event, he presented a Lifetime Achievement Award to Anthony Quinn at the Providence Convergence Film and Video Festival, held, in part, at the Biltmore. At another film festival held at the hotel, Cianci introduced Antonio Banderas and Melanie Griffith to an adoring crowd of fans in the Garden Room, but offended Griffith (albeit, delighting the press) when he introduced her as "Melanie Griffin."

It wasn't just Hollywood that Cianci hoped to draw to his Renaissance City. The Mayor also had his eye on international sporting events, particularly since the Convention Center had been completed in 1993. When a decorated Italian karate team came to Providence for a competition, their travel agent made an unfortunate gaff. Instead of booking them at a proper hotel, the representative booked the entire team rooms at the little-known "Sportman's Inn."

Despite its name, the "Inn" was not a hotel as such. The popular Fountain Street strip club boasted 24-hour peep shows, live dancing girls, and a few rooms upstairs—though they were not often used for "lodging" per se. When the team's plight was reported to the Mayor's office, Cianci swooped in apologetically and relocated the Italians to the Biltmore, comping their rooms for the unfortunate and unsavory mistake.

Ultimately, even with Cianci's skillful pivots around publicity issues, the reality of downtown Providence—home to a dozen strip joints, seedy nightclubs, and violence-prone barrooms—was not something the Biltmore's marketing team could repackage to the general public and passersby. The hotel was losing money, and fast. Downtown was overrun with the wrong kind of business. In the time that had passed since its reopening in 1979, the hotel's grand facade had started to fray. *The Providence Journal*, the majority owner and last remaining member of the consortium that had saved the hotel in the 70s, decided it was finally time to let go of the weathered landmark. In May 1995, it was announced that the Biltmore Hotel would be sold to Grand Heritage Hotels for the meager price tag of just $7 million.

36

THE MAYOR CHECKS IN

Grand Heritage was building a strong reputation as a lifeline for unique hotels in need of a savior. According to their website, "Grand Heritage was founded in 1989 by John W. Cullen to focus on historic properties that suffered from lack of branding and boutique management expertise." In its portfolio, Grand Heritage boasted ownership of the Stanley Hotel in Estes Park, Colorado, best known as the setting for Stephen King's horror novel *The Shining*.

The sale to Grand Heritage, though only returning half of what *The Providence Journal* had hoped for, was greeted with praise from city officials who feared that the failing hotel would be sold for university dormitories or private housing. Grand Heritage promised to reinvigorate the hotel despite the challenges of Providence's economy, and that pleased Mayor Cianci. After signing the purchasing agreement, Grand Heritage announced that it would be embarking on an expansive makeover of the hotel.

Like its predecessors, Grand Heritage quickly moved to revamp the restaurants within the Biltmore. They pressed forward with rapid renovations, which included closing Stanford's on the ground floor and leasing the restaurant space to a third party. The restaurant was marketed to restaurateurs in the region, and a lease agreement was signed between Grand Heritage and Steve DiFillippo, entrepreneur and founder of the Davio's restaurant chain. It would be the first time that the restaurant was completely separated from the hotel's management.

DiFillippo was inspired by the historic charm of the hotel and was excited to dedicate a portion of the restaurant to a reopened special function space in the historic Falstaff Room. In typical Biltmore fashion, even Boston-based DiFillippo had a personal connection to the hotel; his grandfather, bored in retirement, had taken a part-time job as a custodian there in the 1950s to fill his time.

Davio's, with its diverse food menu, cocktail list, and regular cabaret shows, quickly gained popularity with city officials, the Federal Hill contingent, and, of course, the mayor. Buddy was not picky when it came to the Biltmore. He'd take a seat at the bar whether it was called Doorley's, Goddards, Falstaff, Stanford's, or Davio's. He was as comfortable in a suit and tie in the ballroom as he was with his shirt unbuttoned, sipping a martini and smoking cigarettes in a corner booth downstairs. No matter who the owner was, Buddy Cianci was as much a part of the Biltmore Hotel as its glass elevator and neon sign. To Buddy, the Biltmore felt like home.

There was no shortage of Biltmore memories for Buddy Cianci. Volatile behavior and disturbing incidents aside, some of Buddy's special moments at the hotel were almost endearing. In 1995, shortly after Grand Heritage bought the hotel, the Mayor unveiled his "Mayor's Own Marinara Sauce '' during a birthday bash that he threw himself in the ballroom. Though touted as a family recipe (the acronym spells MOMS, after all), the ingredients included some not-so-traditional additions. "I heard it was his girlfriend's recipe," Steve Lautieri, one of the Biltmore's chefs, mused. "What Italian do you know puts carrots in a marinara sauce?" Buddy claimed the carrots were there to cut down on, in his words, "the agita."

Carrots or not, the sauce became a novelty in Providence and

Buddy Cianci holding a jar of his "Mayor's Own Marinara."
Photo obtained on WikiCommons.

beyond. Providence now could boast having a mayor who had run as both a Republican and a Democrat, had been indicted for kidnapping and torture, *and* had his own marinara sauce. Despite the chaos surrounding Buddy Cianci, he remained beloved by many in Providence. His ratings kept going up. He kept winning elections. Quite literally, the city of Providence kept buying his sauce, and Buddy made sure everyone got a taste—of the marinara, that is. He handed it out as a door prize at his fundraisers and served it during his Christmas dinners. Whether or not it was an authentic Italian gravy is arguable, but what was certain was that Buddy was proud of his marinara. When the producers of the hit TV series, *The Sopranos*, wanted to use "Mayor's Own Marinara" for a promotional event, Cianci turned them down, stating that the series unfairly stereotyped Italian Americans. Fortunately, despite his omnipresence at the hotel, Buddy didn't require the kitchens to use his sauce except at his own private functions. Buddy had been lording over the Biltmore since he'd led the charge to rescue the hotel in 1975. Now, over 20 years later, he would become a true fixture. In September 2000, Buddy Cianci moved in to the Biltmore Hotel.

Before arriving with his suitcases, the mayor had presided at 33 Power Street, a swanky brick carriage house on Providence's historic East Side. The carriage house had been built as a horse stable in 1902 by Marsden Perry, the founder of Union Trust Co., forerunner to Fleet National Bank. Cianci had purchased the home in 1985, after renting it from his friend and business colleague, Bruce Sundlun, the very man whom Cianci had turned to when he wanted to save the Biltmore from ruin. The carriage house had been made infamous on the legendary night in 1983 when Cianci lured Raymond DeLeo to the house, assaulted him, and tried to extort $500,000 from the unwitting victim. Over a decade had passed since that fateful night on Power Street, but Buddy had once again found himself in murky water. As rumors of a federal investigation started to spread across the city, the gossip columns mused that Buddy was probably selling Power Street to liquidate his assets before yet another criminal trial.

Always thinking about ways to politicize his personal life, Cianci proclaimed that he would only be living at the Biltmore temporarily while he made a plan for his next residence. He told the press he planned to live in each neighborhood of Providence for one year at a time. "There are neighborhoods in the City of Providence that, quite frankly, a mayor should live in," Cianci told *The Providence Journal*. "Maybe I could live in South Providence one year, Manton the next. Imagine if I moved into South Providence or into one of these neighborhoods," he mused. "Imagine what the effect would be." His plans to neighborhood-hop never panned out, and Buddy remained a resident of the hotel for nearly two years.

As a resident of the Biltmore, Buddy Cianci made is presence known like no other person had before. He crashed ballroom weddings (often to the delight of the bride and groom). He hung out in the lobby, shaking out-of-towners' hands. He threw parties for himself, and his friends, in the restaurants. He imbibed without shame in Davio's, sometimes getting so intoxicated that he would throw $10 and $20 bills at the cabaret dancers and shout, "Show us what you got!" When union troubles plagued the hotel and workers went on strike, the mayor stepped in as a mediator. The *Journal's* op-ed section wondered if Buddy's interest in solving union disputes had anything to do with preserving his own comfort at the hotel.

Under Grand Heritage's ownership, the Biltmore had become a more business-friendly establishment. With a nod to the technology boom of the times, the new one-bedroom suites got two-line speaker phones and self-adjusting alarm clocks that received signals through a satellite. In early 2000, the owners added a concierge suite on the third floor for VIP guests and a private terrace to the Presidential Suite.

As the tensions grew surrounding criminal investigations, Buddy made use of the upgrades and started operating more and more from the hotel, despite having City Hall just across the street. He fielded campaign calls and press inquiries. He met journalists on his private terrace or in Davio's for interviews, and he watched the news on the room's television set, where his daily appearances around the city often made headlines. The kitchen staff reported that Buddy was a decent tenant, always treating the chefs, waiters, and room service staff with respect. While he was described as "wild," in the same breath they said that Buddy was "a great guy." Buddy also proved to be a good neighbor. He became close with the other residents of the hotel, including the owner's mother, Judy Cullen, who lived on the 15th floor.

Grand Heritage was responsible for investing tens of thousands of dollars to refurbish the vintage neon in the Biltmore's rooftop sign, an iconic image of the hotel that could be seen across the city and beyond. Harkening back to its days as a Sheraton hotel, the sign

Glimpses of the Biltmore sign. Author's private collection.

had not been lit since the hotel closed in 1974. Then, on August 17, 2000, from the roof of the hotel, one could hear the clinking of champagne glasses as chief engineer Steward Richardson flipped the switch, illuminating the iconic sign and casting a red glow down toward Washington Street. $60,000 of refurbished neon hummed into life over the city. Buddy gave a speech and poured Moet into outstretched glasses.

Joseph Sykes, who had operated the Biltmore service elevator for 22 years, had never seen the sign lit during his entire tenure at the hotel. He told a reporter at the *Journal* that he anticipated that it was going to make more work for him, working for a hotel that lit up the whole city. Not only did the sign command attention, but it not-so-coincidentally lit up the rooms at the competing Courtyard Marriott, as well. Stewart Richardson, chief engineer of the hotel at the time, laughed, "We have special spotlights that shine right into their rooms." He was only partially joking.

Outside of the hotel, however, the people of Providence were beginning to see the cracks in Buddy's veneer. During an interview with M. Charles Bakst of *The Providence Journal* in Davio's, Buddy sat munching on a hamburger and defended himself against the recent allegations of corruption and racketeering that plagued him. The FBI had recently raided his office in what was being dubbed "Operation Plunder Dome" and Buddy seemed almost despondent in his reflection of his current position and his time in office. "At my age, at 60, it's not the place that you want to be," Buddy told the reporter in between bites of his lunch. "But when your liberty's challenged, you know…" He trailed off, staring at his hamburger. "I had planned a retirement, planned to be comfortable and all that, but life goes on. You keep saying to yourself, 'Well, I tried my best; the city certainly has changed.'"

Operation Plunder Dome was taking the wind out of Buddy's sails. His 25-year reign at the helm of Providence seemed ready to collapse. The FBI's investigation had revealed the city's involvement in questionable lease arrangements between city officials and Edward Voccola, a commercial property owner and convicted felon. In the spotlight was Buddy Cianci's right-hand man, Frank Corrente, who was being investigated for bribery and extortion. The FBI wanted to know if the mayor had played a part in the foul play. They found the evidence they wanted in testimony from Antonio Freitas, who reported to the FBI that city officials, including Corrente, had accepted an inflated bid from Edward Voccola to rent a school space, turning down an honest and legitimate bid offered by Freitas. Freitas agreed to wear a hidden camera and be wired for conversations he had with city officials, recording over 180 meetings for the FBI that implicated Corrente, Joseph A. Pannone (chairman of the Providence Board of Tax Assessment Review), and other corrupt city officials.

In April 1999, the FBI stormed City Hall and arrested Pannone and his vice chairman, David Ead. They seized dozens of crates of documents from five of the city's offices. Investigators wanted to know how high up the corruption went. They suspected it went all the way to the top. From the Biltmore's Presidential Suite, Buddy watched as witness after witness testified on live TV about the corruption surrounding and within the Mayor's office. In April 2001, after a year-long public trial of multiple city officials, a 97-page, 30-count indictment was unsealed, charging the mayor and five of his closest administrators with racketeering, conspiracy, mail fraud, witness tampering, and extortion of more than $1.5 million.

Providence Mayor Vincent Cianci walks across Kennedy Plaza on the first day of his trial for jury selection during the Plunder Dome investigation. Courtesy of the Kathy Borchers Photojournalism Collection of the Special Collections and University Archives, University of Massachusetts Amherst Libraries.

During the trial, Buddy continued to attend to city matters. His calendar never eased up, with fundraisers, funerals, parties, and political rallies filling his time, but the legal battle was weighing on him. Every day he was asked about the ongoing investigation. Every day he declared his innocence. Mike Stanton, then writing for *The Providence Journal*, described the case as it unfolded in the city: "Lurking beneath the graceful new river-walk bridges and the Venetian gondolas and the brick-and-glass is, the government alleges, a darker reality. Following jury selection, which begins Wednesday in the gray United States courthouse facing City Hall, federal prosecutors will seek to weave a tale of corruption and bribery, revenge and betrayal, as they attempt to prove that Cianci sold out the city he professes to love…Witnesses are likely to testify to allegations of crooked deals and cash payoffs, threats and intimidation, and a racketeering enterprise that Cianci allegedly ran from his trophy-laden corner office at City Hall. The Renaissance City portrayed in the government's 97-page indictment is not the Renaissance of Michelangelo and da Vinci, but of Medici and Machiavelli."

Buddy Cianci, who had run for mayor in 1974 as the "anti-corruption candidate," was watching the noose tighten around his free-wheeling public office. Sitting on the edge of his bed at the hotel, the Mayor shouted into the phone at his public relations staff. Spin this, spin that. But nothing was going his way. He chain-smoked. He drank. He brooded until late in the night at Davio's bar. And then, each morning, he put on his suit and headed out to be with the people of Providence, many of whom stood by his side. "Every day I walk to the trial, I leave the *Journal* building," wrote reporter Charles Bakst, "There's the gleaming Convention Center; they're building the handsome sky bridge to the great new mall near the relocated rivers. I stroll past the gorgeous outdoor skating rink, a jewel amid the skyscrapers. Then I go to the trial and listen to garbage and wonder what more we'll learn here, or later. Is Cianci a brilliant leader moving Providence forward? Or is he scum?"

The whole country wanted to know the answer. One of the nation's most popular talk show hosts, radio legend Don Imus, even came to Providence to hold a live broadcast about the trial from the Biltmore. Eight hundred guests packed the ballroom to hear Imus grill the mayor on the details of the case. The interview included jabs at the Mayor, asking him if "opening the mail" was part of his job description, a reference to the allegations of money laundering that was a key part of the trial. Millions of listeners tuned in to the irreverent interview, where Imus stated bluntly: "Obviously he's guilty. The question is, can they prove it?" Buddy shot back that he had pleaded not guilty, and he still expected to be exonerated.

On June 27, 2002, Providence politics, which did not often make national news, hit the front page of *The New York Times's* New England edition: "Providence Mayor Is Guilty of Corruption." No amount of political spin could rescue Buddy this time. After an extensive investigation and trial, the now infamous mayor was convicted of racketeering conspiracy in Rhode Island's Superior Court. The first line of the *Times* article said it all: "The colorful career of Mayor Vincent A. Cianci Jr. turned a shade darker today when a federal jury found him guilty of racketeering conspiracy charges stemming from the government's contention that his corner office in City Hall was the base for a heavy-handed but effective crime operation." Buddy read the paper in the Presidential Suite and considered his options. It was an election year, and he had had every intention of running again. Providence was *his* city, after all. But there was no telling what his sentence would be, or whether or not he'd win an appeal. He sipped his coffee. He called his political strategists and his lawyer. His team across Washington Street waited. And then, picking up the phone on the bedside table, he made the call.

The next day, standing in a crowded anteroom at City Hall, eyes red from lack of sleep, Buddy Cianci addressed a sea of reporters and staffers in front of him. "I will never forget your love and loyalty,"

Cianci said. "But as the legal proceedings continue for an indefinite period into the future, I must make a decision regarding my political future today. I will not seek reelection as mayor." Gasps filled the room. Walter Miller, one of Cianci's most loyal supporters, burst into tears and had to be led from the room by his coworkers. According to a report of the event by the Journal, after Buddy's announcement, the phones in his office rang off the hook with supporters calling to voice their love of the longtime mayor. The fax machine overflowed with messages: "I'm heartbroken," "We will always love you," and, "Sad day for Providence."

Before Buddy's sentencing date, Grand Heritage's owner, John Cullen, and his mother threw their beleaguered tenant a party at the hotel. Two hundred of Cianci's closest friends and supporters were in attendance, entertained by a brass band covering Cianci's favorite crooner-hits. When Cianci took the stage late in the evening, he only spoke of fond memories and the city he deeply loved. "This is a magnificent hotel," Buddy boomed, smiling at his friends. "The people here are like family." He talked about how, as a single man living at the hotel, he never felt lonely. Particularly during the holiday season, he added, the Christmas decorations filled him with joy. "You have people here who are extremely kind, and the owners are wonderful," he added. "I'm proud to live here." The ballroom filled with applause. Some even dabbed their eyes. Everyone knew what no one wanted to say: the Comeback Mayor was, for the first time in his 25-year career, probably not coming back. A few weeks later, Vincent A. Cianci was sentenced to serve five years in federal prison. He was forced to resign from the mayorship immediately following the sentencing, marking the end of an era for the city of Providence.

If the Biltmore Hotel is haunted, undoubtedly it is by the ghost of Buddy Cianci. No one person in the history of the hotel spent more time haunting the hotel during his lifetime, let alone after death. Buddy was obsessed with the hotel. It was as much a part of his life as the clothes he wore or the cigarettes he smoked. He schemed and planned, and drank and ate, and wined and dined, and schmoozed and schemed within the walls of the Biltmore. He never turned his back on the hotel, and more than once stuck his neck out for it. On the day that Buddy left for prison, he took the elevator down from the Presidential Suite to the front desk and placed his key on the counter. He told the hotel manager "I'll be back soon." When he died in 2016, his open casket wake was held just across the street in City Hall. Once the casket closed, it's possible Buddy did what he had done so many times in life: slipped quietly out the side door of City Hall and crossed Washington Street, heading straight to the bar at his favorite hotel.

37

THE 21ˢᵀ CENTURY

A t the turn of the 21ˢᵗ century, Providence was leaning into the future with renewed optimism. The economy had made strides. Downtown was glittering with a new sports arena, convention center complex, a restored waterway—the result of uncovering and dredging the rivers that ran through downtown— and a new train station. Trains were once again running regular service to the city from New London, New Haven, New York, and Boston. Diverse and exciting nightlife was reinvigorating the downtown neighborhoods and highly reviewed restaurants were flourishing. Most importantly, people were returning to the city from the suburbs and a demand for housing was on the rise. The efforts of Providence's committed business community, coupled with the vision and dedication from City Hall, had paid off. The Biltmore, too, was reaping the benefits.

As part of a $6 million renovation in 2003, the hotel welcomed three new high-end tenants: McCormick and Schmick's seafood restaurant, Paul Mitchell day spa, and Garrison Confections, a gourmet chocolatier. Grand Heritage installed the new businesses in the hotel with the goal of attracting more affluent clientele, aiming to turn the hotel into a destination-style resort. McCormick and

The Biltmore in the 21st Century.
Photographed by Damian Marc, damianmarcphotography.com.

Schmick's in particular was a highly anticipated upgrade to Davio's, which closed the year before. The spa, which was renovated to the tune of $1.2 million, included two stories of full-service massage rooms, water fountains, and salons. The largest Starbucks in New England, equipped with its famous "free WiFi for all," graced the glass-front ground floor of the hotel and had an entrance linking it directly to the spa. The chocolatier, opening its first storefront as part of the Biltmore upgrade, had moved its production facility from New York to Providence in order to meet the needs of the Biltmore.

To make the upgrades, Cullen refinanced, taking on a loan of more than $30 million from GMAC insurance.

America was at a political crossroads and the Biltmore provided a stage for the show. In 2008, Michelle Obama spoke at a luncheon in the ballroom entitled "Women for Obama" in support of her husband Barack's run for presidency. Her speech delineated how proud she was to be an American in that moment, and how excited she was to be in a country that could dream of electing a Black president. She was joined by her brother, Craig Robinson, the then basketball coach at Brown University. After Obama's historic presidential win, Vice President Joe Biden visited the Biltmore on several occasions in support of Rhode Island Senator Sheldon Whitehouse's political campaigns. Rhode Island, too, was riding the winds of change. In 2014, when the state elected its first female governor in the most expensive gubernatorial race in the state's history, Gina Raimondo took the stage in the Biltmore ballroom to celebrate her win. "I'm going to lead the comeback of this great state," Raimondo declared over the cheering of hundreds of supporters. She had no idea what lay ahead.

With Providence on the upswing, Cullen and his investors expected to see the Biltmore's returns skyrocketing. However, with downtown prosperity came more competition. Over the first decade of the 21st century, four new hotels sprouted up around the city, as well as several boutique inns. The Biltmore was no longer the only show in town when it came to luxury accommodations, and interest in hotels of the Biltmore's size and grandeur was on the decline. Visitors tended toward either new, modern hotels or small, bespoke accommodations and quirky B&Bs. The Biltmore did not fit in either category. The biggest blow, perhaps, came with the Great Recession of 2007. As America's economy went into a tailspin, the tourism industry took a nosedive. Between local competition and national economic woes, the hotel's owners fumbled the finances. In 2009 and 2010, owners John Cullen and Arnold "Buff" Chase missed a number of loan payments on the mortgage. The missed payments prompted lender US Bank to push the property into receivership, a form of bankruptcy in which a trustee seeks to raise funds to pay off debts of a business.

What started as a grand resuscitation of the landmark hotel ended in a breathless sputter. In 2011, the hotel was taken over by the state, only to be sold out of receivership to Finard Coventry Hotel Management for $16 million. For a brief moment, it seemed the hotel might be on stable ground. When the sale was announced, Todd Finard, principal of the group, told the Journal that they were "delighted to become stewards of the iconic hotel." The honeymoon did not last long. Finard quickly realized they were in over their heads and brought in the Hilton chain to assist them. In December 2014, the Biltmore entered what was supposed to be a 15-year partnership with Hilton Worldwide as the fourth hotel in their Curio Collection, a brand of independent hotels known for their historic significance. The Hilton arrangement retained Finard Coventry Hotel group but provided guests with Hilton amenities such as use of their online booking system and the option to receive Hilton reward points. In the arrangement, Finard paid Hilton fees for the affiliation but retained the Biltmore brand. The Finard and Hilton partnership was fleeting. Just three years later, the hotel would once again be sold.

38

THE BILTMORE GRADUATES

To the people of Rhode Island, the Biltmore is the Biltmore. It doesn't matter who owns it, or what additional surname is added to the title. The names Providence Biltmore, Sheraton Biltmore, the Biltmore Hotel and Motor Inn, Biltmore Plaza, and the Omni Biltmore all served a singular unifying purpose: to maintain the iconic brand of the historic hotel. For 97 years, it was always just that, the Biltmore. Until it wasn't.

In April 2019, something radical happened. For the first time in its history, the hotel was stripped of its Biltmore name and formally renamed the "Graduate Providence." Two years prior, the Biltmore hotel had changed hands yet again, this time being purchased by the Chicago-based hotel and real estate firm, Adventurous Journeys (AJ) Capital Partners. The hotel went for an impressive price of $43.6 million.

AJ Capital Partners' self-stated mission, to "humanize hospitality through handcrafted projects made by people for people," promised to deliver to Providence a reenergized hotel that "evokes emotional connections and becomes a backdrop for enriching life experiences." All considered, AJ Capital Partners' mission seems to align with the initial intent of the Chamber of Commerce when they imagined

AJ Capital Partners officially renamed the Biltmore the Providence Graduate.
Courtesy of the Graduate Providence.

a grand hotel for Providence all those years ago. The new owners also appreciate the historic significance of the hotel. However, even though they announced early on that they would keep the neon "Biltmore" sign on the roof as a nod to the historic roots, the hotel would no longer carry the Biltmore name. Needless to say, Providence had something to say about it.

In 1922, Rhode Islanders had written to *The Providence Journal* to scrutinize the foreign sounding "Biltmore" that was rumored to be attached to the spectacular new construction on Butts Block. They demanded to know why a more "Rhode Island" sounding title couldn't be found for the building. Ninety-five years later, another editorial graced the opinion section of the *Journal*. Only this time, it was in defense of protecting the Biltmore legacy. Penned by Dick Brush, former GM to the hotel, the strongly worded letter heeded warning to the new owners: "The Biltmore has long held a central place in the political, economic, social, and cultural life of Providence and Rhode Island," Dick wrote. "Many of us have been to political rallies, business meetings, proms, and dinner parties there. Many of us said or heard the words 'I'll meet you in the lobby of the Biltmore'... I hope the new owners will operate with an understanding of the hotel's significance as it nears its centennial year. Although the hotel has an out-of-state owner, in a sense, it belongs to all Rhode Islanders."

AJ Capital Partners quickly moved to allay some of the city's fears. They announced planned renovations, which included a new rooftop restaurant for the 18th floor—where L'Apogee had been. They also shared plans to restore and reopen the glass elevator that had been defunct for nearly 25 years. The hotel renovated and redecorated its lobby, meeting spaces, and rooms, adding Rhode Island–inspired wallpaper, artwork, and furnishings. Even the Comeback Mayor got a nod—each of the rooms were adorned with paintings and pictures of Buddy Cianci. This latter change did not last long. Soon, complaints came in about the former mayor's likeness adorning the walls. "No one who is proud of Providence or working hard for our future finds it 'quirky' to be reminded of the corruption, crime, fear, and dishonesty that gripped our community for decades under Cianci's administration," wrote Kath Connolly, a prominent public engagement consultant in the city, in a letter to the hotel's management. "Cianci was a brilliant, colorful, and witty man. He was also a rapist, a felon, a megalomaniac, and a bully. His legacy is not clever, cute, or one we seek to champion to visitors." The controversial mayor's likeness was removed from the rooms after just three months on display and the portraits were donated to the Cianci Educational Foundation.

After substantial changes to the interiors, AJ Capital Partners reopened the Biltmore officially as the Graduate Providence with much fanfare. The public couldn't deny it: they had done a beautiful job on the hotel. Scott Williams, the hotel's newly appointed General Manager, told the *Journal* that the company had gone to great lengths to ensure that the decor and design of the Graduate had ties to the community, and was a reflection of the city it inhabited. The purpose, he said, was to ensure that guests did not just have a pleasant stay, but that they had an exceptional experience.

Perhaps most importantly, the Graduate retained the existing staff. Legacy employment, of which the hotel was proud, did not falter. When management did an informal tally of the number of cumulative years that the existing staff had worked at the hotel, the number topped 1200 years of service to the Biltmore between them. Many people who had worked at the hotel since it was a Sheraton continued to serve the hotel, and the spirit of the Biltmore felt more energized than it had in a long time. Reservations for events, weddings and parties poured in. The hotel was poised to have a banner year.

Then, in March 2020, the entire world seemed to stop spinning. Everything at the hotel came to a screeching halt.

39

FINDING MR. POTATO HEAD:
LIFE DURING THE COVID-19 PANDEMIC

M ichael Babb first arrived in Rhode Island with his parents in
the spring of 2010. He was looking at colleges—something
far away from his New Jersey home—but nothing yet had
struck a chord. Even as a teenager, Michael loved architecture and
history, and as the family car turned up the cobblestone curve of
Weybosset Street, he had his "aha" moment. He knew this was a city
he wanted to be in. As his father maneuvered the car down Dorrance Street, Michael saw it for the first time: the Biltmore's neon
sign. Something inside him changed. Forever.

As they parked and walked to the Biltmore, where his parents had
booked an overnight before his campus tour of Johnson & Wales
University, Michael gawked at the blazing red Biltmore sign, noting
that you could see it from almost any angle in the city. Rounding
the corner and crossing the threshold of the front entrance, Michael,
not unlike hundreds of thousands of Biltmore guests before him,
stopped in his tracks. "The grand staircase, the glass elevator, the
glimmering chandeliers," Michael said in an interview. "It was prac-
tically an out-of-body experience." From that moment on, he was

hooked. John McEntee Bowman was no doubt smiling down on Michael that day; another person was being drawn in by the grandeur of the finest hotel in Rhode Island history. It was the exact reaction that Bowman had so meticulously curated on opening day in June 1922. And the wow factor remained.

Fast forward 10 years. Michael Babb was a college graduate, but more important to Michael was the fact that he had recently received his first "Manager of the Year" award for his exceptional work over eight and a half years as an employee of the Biltmore Hotel. The hotel had just reopened as the Graduate, and Michael says that he and the staff were "riding high," anticipating a record-breaking year in events and banquets for the 2020 season.

Then, whispers of a highly contagious disease outbreak started to be heard. First in global news reports, then, on local cable. What started off feeling like a distant problem in a faraway land was suddenly knocking at the door in Providence. Michael sat in his office on a cold day that March as the phones rang off the hook. Cancellation after cancellation. Weddings, graduation dinners, corporate events. Everyone wanted to push out their events or cancel them outright. News of the rising death toll, coupled with a complete ignorance about how and why the virus was spreading, terrorized the nation. Conflicting messages from the government added to the chaos. Individual businesses struggled with the lack of consistent information about what to do next.

Graduate Hotels' Regional Director of HR came down to Providence from the Boston office. The staff were assembled in the grand ballroom, instructed to take an appropriate distance from one another for safety, and asked to wait while hotel leadership met in the executive office. "The toughest day I have ever had in my career was the day I had to sit with every single department head and every hourly staff member and tell them that we were closing, and we didn't know when we would be reopening," Scott Williams shared during a 2022 interview. That day, the entire staff of the Graduate

Providence was furloughed indefinitely. The entrances were quickly locked from the inside, and the lights turned off in the public spaces. In the car on the way home, Michael sobbed. Life without the Biltmore was just unimaginable.

When the days turned to weeks and weeks turned to months, Michael and many others at the hotel began to wonder if they'd ever get their jobs back. The city was a ghost town. Adding to the intensity of the situation, protests broke out nationwide in the wake of the killing of George Floyd at the hands of a ruthless cop. Storefronts in downtown Providence were boarded up as tensions rose. The front door of the Biltmore was quickly covered with plywood. It was too much for many of the hotel's longest-standing employees. Some could not even bear to pass the building in their cars.

Boarded up and shuttered as it was, a few interesting things were taking place inside. Scott Williams and two members of his team, his assistant general manager and the head of engineering, maintained the hotel during the closure. The three employees kept the building functioning with rotating shifts—24 hours on, 48 hours off. On shift, Scott roamed the hotel, going from room to room to turn lights on and off and run water through the pipes. Each shift included a three-floor maintenance check of every room, with each room getting attention once per week. In addition to the standard checklist, the team of three assigned themselves other projects to keep busy. In one instance, Scott found an extension ladder and set about repainting the gold leafing along the trim of the 17th-floor ballroom. The paint job took almost a year to complete, but Scott figured he had the time.

With no one else in the building, the hotel began to feel incredibly desolate, and pretty creepy. Scott and the others set up mini apartments in their offices, equipped with beds, linens, workout gear, and recreational items. On slower days, Scott took his longboard up to the ballroom, put on some music, and skateboarded around the varnished dancefloor. Other than the fact that he did not see any ghosts, Scott says the whole experience was a lot like the movie *The Shining*.

Other than maintenance checks and exercise, to keep themselves entertained during the earlier months of the pandemic, Scott and his two colleagues devised a game they called "Find Mr. Potato Head." The game was pretty simple: someone hid a Mr. Potato Head doll somewhere in the hotel. Over the course of the next week, someone else would inevitably find it. Checking the pipes in an upper floor bathroom, Scott opened a shower curtain one day and found Mr. Potato Head sitting in a bathtub. Another time, he popped up from behind a stack of plates in the cafeteria. If you were so lucky as to find Mr. Potato Head, your job was to hide him again, somewhere different. The game went on for months.

Interestingly, this was not the first time that Mr. Potato Head ventured into the Biltmore Hotel. Created in 1952, Mr. Potato Head was the first toy ever advertised on television and was one of the early toys that made the Hasbro toy company a success. Headquartered in Providence, Hasbro teamed up with the city at the very beginning of the 21st century to help reinvigorate Providence's tourism appeal. The campaign was entitled: "Rhode Island: the birthplace of fun." The idea was to establish the state as a family-friendly destination for travelers near and far. The gimmick: larger than life Mr. Potato Head statues installed throughout the state. Fifty massive statues were commissioned for the project, each attached to a 600-pound concrete base. The themed statues incorporated historical and cultural traits from the Ocean State: "The Independent Potato," bronzed and striking the pose of the famous Independent Man statue atop the State House, could be found at 30 Exchange Terrace; "Italian Potato Chef" was stationed in front of Angelo's Restaurant on Atwells Avenue; "Edgar Allen Poe-tato" was installed at the Rhode Island Convention Center; and "Fred the Friendly Fisherman" clad in a slicker and bearing a bucket of quahogs and a lobster trap, sat at the South County Tourism Office in South Kingstown. Of course,

Mr. Potato Head hiding out in the ballroom during the COVID-19 pandemic.
Photo courtesy of Scott Williams.

the Biltmore couldn't be left out. The hotel sponsored one of the statues and had it installed in their picture window on the ground floor. The statue was labeled "The Light from Within," a perfect foreshadowing to the role that Mr. Potato Head would take on 20 years later as the clever peek-a-boo pandemic companion for Scott Williams and his team.

Without any clear idea of if or when the hotel would reopen, Michael Babb began to look elsewhere for work. He even went on a few interviews. "In the end, though," the 28-year-old recounted with a sigh, "I just didn't want to work anywhere else." The resounding theme of the Biltmore's history is that once you are in the Biltmore's orbit, you never want to leave. Over nearly a decade of working at the hotel, Michael shrugs when he is asked about famous guests or celebrities that he's met. Those are not the highlights of his career. When asked what has kept him coming back to the Biltmore, Michael says candidly, "The staff. Working with these people, this level of excellence, it's a privilege. Coming to work here was like getting adopted into a family. We have Christmas parties at each other's houses, we go out together after work. This is family first, work second. The things that you really need to know to be exceptional in this business, they don't teach you in school. I learned it here, from these people." Though after a moment's reflection he added, "But one time Jack Black was filming a movie here. That was pretty cool."

At Graduate headquarters in Chicago, the hotel's owners were not sitting idly by while the pandemic locked them down. In partnership with a personal friend, Paul Blair—more popularly known as the Grammy-award winning producer DJ White Shadow—AJ Capital Partners' owners came up with an idea to incubate a new kind of talent in their hotels. This idea grew quickly into an action plan, and by the time the hotel was ready to reopen, the Sweet Dreams Society had been born.

According to the Graduate's website, the Sweet Dreams Society is "helping emerging artists turn their dreams into reality." Led by White Shadow and his friends at AJ Capital Partners, the Graduate Sweet Dreams Society is "an immersive artist-in-residence program and creative community, hosted at hotels across the country." Under the mentorship of White Shadow, artists are selected to set up studios and workspaces in Graduate hotels for a designated period of time. They are invited to use the hotel's studio space to create one or more capstone projects that can then be showcased by the hotel. Kicking off the program in Providence, the Graduate welcomed the hotel's first official artist-in-residence to inhabit the first-floor gallery. The studio and program do not generate revenue for the hotel, but aims to give local artists a leg up as they build their portfolio and network in the community.

After the hotel reopened in 2021, it selected its first official artist-in-residence, a photographer, musician, and sculptor named David Lee Black. Conjuring creative energy in the confines of the Biltmore's lobby-level gallery, Black drew upon the seemingly galactic energy that fills every crevice and curve of the hotel's architecture. At a gallery opening, just weeks before the centennial anniversary of the hotel, Black transformed the hotel's historic Garden Room into the backdrop for a grand spectacle—a paradoxical masterpiece of old and new. Lining the towering walls were Black's photographs and sculptures, a carefully curated mixture of haunting and whimsy. The stoic easels, though the obvious centerpieces of the show, were nearly lost in the background to the pounding soundtrack of the Providence Drum Troupe, followed by stomping circus performers and cheering acrobats, all of which exploded into the room mid-evening. A woman on four-foot stilts shimmied by the bar, while a flailing, oversized Martian-like creature stumbled around, seemingly mesmerized by the saxophone player. Black's friends and guests were just as much a part of the exhibit as his photographs, and they did not disappoint. Rather than make a mockery of the historical significance of the Garden Room, the circus that

Artist-in-residence, David Lee Black, in his Biltmore studio. 2021.
Photo courtesy of David Lee Black.

unfolded seemed to leap from the walls themselves, an unleashing of the hotel's secrets that yearned to be set free. If the Biltmore's walls could talk, they would speak the language of David Lee Black and his band of merrymakers.

Black's Sweet Dreams Society event was perfectly Biltmore in every way. It was scandalous, it was salacious, it was loud. But at the same time, it was merriment and joy in its most simple iteration. Much like the exquisite architectural genius of the hotel, the spectacle of Black's event could easily be dismissed as frivolous when, in fact, it is so much more. Each detail lovingly crafted, each viewpoint carefully considered, Black's art and the art of his community provided a perfect overlay to the opulence of the grand hotel. Black will forever be remembered in the Biltmore's history as its first official artist-in-residence, and he has left very big shoes to fill for the next creator who comes along.

When the Graduate Providence first reopened, it opened with just 30 staff members, compared to the 160 it had before the crisis began. With the availability of vaccines, optimism that the pandemic would be ending started to rise. Hotels all over the state started to see a return of wedding bookings. Scott Williams told the *Journal* he had "no idea" when the hotel would return to being as fully staffed as they had before the closure, but he was optimistic. "They're coming back, they're coming back in droves," he said, excitedly. "People want to travel again, they're excited to stay at the Graduate, to see what we've done with the place. And it's not just business travelers or people from out of state—no. Now we are seeing a resurgence of locals coming to Providence to catch a show or have a nice dinner. They're coming from South County, from Cumberland, all over. People just want to get out and stay somewhere nice."

As the world begins to bounce back from the COVID-19 crisis, what happens to the hotel is as much in the hands of its new owners as it is in the city's. In interviews in 2021, on the eve of the hotel's centennial, the legacy of the Biltmore came through crystal clear:

excellence. Excellence in everything, from the person who greets you at the door to the fixtures in the guestrooms. Excellence was what was promised by the Chamber of Commerce to the city of Providence in 1922. The tremendous service that the von Trapps raved about and Jackie O counted on still wows Michael Babb today. Of course, the hotel has had its rough patches. A review of guest experiences over the years will produce a range of testimonies, from absolute disgust to total elation. Change is inevitable. These days, when the legendary flambé dessert course comes out at the end of a Biltmore ballroom wedding, just as it has for over 80 years, it comes out to the musical accompaniment of Pit Bull's *Fireball* instead of a 15-piece orchestra. But, according to Babb, it still takes the crowd's breath away. Just like it has for decades.

The resounding story of the Biltmore over 100 years has been the story of its people: the 1,800 people who invested in the hotel at its beginning, the hundreds of thousands of guests who have woven their life stories into the fabric of the hotel, and, most importantly, the many thousands who have worked in its restaurants, guest rooms, offices, and kitchens. The Biltmore is Providence's hotel; it belongs to its people. The fate of the hotel will forever be up to its stewards, the people of Providence, to maintain the grand old structure and its important history. For now, it seems assured that it will remain a beautiful destination in the heart of the Renaissance City for a long time into the future.

When Scott Williams reflected on the challenges of the past two years, he paused for a moment and said, "I think people are realizing now, more than ever, what we almost lost. What we had taken for granted. They're realizing that we need to support the arts, we need to shop locally, we need to support the businesses in our community that we love. Because if we don't, they'll go away. And we will be left with none of the things that make this city such a wonderful place."

Here's to never taking the Providence Biltmore, or our city's history, for granted. Here's to another 100 years.

NOTES AND SOURCES

1 DREAMING OF A FIRST-CLASS PUBLIC HOUSE

McLoughlin, W. G., *Rhode Island: A History.* W. W. Norton & Company, 1986.

W.A. Craick, "The Greatest Hotel Man In The World," *Maclean's,* February 1, 1917.

"Hit By Hot Iron From The Sky." *The New York Times.* July 21, 1921.

"Committee of 100 Hears Addresses." *The Providence Journal.* October 22, 1915.

"E.F. Albee May Help Erect New Hotel Here." *Providence Daily Journal.* June 11, 1919.

"Hotel Site Option Procured In City." *The Providence Daily Journal.* October 18, 1919.

"New Hotel Will Be Open in a Year." *The Providence Daily Journal.* October 29, 1919.

"First Class Hotel Here Now Certain." *The Providence Daily Journal.* October 22, 1919.

"Hotel Question Still Undecided." *The Providence Journal.* November 1, 1919.

"Negotiations for Hotel Completed." *The Providence Journal.* November 6, 1919.

"Hotel Corporation Plans Progressing." *The Providence Journal.* November 7, 1919.

"Purchase of Hotel Site is Arranged." *The Providence Journal.* November 15, 1919.

"New Hotel's Cost About $3,500,000." *The Providence Journal.* December 4, 1919.

"Letters on current topics from Sunday Journal readers." *The Providence Journal.* November 9, 1919.

"I remember…" *The Providence Journal.* January 18, 1948.

2 BE A BOOSTER!

"Two Days More for Hotel Drive." *The Providence Journal.* April 7, 1920.

"Don't Let The Biltmore Fail." Advertisement. *The Providence Journal.* April 4, 1920.

"Why the Providence Biltmore May Not Be Built." Advertisement. *The Providence Journal.* April 4, 1920.

"Biltmore Drive Lacks Impetus." *The Providence Journal.* April 20, 1920.

"Providence Biltmore Hotel Building At Which At Cost of $5,000,000 Is Now Assured." *The Providence Journal.* February 14, 1920.

"Promoters of Providence Biltmore Hotel May Sign Agreement Today." *The Providence Journal.* February 12, 1920.

"Work on Big Hotel Here Opens April 1." *The Providence Journal.* January 22, 1920.

"Goodbye Providence, See You In The Morning." Advertisement. *The Providence Journal.* March 12, 1920.

"To-Day." Advertisement. *The Providence Journal.* March 16, 1920.

"A Sound Investment, A Civic Need." Advertisement. *The Providence Journal.* March 10, 1920.

"Share in the Pride. Share in the Profit." Advertisement. *The Providence Journal.* March 17, 1920.

"Team 4 Will Finish Shingling The Roof of The Providence Biltmore This Forenoon." Advertisement. *The Providence Journal.* March 20, 1920.

"New Hotel Stock Drive Opens Soon." *The Providence Journal.* March 12, 1920.

"This Is The Time To Invest." Advertisement. *The Providence Journal.* March 17, 1920.

"Thomas Carville First New Hotel Stockholder." *The Providence Journal.* March 17, 1920.

"Why Call It The Biltmore." Advertisement. *The Providence Journal.* March 11, 1920.

"New York Subscriptions Assure Biltmore Hotel for Providence." *The Providence Journal.* May 7, 1920.

"The Zero Hour Club." Advertisement. *The Providence Journal.* May 2, 1920.

"Providence Biltmore a Chamber of Commerce Achievement," Providence Magazine, Vol. 34, No. 6, June 1922.

3 PALACES OF THE PEOPLE

Sandoval-Strausz, A. *Hotel: An American History.* Yale University Press. 2008.

The Hotel World, The Hotel and Travelers Journal. Volume 92. 1921.

The Hotel World, The Hotel and Travelers Journal. Volume 95. 1922.

Satow, J. *The Plaza*, p.12

"Biltmore Opening Guests Are Invited." *The Providence Journal.* June 4, 1922

"Biltmore Hotel To Have Formal Opening Tonight." *The Providence Journal.* June 6, 1922.

"Opening of the Providence Biltmore Marks New Epoch In City's History." *The Providence Journal.* June 7, 1922.

4 OPENING DAY

"Big Party From New York Coming For Biltmore Opening." *The Providence Journal*. June 2, 1922.

"Biltmore Hotel To Have Formal Opening Tonight." *The Providence Journal*. June 6, 1922.

"Here's A Useful Souvenir." Advertisement. *The Providence Journal*. June 7, 1922.

"Providence Biltmore." Advertisement. *The Providence Journal*. June 6, 1922.

"Our New Hotel." Advertisement. *The Providence Journal*. June 18, 1922.

"High Class Photographic Studio To Open In The Hotel Biltmore." *The Providence Journal*. June 4, 1922.

"When You Inspect The New Biltmore Hotel." Advertisement. *The Providence Journal*. June 7, 1922.

5 THE RISE AND FALL OF DUTEE FLINT

Comstock, F. "Dutee Wilcox Flint—The Meteoric Rise and Disastrous Fall of a Ford Dealer and Confidant of Henry Ford." *Hemmings Magazine*. January 1, 2014.

"Opening of the Providence Biltmore Marks New Epoch In City's History." *The Providence Journal*. June 7, 1922.

"Regatta Committee Plans Double Header." *The Providence Journal*. March 30, 1925.

"Dutee Flint Dies." *The New York Times*. April 2, 1961.

"Dutee Wilcox Flint." Rhode Island Radio. *61 Thrift Power*. www.61thriftpower. com

6 "THE HOTEL IS OURS."

"Biltmore Hotel Formally Opened." *The Providence Journal*. June 7, 1922.

"Open To-Day. A Proud Day for Providence." Advertisement. *The Providence Journal*. June 6, 1922.

"State's Most Prominent Citizens Gathered in Main Dining Room at Formal Opening of Biltmore." *The Providence Journal*. June 7, 1922.

"You Have Been Too Good To Us." Advertisement. *The Providence Journal*. June 6, 1922.

The Hotel World, The Hotel and Travelers Journal. Volume 95. 1922.

7 MYSTERY OF BETTY BEESWAX

Jeffers, H. Paul. *Gentleman Gerald*. St. Martin's Press. 1993.

"Mystery Woman in Chapman Case." *The Providence Journal*. March 26, 1926.

"Police Declare Pals' Negligence Betrayed Chapman." *The Providence Journal.* February 9, 1925.

"Gerald Chapman, Criminal Celebrity, Might Have Been Artist or Poet." *The Providence Journal.* March 25, 1925.

"Missing Witness Sought by Groehl." *The Providence Journal.* March 23, 1926.

"Murderers Gun Identified As One Owned By Chapman." *The Providence Journal.* April 2, 1925.

"Poem By Chapman Given to Public. *The Providence Journal.* March 5, 1926.

"Romantic Glamour Torn from Chapman." *The Providence Journal.* March 28, 1925.

"Two Killed One Shot in $93,000 Hold Up." *The Providence Journal.* October 30, 1925.

8 BOOTLEGGERS AT THE BILTMORE

Krajicek, D. "Rhode Island Rumrunner." *NY Daily News.* March 25, 2008

Okrent, Daniel. *Last Call: The Rise and Fall of Prohibition.* New York: Scribner, 2010.

"State's Most Prominent Citizens Gathered in Main Dining Room at Formal Opening of Biltmore." *The Providence Journal.* June 7, 1922.

"Says 20 Million Defy Liquor Laws." *The Providence Journal.* June 7, 1927.

"Izzy Einstein Found Providence Wide Open." *The New York Times,* September 11, 1922.

"Rumrunners Buy Back Liquor Boats." *The Providence Journal.* January 3, 1924

"Biltmore takes you back to the way it used to be." *The Providence Journal.* October 1, 1982.

"Patriarca, Cosa Nostra Boss Looks Like Movie Bad Man." *The Boston Globe.* June 21, 1967.

"Gem Hold Up Suspect Seized At Racetrack." *The New York Times.* August 14, 1938.

"Inquiry Demanded in Hurley Pardon." *The New York Times.* December 24, 1938.

"Patriarca: Showdown Near." *The Boston Globe,* June 21, 1967.

"Underworld Chief? 'Prove It,' He Says." *The Boston Globe.* February 26, 1967.

"Patriarca Prefers Privacy." *The Boston Globe.* March 9, 1968.

"Raymond Patriarca, 76, Dies. New England Crime Figure." *The New York Times.* July 12, 1984.

"Danielson and Putnam News." *Norwich Bulletin.* August 11, 1922.

"Bound Over For Attempt To Bribe State Police Officers." *Norwich Bulletin.* August 9, 1922.

"Police Hold Agent on Bribery Charges." *The Providence Journal.* August 10, 1922.

"Barnett C. Hart Held For Bribery." *The Providence Journal.* August 13, 1922.

"Claim Bank Notes Offered When Beer Trucks Are Seized." *The Hartford Courant.* August 8, 1922.

Cohen, S. "No Unescorted Ladies Will Be Served." JSTOR Daily. March 20, 2019.

9   THE LONG WALK HOME

Franck, P. *Prides Crossing: The Unbridled Life and Impatient Times of Eleonora Sears.* September 1, 2009.

"Eleonora Sears Wins 44 Mile Hike." *The New York Times.* December 15, 1925.

"Eleonora Sears Walking From Providence to Boston on a Bet." *The New-York Tribune.* December 14, 1925.

"Man Who Bet With Miss Sears Not On Hand." *The Boston Daily Globe.* December 14, 1925.

"Eleonora Sears Walks To Boston, Wins Her Wager." *The Providence Journal.* December 15, 1925.

"Eleonora Sears, Brahmin Bad Girl on the Tennis Courts (and Polo Field and Squash Court...)" *New England Historical Society. Website.* 2022.

10   THE SKY'S THE LIMIT

"Duane Wallick To Manage Biltmore Succeeds Daily." *The Providence Journal.* January 9, 1923.

"Stork Leaves Baby Monk at Zoo of Providence Biltmore Hotel." *The Providence Journal.* May 14, 1930.

"These Lucky Ones Live Life of Riley." *The Providence Journal.* July 4, 1930.

"Unknown Species of Fowl Found Strolling Downtown in Blizzard." *The Providence Journal.* January 20, 1936.

11   LINDY FEVER

"Biltmore To Open With Aviation Ball." *The Providence Journal.* May 18, 1922.

"Lindbergh Cheered by 300,000 Flying 'We' Into Providence: Women Faint..." *The New York Herald Tribune.* July 22, 1927.

"Providence Gives Lindbergh Ovation." *The New York Times.* July 22, 1927.

"Frenzied Thousands Accord Lindbergh Greatest Reception In History of State." *The Providence Journal.* July 22, 1927.

"Dunne Sees Moral in Lindbergh Visit." *The Providence Journal.* July 23, 1927.

"Lindbergh Greets Nearby Cities On Flight To Boston." July 23, *The Boston Globe.* 1927.

"Providence Awaits Flyer, Due There at 1 o'clock." *The Boston Daily Globe.* July 21, 1927.

"Second Aero Ball Brilliant Success." *The Providence Journal*, April 14, 1923.

12 TO LIVE, TO LOVE, AND TO LABOR

"History of the Biltmore." Courtesy of *Graduate Providence*. 2022.

"Baseball, Boxing and Racing." *The Providence Journal.* April 10, 1923.

Historical Note on Thomas F. MacMahon Papers. *Rhode Island Historical Society*.

Highlights of R.I. Labor History. Rhode Island Labor History Society. RI AFL CIO. 2022.

Interview with Dick Brush. February 3, 2021.

"Elizabeth Baxter Dies in 62nd Year." *The Providence Journal.* November 2, 1949.

"Suicide Was To Be Married On Monday." *The Boston Globe.* October 30, 1925.

"Molly Gray, Dancer, Weds W.J. Ryan, Hotel Manager." *The Providence Journal.* August 4, 1922.

"Hotel Aide Fined $1250." *The Providence Journal.* November 21, 1959.

"Ethel Barrymore Sues Colt For Divorce After Long Separation." *The Providence Journal.* June 26, 1923.

"Down the Spillway." *The Sun.* September 18, 1934.

"Providence Chef Greets Fiance." *The Providence Journal.* September 24, 1937.

"DeKay Brought Here for Trial." *The Providence Journal.* June 22, 1925.

"Former Governor Beekman On Stand All Day…" *The Providence Journal.* November 23, 1922.

"Polygamist Starts Two Year Sentence." *The Providence Journal.* February 10, 1938.

"Has $50 to Meet $149,978 Decree." *The Providence Journal.* September 23, 1926.

"Friends Honor Hotel Workers." *The Providence Journal.* July 16, 1930.

"Happy Ending for Troublous Courtship." *The Providence Journal.* September 30, 1937.

"Every point of excellence…" Advertisement. *The Providence Journal.* November 20, 1932.

Interview with Joan S. Hicks. April 5, 2021.

"Bed Time Tail Bouncer Wins First Victory Over Starlings." *The Providence Journal.* January 29, 1933.

13 THRICE SCORNED

Bicknell, W. *History of Rhode Island and the Providence Plantations. Volume 5.* American Historical Society. 1920.

"Wedding Saves Life." *The People's Banner*. Nov. 6, 1902

"Dr. Cupid Was No Quack." The Evening World, Night Edition. November 10, 1902

"Morphine Claimed Victim." *The Providence Sunday Journal*. March 4, 1906.

"What Became of $40,000?" *The Providence Journal*. May 8, 1942.

"Copy of Will Not Probated." *The New-York Daily Tribune*. February 8, 1903.

"Widowed Bride Lost Wealth." *The New York Times*. February 8, 1903.

"Socials." *The Providence Journal*. May 2, 1908.

"In Memoriam." *The Providence Journal*. January 15, 1921.

"Benno Wolf's Will." *The Providence Journal*. January 21, 1905.

"Death Bed Bride Gets Big Fortune." *The Providence Journal*. September 15, 1906.

"Mrs. Gibson Seeks Abatement of Tax." *The Providence Journal*. February 22, 1908.

"Mrs. Gibson Loses Suit." *The Providence Journal*. March 23. 1905.

"Socials." *The Providence Journal*. July 21, 1911.

"Socials." *The Providence Journal*. February 7, 1913.

"Visitors Throng Beaches at Pier." *The Providence Journal*. July 8, 1916.

"Old Wolfe Estate Here to be Boarded Up." *The Providence Journal*. April 12, 1934.

"Socials." *The Providence Journal*. July 4, 1919.

"Antiques Stolen From Home Here." *The Providence Journal*. June 5, 1930.

"Agree on Settlement." *The Providence Journal*. October 8, 1942.

"Henrietta Gibson Stricken Suddenly." *The Providence Journal*. September 13, 1942.

"Will Suit Trial Gets Underway." *The Providence Journal*. November 25, 1941.

14 FANNING THE FLAMES

Comstock, F. "Dutee Wilcox Flint—The Meteoric Rise and Disastrous Fall of a Ford Dealer and Confidant of Henry Ford." *Hemmings Magazine*. January 1, 2014

Farley, Richard. The Great American Racetrack War. *Town and Country*. June 2017

"O'Hara Arrested After Radio Address Accusing Governor of Shakedown." *The Providence Journal*. October 27, 1937.

"O'Hara Resigns…" *The Providence Journal*. February 10, 1938.

"Deputy Sheriffs Batter Way Into Track's Office in Hotel, Seize Records." *The Providence Journal*. February 9, 1938.

"Live Where Friendly Hospitality is the Watchword." Advertisement. *The Providence Journal*. June 10, 1938.

15 ANTIDOTES TO NATIONAL DEPRESSION

"Providence Biltmore Lunch Room." Advertisement. *The Providence Journal*. July 25, 1930.

"Come and Be Entertained!" Advertisement. *The Providence Journal*. March 9, 1930.

"Be A High Hat if You Want To." Advertisement. *The Providence Journal*. January 5, 1932.

"So long, Frank." *The Providence Journal*. May 20, 1998.

"Biltmore takes you back to the way it used to be." *The Providence Journal*. October 1, 1982.

"Eva LeGallienne Frowns Upon Boondoggling in the Theatre." *The Providence Journal*. November 16, 1935.

"Auto Delegates Feted at Dinner." *The Providence Journal*. June 19, 1930.

"Food Drive Total is Raised to $4192." *The Providence Journal*. January 11, 1933.

"Few Favor Cuts in Racing Days at Narragansett." *The Providence Journal*. October 11, 1935.

The A. & L. Tirocchi Dressmakers Project website, Rhode Island School of Design and Brown University. http://tirocchi.stg.brown.edu/514/index.html

Murray, J. "Textile Strike of 1934." *North Carolina History Project*. 2022.

"Union, Hotels Settle Strike." *The Boston Daily Globe*. May 3, 1937.

"Air Conditioning in Hotel Approved." *The Providence Journal*. June 13, 1936

"Babe was a hit with R.I. hurler and 4,000 fans…" *The Providence Journal*. August 7, 1998.

"Biltmore Reports Deficit of $82,000." *The Providence Journal*. January 21, 1932.

"Biltmore Hotel Loss is Larger." *The Providence Journal*. March 27, 1934.

"Prov. Biltmore Might Reorganize." *The Providence Journal*. April 14, 1935.

"Providence Biltmore Hotel Files Reorganization Plea." *The Providence Journal*. March 13, 1936.

"Biltmore Hotel to be Reorganized." *The Providence Journal*. March 12, 1936.

"Prov. Biltmore Will File Data." *The Providence Journal*. April 8, 1936.

"The JFK Assasination: Forty Years Later." *The Providence Journal*. November 22, 2003.

16 HELL OR HIGH WATER

"Hurricane Damage To New England Business Exceeds Expectations." *Women's Wear Daily*. Sep 23, 1938.

"In the Wake of Hurricane and Flood Across Devastated New England." *The Hartford Courant*. September 4, 1938.

"At Least 544 Killed." *Boston Daily Globe.* September 1, 1954.

"The Hurricane of '38; Anniversary of '38" *The Providence Journal.* September 20, 1998.

"RI Marks Hurricane's 70th Anniversary." *Associated Press.* September 21, 2008.

17 PREPARING FOR WAR

"German Plates Used at Banquet Arouse Anger of Jewish Diners." *The Providence Journal.* July 29, 1936.

"Blackout Plunges Half Million Into Darkness." *The Providence Journal.* April 9, 1942

"Maple Leaf Fund Chapter Planned." *The Providence Journal.* August 15, 1941.

"Rubber Salvage Drive Speeded." *The Providence Journal.* June 18, 1942.

"2 Opera Singers in Park Program." *The Providence Journal.* August 21, 1942.

"Gas Ration Officials Told By OPA to be Hard-Boiled." *The Providence Journal.* July 14, 1942.

"Biltmore Might Become Hospital." *The Providence Journal.* Oct. 16, 1942

"Worcester Academy." Advertisement. *The Providence Journal.* June 16, 1942.

"Rhode Islanders in Service." *The Providence Journal.* Oct. 31, 1943

"Officers Club to Expand." *The Providence Journal.* June 13, 1944

"Tale of Romance is Told By Baroness Von Trapp." *The Providence Journal.* Dec. 14, 1941

18 STATE SECRETS IN SUITE 1009

"FBI Arrests Antoine Gazda and Baroness." *New York Herald Tribune.* December 10, 1941.

"Alien Freed in Custody of War Office." *The Sun.* March 19, 1942.

"The Surprising Antoine Gazda." *The Providence Journal.* March 21, 1943.

"The Surprising Antoine Gazda." *The Providence Journal.* March 28, 1943.

"The Surprising Antoine Gazda." *The Providence Journal.* April 4, 1943.

"The Surprising Antoine Gazda." *The Providence Journal.* April 11, 1943.

"Personal and Social." *The Providence Journal.* March 25, 1944.

"Personal and Social." *The Providence Journal.* December 1, 1945.

"Antoine Gazda, Developer of Anti-Aircraft Gun, Dies." *The New York Times.* September 24, 1957.

19 A NAME IN LIGHTS

"Biltmore Hotel Earns Less in '44." *The Providence Journal.* April 27, 1945.

"Biltmore Profits for 1946 Increase." *The Providence Journal.* April 16, 1947.

"Biltmore Hotel Inc. Is Dissolved By Vote of Its Shareholders." *The Providence Journal.* June 23, 1948.

"Sheraton Group Takes Biltmore." *The Providence Journal.* February 1, 1947.

"Sheraton Corporation To Buy Controlling Interest In Crown and Biltmore Hotel Holdings." *The Providence Journal.* January 5, 1947.

"Sale of Biltmore Set for Next Week." *The Providence Journal.* January 24, 1947.

"Magnates Began With Souvenirs." *The Providence Journal.* January 5, 1947.

"Sheraton Group Buys Providence Biltmore." *The Boston Daily Globe.* January 5, 1947.

"Providence-Biltmore Sold in $3,000,000 Deal." *The New York Herald Tribune.* January 13, 1947.

"Providence Biltmore Bought By Sheraton." *The New York Times.* January 14, 1947.

"Sheraton Hotels Lead With Superb Television." Advertisement. *The Boston Daily Globe.* June 6, 1948.

"Sheraton Corporation History." *International Directory of Company Histories*, Vol. 3. St. James Press, 1991.

"514 Broadway." A. & L. Tirocchi Dressmakers Project. Rhode Island School of Design Museum. Website copyright 2001.

20 THE WOMAN AT THE WINDOW

"Mrs. C. Hovey Jr. Killed." *The New York Times.* Sept. 6, 1949.

"Mrs. Chandler Hovey Falls to Death From Window of Hotel." *The Boston Daily Globe.* September 6, 1949.

"Hub Woman Dies in Eleven Story Fall." *The Providence Journal.* September 6, 1949.

21 "MR. BILTMORE"

"Fred Stone Wins Fresh Laurels at Providence Biltmore." *The Boston Daily Globe.* July 2, 1940.

"Mrs. Dahl Tells How to Win Friends and Influence Franco." *The Providence Journal.* July 23, 1940.

"For the Love of Mike." *The Providence Journal.* November 12, 1944.

"Esther Merriman Makes Her Debut." *The Providence Journal.* November 27, 1930.

"The Most Important Musical Note of the Season." Advertisement. *The Providence Journal.* August 15, 1937.

"Business of Being a Comedian is Serious Matter to Ed Wynn." *The Providence Journal.* October 3, 1932.

"Cocktail Time at The Biltmore with Rita Bell." Advertisement. *The Providence Journal.* January 10, 1936.

"Hildegarde Takes Over Garden Room of Sheraton Biltmore." *The Providence Journal.* September 26, 1950.

"Stevenson's RI Itinerary for Oct. 6 Announced." *The Providence Journal.* September 25, 1956.

"New Rudy Vallee Is Coming This Week." *The Providence Journal.* January 21, 1951.

"It Is Really The Season For Family and Friends." *The Providence Journal.* December 6, 1974.

"Dinner Opens United Fund Drive in State." *The Providence Journal.* October 7, 1960.

"Airline Hostesses for TWA." Advertisement. *The Providence Journal.* April 3, 1960.

"After Fifty Years, The Job Still Holds Surprises." *The Providence Journal.* September 18, 1998.

"Four decades in service to a grand hotel." *The Providence Journal.* December 29, 1990.

"A fond farewell to Mr. Biltmore" *The Providence Journal.* March 23, 2003.

Interview with Dick Brush. April 2021.

Interview with Steve Lautieri. May 2021.

22　PROGRESS AND PROFIT

"Hotel Gives Dinner Proceeds To Aid Restoration Project." *The Providence Journal.* December 2, 1960.

"Innkeeper." *The Providence Journal.* September 15, 1963.

"School Segregation Lawyer Speaks at NAACP Dinner." *The Providence Journal.* July 4, 1962.

Green, V. *The Negro Motorist Green Book.* Smithsonian Digital Archives. 2022.

"Numerous sites in Rhode Island appear in historic 'Green Book'." Michelle San Miguel for NBC 10 News. February 21, 2019.

"Ill Fitted Hotels See Poor Lure." *The Providence Journal.* November 14, 1954.

"Evoking memories of R.I.'s Racial Divide." *The Providence Journal.* February 20, 2011.

Cohen, S. "No Unescorted Ladies Will Be Served." JSTOR Daily. March 20, 2019.

"Male Bars Contested in Court." *The Providence Journal.* July 19, 1974.

"Israel Will Appeal Tavern Ruling." *The Providence Journal.* July 25, 1974.

23　THE GOLDEN TICKET

Schrott, A. *My Life's Journey.* 2012. Courtesy of the Schrott Family Private Collection.

"Sculpture Chef Wins Prize." *The Providence Journal.* May 30, 1954.

MJ Roundtree. Obituary. *The Providence Journal.* December 21, 1975.

"Taste of Providence—A Feast for the Eyes." *The Providence Journal.* June 4, 2003.

Interview with Jimi Pugliese. May 2021.

24 BREAKFAST AT THE BILTMORE

"WJAR-TV's Nancy Dixon." *The Providence Journal.* April 20, 1955.

"WJAR's Johnny King." *The Providence Journal.* July 20, 1955.

Interview with Dick Brush. May 2021.

Research notes also provided by the Rhode Island Historical Society. June 2022.

25 (I CAN'T GET NO) SATISFACTION GUARANTEED.

The Beatles. Ed Sullivan Artist Page. www.edsullivan.com/artists/the-beatles/

The Rolling Stones. Ed Sullivan Artist Page. www.edsullivan.com/artists/the-rolling-stones/

Rhode Island Rocks archives. www.rirocks.net

Interview with Jimi Pugliese. May 2021.

26 THE KENNEDYS' HOTEL OF CHOICE

"Candidate Is Two Hours Late In Arriving." *The Providence Journal.* November 7, 1960.

"The JFK Assassination: Forty Years Later, *The Providence Journal*, November 22, 2003, by Scott MacKay

27 MOTOR INN, MONEY OUT

"Secrets of the Belvedere Hotel." *Baltimore Magazine.* December 2003.

"Reception is Scheduled for new Biltmore Manager." *The Providence Journal.* August 30, 1969.

"Downtown Plan Credits Given." *The Providence Journal.* May 2, 1960.

"Patriarca Showdown Near." *The Boston Globe.* June 21, 1967.

"Patriarca, Cosa Nostra Boss, Looks Like A Movie Bad Man." *The Boston Globe.* May 20, 1967.

"Underworld Chief? Prove It, He Says." *The Boston Globe.* February 26, 1967.

"Say The Secret Word: Food." *The Providence Journal.* November 10, 1974.

Stanton, M. *The Prince of Providence.* Random House. 2004.

"Jewelry Show Judged Successful." *The Providence Journal.* November 3, 1974.

"Downtown area's decline blamed on merchants." *The Providence Journal.* September 19, 1974.

"Doorley To Run Again, Spurns City Committee." *The Providence Journal.* March 14, 1974.

"New York Development Firm Eyeing Biltmore Hotel." *The Providence Journal.* October 8, 1975.

"$1.1 Million is Asked for Biltmore Hotel." *The Providence Journal.* October 31, 1975.

"Interface Team Hopes to Save Union Station." *The Providence Journal.* March 2, 1975.

28 "SELL AND GET OUT"

"Doorman Faithful to Biltmore." *The Providence Journal.* January 24, 1974.

"Owners of Biltmore Just Want to Get Out." *The Providence Journal.* January 16, 1975.

"Biltmore Buyer List Growing." *The Providence Journal.* November 6, 1975.

"Sale of Biltmore possible soon." *The Providence Journal.* July 25, 1975.

"Home for elderly in Biltmore eyed." *The Providence Journal.* January 31, 1975.

"Biltmore sale talks in final stages." *The Providence Journal.* November 22, 1975.

"Biltmore sued for $50,000." *The Providence Journal.* March 4, 1975.

"Biltmore talks continue." *The Providence Journal.* December 19, 1975.

"Abrupt Biltmore closing shocks its tenants." *The Providence Journal.* January 15, 1975.

"Biltmore may become Copley Plaza 'sister'." *The Providence Journal.* September 30, 1975.

"A resolute Cianci starts acting like a mayor." *The Providence Journal.* January 12, 1975.

"Give the Biltmore a deadline." *The Providence Journal.* January 18, 1975.

"Debt-ridden Biltmore closes." *The Providence Journal.* January 15, 1975.

"Downtown planners look southward." *The Providence Journal.* April 6, 1975.

"Final offer reported for Biltmore." *The Providence Journal.* December 12, 1975.

"Biltmore sued by electric co." *The Providence Journal.* January 30, 1975.

"Biltmore opens doors briefly." *The Providence Journal.* October 18, 1975.

"Tax incentive plan encourages building repairs." *The Providence Journal.* December 31, 1975.

29 THE 21ST PROVIDENCE GROUP

"Cianci Headquarters Has Humid Opening." *The Providence Journal.* June 22, 1974.

"4 firms buy Biltmore and plans are made to restore its glory." *The Providence Journal.* September 3, 1976.

"Parties 'agree' on Biltmore purchase." *The Providence Journal.* January 24, 1976.

"Biltmore deadline moved up to Aug. 14." *The Providence Journal.* July 31, 1976.

"Biltmore final sale expected." *The Providence Journal.* September 1, 1976.

"Biltmore is sold to group planning major restoration." *The Providence Journal.* September 3, 1976.

"Biltmore: Key to a vital city." *The Providence Journal.* August 29, 1976.

"Biltmore wins first okay for tax break." *The Providence Journal.* July 18, 1976.

"Biltmore Hotel renewal a community effort." *The Providence Journal.* July 16, 1976.

"Biltmore plan seen big boost to Providence." *The Providence Journal.* July 17, 1976.

"Cianci seeks federal aid for Biltmore Hotel work." *The Providence Journal.* July 22, 1976.

"Cianci says trip to D.C. satisfactory." *The Providence Journal.* July 23, 1976.

"Proposed tax break for Biltmore incurs wrath of city councilman." *The Providence Journal.* July 14, 1976.

"$3 million federal loan for Biltmore Hotel development disclosed at Capitol hearing." *The Providence Journal.* August 26, 1976.

"Textron still seeking Biltmore operator." *The Providence Journal.* March 24, 1976.

"Senator Pastore seeks grants for 2 cities." *The Providence Journal.* June 25, 1976.

"*The Providence Journal*'s conflict of interest." *The Providence Journal.* August 5, 1976.

"Old Biltmore fixtures go on sale tomorrow." *The Providence Journal.* January 12, 1977.

"Downtown uplift for Providence." *The Providence Journal.* January 2, 1977.

30   THE BILTMORE REIMAGINED

"Biltmore's 'renaissance' man promises Rhode Islanders posh pizzazz for their money." *The Providence Journal.* September 5, 1976.

"Copley concept still eyed for the Biltmore." *The Providence Journal.* March 4, 1976.

"Hotel group seeks OKs on fire code." *The Providence Journal.* March 30, 1977.

"Glass elevator gets first OK." *The Providence Journal.* April 21, 1977.

"Revised stairway exit route for Biltmore gets approval." *The Providence Journal.* July 21, 1977.

"Fire exit for hotel scored by board." *The Providence Journal.* June 16, 1977.

Tremain, A. *Without Reservations.* Peppertree Press. 2010.

"From Palm Beach to New Delhi, Alan Tremain led a life of luxury in running hotels, and now he's put those memories into a book." *Palm Beach Post.* April 7, 2012.

"The hotel is designed to be 'a little wild' for Providence." *The Providence Journal.* June 12, 1977.

"Biltmore plans combine elegance and nostalgia." *The Providence Journal.* June 12, 1977.

"Building firm signs Biltmore renovation pact of $7.2 million." *The Providence Journal.* September 28, 1977.

"Biltmore Hotel's grand new lobby to greet visitors at their own level." *The Providence Journal.* March 8, 1978.

"Biltmore Plaza begins work on glass-enclosed elevator." *The Providence Journal.* December 21, 1978.

"Hotel reopening set early in 1979 instead of Dec. 1." *The Providence Journal.* November 4, 1978.

31   RESTORATION FOR THE PEOPLE

"The Dunfeys refocus Biltmore's image." *The Providence Journal.* March 14, 1982.

"The wine had little chance to age." *The Providence Journal.* July 15, 1982.

"The race does not go to the swift on Bastille Day." *The Providence Journal.* July 15, 1983.

"Group purchases ailing Biltmore Hotel." *The Providence Journal.* July 28, 1984.

"Dunfey brothers give Biltmore classical touch." *The Providence Journal.* February 18, 1982.

"Bush to attend two fundraisers for Susan Farmer." *The Providence Journal.* August 12, 1986.

"Biltmore takes you back to the way it used to be." *The Providence Journal.* October 1, 1982.

"Barbara Bush a special lady, but she has a common." *The Providence Journal.* June 18, 1989.

"Dunfey Hotels Are Run As a Family Affair." *The New York Times.* June 15, 1979.

Interview with Dick Brush. April 2021.

32   DINING OUT OF ORBIT

"Kissing off those who link rock with Satan." *The Providence Journal.* August 19, 1990.

"Frank Black to belt it out again in RI." *The Providence Journal.* March 20, 1996.

"Cianci witness balks at testifying." *The Providence Journal.* February 18, 1984.

Stanton, M. *The Prince of Providence.* Random House. 2004.

"John Kennedy Jr. ends 4 quiet years at Brown." *The Providence Journal.* June 7, 1983.

"Kennedy name fills air in winning, losing camps." *The Providence Journal.* September 15, 1988.

Interview with Dick Brush. April 2021.

33 THE CURIOUS CASE OF CLAUS VON BULOW

"Fatal Charm: The Social Web of Claus von Bulow." *Vanity Fair*. August 1985.

"Providence hotels, eateries glad about von Bulow." *The Providence Journal*. February 15, 1985.

"Von Bulow verdict: Innocent, 'I am very relieved.'" *The Providence Journal*. June 10, 1985.

"Stepchildren insist he is guilty." *The Providence Journal*. June 11, 1985.

"Reporter's notebook." *The Providence Journal*. April 16, 1985.

"Andrea stays away from the limelight." *The Providence Journal*. April 13, 1985.

"High society trial fails to draw big spenders." *The Providence Journal*. May 25, 1985.

34 OMNI HOTELS

"The Biltmore leads the list of revamped restaurants." *The Providence Journal*. January 14, 1987.

"Biltmore launches a plan to cut losses New managers hope salesmanship will let hotel break even by '85." *The Providence Journal*. September 5, 1982.

"Suite for the two in tuxedos." *The Providence Journal*. December 12, 1990.

"The attire is formal for Pete and Penny." *The Providence Journal*. December 8, 1990.

"Nigerian guilty of selling heroin to drug agents." *The Providence Journal*. October 26, 1985.

"Update on $100,000 champagne bottle." *The Providence Journal*. December 22, 1991.

"Woman trapped for 3 hours in glass elevator." *The Providence Journal*. December 5, 1985.

"Couple climb to safety as Biltmore elevator jams." *The Providence Journal*. December 10, 1985.

"The night the astronaut became a commodore." *The Providence Journal*. May 4, 1986.

"After Cats, Junkyard bash." *The Providence Journal*. March 1, 1987.

"Joy of Children's Giving Tree." *The Providence Journal*. January 27, 1985.

"Investors to buy Biltmore Hotel." *The Providence Journal*. July 27, 1984.

Interview with Michael Fournier. June 2021.

"Maya Angelou's unforgettable visit." *The Providence Journal*. June 13, 2014.

35 HOLLYWOOD AT THE BILTMORE

"You could build five three-story houses in here." *The Providence Journal*. October 20, 1997.

"When Matt Dillon comes to town." *The Providence Journal*. November 27, 1997.

"It's a star studded night for film's East Coast premiere." *The Providence Journal.* July 15, 1998.

"Film festival to honor Anthony Quinn's career." *The Providence Journal.* May 1, 1998.

"A Chong with no Cheech." *The Providence Journal.* January 18, 1990.

"A Chef for all Seasons." *The Providence Journal.* January 17, 1990.

"Premiere brings out the stars." *The Providence Journal.* December 12, 2003.

"Stuck on You screening set for Woonsocket." *The Providence Journal.* November 28, 2003.

"Banderas, Griffith steal the show." *The Providence Journal.* April 20, 2002.

36   THE MAYOR CHECKS IN

"Cianci gets $1.1 million for home—Fla. businessman buys the historic East Side carriage house." *The Providence Journal.* September 2, 2000

"Biltmore's refurbished sign lights up Providence skyline." *The Providence Journal.* August 18, 2000.

"Mayor to market marinara." *The Providence Journal.* May 3, 1995.

"Davio's owner has big plans for the Biltmore." *The Providence Journal.* March 5, 1997.

"Biltmore Hotel getting ready for a major lift." *The Providence Journal.* October 5, 1995.

Interview with Steve Lautieri. June 2021.

"Welcome to Casey's cabaret." *The Providence Journal.* September 9, 2008.

"Crowd tuns out for Buddy in the Morning." *The Providence Journal.* May 11, 2002.

"Cianci tells Biltmore staff: I'll be back." *The Providence Journal.* August 28, 2002.

"The Plunder Dome Verdict." *The Providence Journal.* June 26, 2002.

"Cianci era ends…" *The Providence Journal.* September 7, 2002.

"Longest serving mayor…" *The Providence Journal.* September 7, 2002.

"Probes of ethics charges ordered." *The Providence Journal.* March 3, 2004.

Stanton, M. *The Prince of Providence.* Random House. 2004.

"Buddy's world: A conversation with Providence's mayor." *The Providence Journal.* September 30, 2001.

"The Cianci Wake." *The Providence Journal.* February 7, 2016.

37   THE 21ˢᵀ CENTURY

"Omni Biltmore hotel sold to restoration company." *The Providence Journal.* May 18, 1995.

"Biltmore celebrating 90 years ahead of renovation." *Associated Press.* Jun 20, 2012.

"Biltmore upgrade includes new tenants." *The Providence Journal.* August 13, 2003.

"Candidate Obama's wife visiting RI today." *The Providence Journal.* February 20, 2008.

"Biltmore: Rooms for improvement." *The Providence Journal.* March 27, 2000.

"The all new, totally fresh Rhode Island." *The Providence Journal.* January 10, 2003.

"Biden says America will leap forward over China." *The Providence Journal.* February 23, 2012.

"Biden to stop in R.I. for Whitehouse." *The Providence Journal.* February 22, 2012.

"Providence Biltmore hotel now in receivership." *The Providence Journal.* April 7, 2011.

"RI Elects first female governor." *The Providence Journal.* November 5, 2014.

"Providence Biltmore sells for $16 million." *The Providence Journal.* May 31, 2012.

"Biltmore hotel in receivership." *The Providence Journal.* April 8, 2011.

"Judge OKs sale of Providence Biltmore: new owners." *The Providence Journal.* February 16, 2012.

"Biltmore, Hilton to partner." *The Providence Journal.* December 17, 2014.

"Cianci says Biltmore, union likely to settle." *The Providence Journal.* April 4, 2002.

38 THE BILTMORE GRADUATES

"Plan to restore Biltmore elevator OK." *The Providence Journal.* April 10, 2018.

"Artist's cheery prints make grade." *The Providence Journal.* August 28, 2019.

"On second thought, Cianci won't stay." *The Providence Journal.* June 12, 2019.

"New era for Biltmore." *The Providence Journal.* October 25, 2017.

"Graduate studies…" *The Providence Journal.* June 8, 2019.

"Letters to the Editor." *The Providence Journal.* October 29, 2017.

"Graduate hotel closes due to virus." *The Providence Journal.* March 21, 2020.

39 FINDING MR. POTATO HEAD: LIFE DURING THE COVID-19 PANDEMIC

Interview with Michael Babb. May 2022.

Interview with Scott Williams. May 2022.

Interview with David Lee Black. May 2022.

AMANDA QUAY BLOUNT is a New Jersey native but lives in Rhode Island with her husband, daughter, their pet rabbit, Arthur, and the family dog, Rye. When she isn't researching and writing historical fiction and nonfiction, Amanda runs a nonprofit organization and is a strategic planning consultant. She has traveled extensively around the world, collecting stories along the way. Amanda believes it is a profound privilege to be able to tell other people's stories through her writing and is grateful for the opportunity to share some of these stories with the world. *Meet Me At The Biltmore* is Amanda's first published book.

Let's keep the story going: www.biltmorebook.com

CPSIA information can be obtained
at www.ICGtesting.com
Printed in the USA
LVHW042136100423
743977LV00003B/634

9 781958 217221